This book proposes a theory of collective and national identity based on culture and language rather than power and politics. Applying this to what he calls Germany's "axial age," Bernhard Giesen shows how the codes of nineteenth-century German identity in turn became those of the divided Germany between 1945 and 1989. The identity he describes derives from the ideas of German intellectuals, from the uprooted Romantic poets to the influential German mandarins. Carried by the emerging bourgeoisie, it was constructed on the tensions between power and spirit, money and culture, and the sacred and profane. It also took four distinct forms: the nation as the invisible public of Enlightenment patriotism, the nation as the Romantics' aesthetic holy grail, the Left Hegelian nation at the barricades of democracy, and the nation as an extension of the Prussian state.

BERNHARD GIESEN is Professor of Sociology at Justus-Liebig University, Gießen, in Germany. He has held visiting positions at the European University Institute, Florence, Italy, and at the University of Chicago, New York University, and the University of California, Los Angeles. He has published several books of social theory, including, with J. Alexander, R. Münch and N. Smelser (eds.), *The Micro–Macro Link* (1987).

Intellectuals and the German Nation

Cambridge Cultural Social Studies

Series editors: JEFFREY C. ALEXANDER, *Department of Sociology, University of California, Los Angeles, and* STEVEN SEIDMAN, *Department of Sociology, University at Albany, State University of New York.*

Titles in the series

ILANA FRIEDRICH SILBER, *Virtuosity, charisma, and social order*

LINDA NICHOLSON AND STEVEN SEIDMAN (eds.), *Social postmodernism*

WILLIAM BOGARD, *The simulation of surveillance*

SUZANNE R. KIRSCHNER, *The religious and Romantic origins of psychoanalysis*

PAUL LICHTERMAN, *The search for political community*

ROGER FRIEDLAND AND RICHARD HECHT, *To rule Jerusalem*

KENNETH H. TUCKER, *French revolutionary syndicalism and the public sphere*

ERIK RINGMAR, *Identity, interest and action*

ALBERTO MELUCCI, *The playing self*

ALBERTO MELUCCI, *Challenging codes*

SARAH M. CORSE, *Nationalism and literature*

DARNELL M. HUNT, *Screening the Los Angeles "riots"*

LYNETTE P. SPILLMAN, *Nation and commemoration*

MICHAEL MULKAY, *The embryo research debate*

LYNN RAPAPORT, *Jews in Germany after the Holocaust*

CHANDRA MUKERJI, *Territorial ambitions and the gardens of Versailles*

LEON H. MAYHEW, *The New Public*

VERA L. ZOLBERG AND JONI M. CHERBO (eds.), *Outsider art*

SCOTT BRAVMANN, *Queer fictions of the past*

STEVEN SEIDMAN, *Difference troubles*

RON EYERMAN AND ANDREW JAMISON, *Music and social movements*

MEYDA YEGENOGLU, *Colonial fantasies*

LAURA DESFOR EDLES, *Symbol and ritual in the new Spain*

NINA ELIASOPH, *Avoiding politics*

Intellectuals and the German Nation

Collective Identity in an Axial Age

Bernhard Giesen
Translated by Nicholas Levis and Amos Weisz

PUBLISHED BY THE PRESS SYNDICATE OF THE UNIVERSITY OF CAMBRIDGE
The Pitt Building, Trumpington Street, Cambridge CB2 1RP, United Kingdom

CAMBRIDGE UNIVERSITY PRESS
The Edinburgh Building, Cambridge CB2 2RU, United Kingdom
40 West 20th Street, New York, NY 10011–4211, USA
10 Stamford Road, Oakleigh, Melbourne 3166, Australia

Originally published in German as *Die Intellektuellen und die Nation*
by Suhrkamp Verlag 1993

First published in English by Cambridge University Press 1998 as
Intellectuals and the German Nation

Printed in the United Kingdom at the University Press, Cambridge

Typeset in Times 10/12.5 pt [SE]

A catalogue record for this book is available from the British Library

Library of Congress Cataloguing in Publication data

Giesen, Bernhard, 1948–
[Die Intellektuellen und die Nation. English]
Intellectuals and the German nation: collective identity in an axial age / Bernhard Giesen: translated by Nicholas Levis.
p. cm. – (Cambridge cultural social studies)
Includes bibliographical references and index.
ISBN 0 521 62161 5 (hardback); 0 521 63996 4 (paperback)
1. Intellectuals – Germany – History – 19th century.
2. Intellectuals – Germany – History – 20th century. 3. Nationalism – Germany – History – 19th century. 4. Nationalism – Germany – History – 20th century. 5. Germany – Historiography. 6. Germany – History – 1945–1990. 7. Philosophy – History. 8. Hegel, Georg Wilhelm Friedrich, 1770–1831. I. Title. II. Series.
DD204.G5413 1998
320.54′0943–dc21 97-27897 CIP

ISBN 0 521 62161 5 hardback
ISBN 0 521 63996 4 paperback

Contents

Preface

Anyone who writes a study on intellectuals and the nation, and therein treats the intellectuals as the inventors of German identity, is necessarily referring to himself in several ways. For all the efforts at distance and abstraction, the presentation of the historical material herein is inescapably determined, much like the general theoretical considerations on the relationship of intellectuals to national identity, by contemporary perspectives of more recent history, and by the self-understanding of German intellectuals in the present day. It is possible to reflexively compensate for such perspectivity, but it cannot be avoided entirely.

The present work arose in the course of a research project on "National and Cultural Identity as a Problem of Early Modern and Modern Europe" at the University of Gießen. I am especially indebted to my assistants, Christian Kritschgau and Kay Junge, for the difficult work of evaluating historical sources, and for their criticism and wealth of bibliographical recommendations. The manuscript would never have been completed so quickly without them. Many friends and colleagues contributed to this book's deliberations directly through criticisms and suggestions. This applies especially to Shmuel N. Eisenstadt, whose idea of an "Axial Age" exercised decisive influence upon this study, and who read, and critically evaluated, large sections of the manuscript – as did Helmut Berding, Jörg R. Bergmann, Günther Oesterle and Wolfgang L. Schneider. For extensive discussions on the theses of this study, and for a large number of critical suggestions, I would like furthermore to thank Jeffrey C. Alexander, Reinhard Bendix, Randall Collins, Klaus Eder, Harold Garfinkel, Reimer Gronemeyer, Karl Otto Hondrich, Klaus Kröger, Claus Leggewie, Iván Szelény, Johannes Weiß and Conrad Wiedemann.

Finally, I am grateful to all the members of the research team in Gießen, especially P. Fuchs and S. Ruwisch for their criticism and specific analyses, and D. Schimmel, G. Barr, and L. Karschies for their help in the technical preparation of the manuscript.

This translation is published with the support of the Exxon Foundation and of Inter Nationes, Germany.

Introduction: the nation in social science and history

This book deals with the national identity of the Germans. As a consequence of German unification, and in the midst of a renaissance of national movements in eastern and central Europe, the issue has gained a currency that sophisticated academic research often finds suspect. The present study establishes a necessary distance from the simply current – not merely because it arrives at the present only after a journey through the past, but also, and primarily, because the origins of national identity are reconstructed here within an explicit theoretical framework. This sort of theoretical framework may seem rather elaborate for historical material – and those uncomfortable with theory should proceed directly to chapter 2 – but it provides the possibility of comparison, and places the rise of German identity in the context of general problems of Modernity. Our examination therefore begins with an overview of various scholarly perspectives on the issue of "nation" as such; and the following chapter constitutes a general theoretical essay on the construction of collective identity.

1) In the nineteenth century, Europe discovered the nation as the foundation of political sovereignty, social organization, and historical orientation.[1] The nation came to be considered the paramount "collective subject" of history, not only in projections of "future history," but just as much in the reconstruction of the historical past. Other forces – dynastic interests, individual ambition, and the struggle among denominations – had, in this view, been able to prevent, for a very long time, the discovery of the nation and its achievement of self-consciousness. But the transition from a sort of somnolent existence to the actions of a self-aware nation seemed inevitable. Similar to the way in which an individual subject undergoes a process of maturation before achieving self-determination and self-sufficient action,

nations were also destined, over the course of history, to achieve the realization and determination of their identity. The Hegelian background of this model of history can hardly be ignored, especially as expressed in writings of German historians. The identity of the nation became the reference point for political action and economic interest, for cultural reflexion and pedagogic effort. The nation–state represented a reconciliation of territorial statehood with the necessity of democratic legitimation in a fashion that no longer required individual assent to authority. Because the people as a whole were sovereign, they no longer needed to safeguard in detail a presumed conjunction of power with the will of the people. A middle level between regional markets and the all-encompassing relations of the world market was discovered in the national economy, where the tension between universal economic rationality and particular communal relationships could be moderated, while the legal framework for economic action could at the same time be secured by the state.

This conception, originating in western Europe and embodied in the French Revolution, of the nation as the "normal form" in history and society, was furthermore the defining force in an important tradition of the scholarly analysis of nations: a tradition stretching from early national historical writing in France and Germany, from Treitschke, Maurras and Barrès, to the modernization theory prevalent in the years after the Second World War.[2] The current sprang from an emphatically charged historical metaphysics, impervious to any empirical–historical examination, wherein the nation poses the categorical frame, within which *its history* can take place as the object of research, but is itself no longer the object of any critical or empirical gaze.

This changed especially with respect to those states of the Third World that became politically independent in the 1960s within borders that had been imposed by foreign interests and the administrative imperatives of colonial powers. "Nation-building" thus became a practical political project, as well as a central research theme of the social sciences.[3] Although the western European nation–state continued serving as the barely questioned "ideal form," a switch in the direction of view and a metamorphosis of attitude was thus completed. While in western Europe the development of national consciousness ran largely parallel to the constitution of national states, and while in central and eastern Europe political history reacted to an already existing, ethnocultural national consciousness, most of the new Third World states were already constituted as "nation"–states *before* a national consciousness could arise beyond the limits of a narrow, European-educated elite. Instead of being nations without states, these were states without nations.[4] The state-carrying elites of Africa and Asia had pursued their struggles for independence with a rhetoric of anticolonial liberation. This rhetoric became even more indispensable after decolonization, however, especially where no other fundamentalist ideologies could be found to replace it.[5] And faced with a choice between socialism and nationalism, the development politics of the West preferred to support efforts toward a national substantiation of the new states. Thus the nation became a political project to be described, advised upon, and programmatically realized with the help of sociology, pedagogy, and political science.

The failure of the attempt to weld together tribal groups evincing extreme ethnic and cultural heterogeneity into nations that could hold together even after the deaths of their charismatic founding figures finally led to a more differentiated view. The explicitly supported, practically approached process of "nation-building" was now supplanted by an empirical and historically sophisticated analysis of "nation-becoming." Certainly the western European model continued to serve as the authoritative starting point for diffusionist or comparative perspectives.[6] But analyses finally began to acknowledge the differences in the historical and sociostructural initial conditions confronting nations-to-be, or in the cultural and institutional backgrounds. History was no longer explained as the result of national emancipation. Instead, nations were explained as the result of history. Starting as a metahistorical, referential frame of analysis, nations thus first became the project of political practice before they were finally treated as the object of historical description and analysis.

2) In contrast to the emphatically charged conception of the "nation" traceable back to German Idealism,[7] the Enlightenment also bestowed a critical perspective on the national, running back to Kant and his idea of "world peace between all reasonable subjects": neither wars between peoples, nor the particularities of national interest, can be rationalized or justified within the framework of a universally applicable and transcendentally substantiated reason and morality. From this universalist perspective history does not appear as the gradual awakening of nations, but as the fading away of national, religious, and feudal-rank differences with respect to a Modernity that overwhelms all borders.[8] Religion is overcome by enlightenment and science; the ruling classes by revolution and democracy; and, finally, borders between nations are overcome and replaced by world peace and the solidarity of mankind.

Although it never disappeared entirely, this antinational Modernism played a limited, peripheral role in the historical scholarship of the nineteenth century. That changed radically, however, as the national emphasis perished in the inferno of the two World Wars of the twentieth century. Especially after the Holocaust and the devastation of Europe through the Second World War, the orientation of politics and history around national interest appeared to be the original sin of Modernity, bound to lead inevitably to history's catastrophic collapse.

The salvation story of national self-discovery thus turned into the prehistory of an exemplary fall from grace, by which postnational politics and historical scholarship were to reorient themselves. The idea of national self-determination was supplanted by that of the nationalist seduction. National identity is thus rediscovered as the transitory result of political construction and propaganda and the role of political and intellectual seducers is brought to the fore. The view of nationalism as the demon of Modernity corresponded to a political praxis that had set out to tame and overcome that demon through enlightenment and education.

But any attempt to reconstruct the intellectual prehistory, especially that of German nationalism, is quickly forced to make distinctions. There is no simple path leading from Luther and Herder to Fichte and Nietzsche, and the connection between them and the racism of Chamberlain or Rosenberg is also by no means unambiguous.[9] A differentiation between "good" nationalism and "bad" nationalism is thus ultimately found necessary; patriotism is contrasted to national chauvinism; and in the end even the automatic connection between nationalism, and fascism or Nazism, is undone.[10] Thus critical research into nations also underwent a reversal of perspective. The variety of national paths to Modernity was discovered, and comparative explanations took the place of moral political verdicts.

3) This sort of comparative research on nations can also be traced back to an eighteenth-century debate. An empirical/descriptive view of national differences had already arisen in Enlightenment Europe, following the reception of Montesquieu's work, focusing not only upon the differences among nations in political institutions, but also differences in everyday behavior between the English and Italians, French and Germans. The characters of peoples, their virtues and qualities, were encyclopedically summarized, and associated with climate and geography. However, this comparative, empirical view of national differences could hardly have held up well, or come to the fore, in the nineteenth century. Only in the comparative research into nations of recent decades did it once again become the defining perspective.

One comparative approach to the research on nations begins by concentrating on the asynchrony with which historical processes reached fruition in each region. The lack of simultaneity among regions on their way into

Modernity is thus raised to a shaping principle of national identity. Pathbreaking nations face latecomers. The interaction between them lastingly defines the formation of each of their national identities.[11] England and France had superiority and a head start in both unification of the territorial state and economic development. This blocked the way, for the "latecomer nations" of eastern and central Europe, to a *political–statist* or economic identification of national particularity.[12]

Much like the twentieth-century newcomer nations of Africa, the late arrivals of Europe had to substantiate their national identity in other areas, using other ideas. Often this involved the idea of *moral* superiority, such as that of the vassal emancipating himself from the oppression of his lord, or of the unspoiled, modest, and "pure" commoners faced with the corrupt and depraved royal court.[13] Most of all, however, peculiarities and distinctions of *culture and language* could serve as substantiations for national identity. From Herder and German Romanticism, this conception can be followed right up to Meinecke's famous distinction between the "state nation" and the "cultural nation," upon which the present work is also based.[14]

Not only will differences between various societies serve herein as our axis of comparison; the asynchrony of development among *various spheres within* society will also be pivotal. In the western European nations, the territorial state formed the borders of a nation that in itself was not yet by any means culturally homogeneous. The contrasts between *Langue d'oc* and *Langue d'oïl* within France, for example, or the divide between Catholic Scots and Reformed English within Britain, were moderated and defused only long after the territorial unification of the state was completed. Conversely, Poles, Germans, Italians and Czechs possessed a common language and literature that crossed over the borders of the principalities, long before their consolidation into nation–states.

A further distinction relates to the historical period within which a culturally grounded national consciousness arises. While the old nation–states of western Europe – much like the Dutch, Swedes, Poles, Russians, and Germans – all possessed such a national consciousness before the nineteenth century, i.e. before the "Age of Nationalism" in a narrower sense, the Czechs, Slovaks, Romanians, Serbs and new nations of Asia and Africa only developed their national consciousness within the context of a globally available idea of national independence.[15] But the new nations of Africa, Arabia, and South Asia had only a limited cultural foundation to fall back upon. In substantiating their national identity, they were at first far more dependent upon formal territorial borders and the administrative apparatus left behind by the colonial powers. Alongside the "*state nations*" of western and northern Europe and the "*cultural nations*" of central and eastern Europe, there arose in 1960 the new "*territorial nations*" of Africa, which, much like the United States of America, do not possess a homogeneous ethnic and cultural foundation.

More precise observation shows, however, that ethnocultural homogeneity is also the rare exception among European nations. Within each nation–state, there is usually a distinction between a state-carrying majority nation, and only partly integrated national and/or ethnic minorities, such as the Basques and Catalans in Spain, Welsh and Irish in Great Britain, Bretons and Alsatians in France. In addition, there are the new ethnocultural minorities that arise through immigration: Pakistanis and West Indians in Great Britain, North Africans in France, Turks in Germany.

This brings up the relation between the *carrier groups* of national identity and groups on the periphery of a society. The tension and dependence between the ruling elites and the economic center on the one side, and peripheral groups on the other, has been researched primarily within the Marxist tradition.[16] According to that view, the dominance of a metropolis over the determination of national identity calls forth aspirations for cultural autonomy as a countering action among peripheral groups. The effort of these "internal colonies"[17] to achieve autonomy and equal status with respect to the metropolitan culture leads to the reconstruction of a "submerged" past, aiming at "national rebirth."

National consciousness as a reaction to the political, economic, and cultural dominance of a metropolis is admittedly not just a European phenomenon, with the Irish or Corsicans for example, but in fact provides the key to explaining the independence movements of Africa and Asia, or the ethnic movements of North America. But a further sociostructural distinction, one that Marxist theorists too gladly overlook, must also be made. It is usually not the impoverished and oppressed masses on the periphery who emerge as the carriers of national identity, but rather the *elites* within peripheral sectors and classes. Although excluded from metropolitan and hegemonic culture, by no means do they represent the lowest end of social stratification. Here traditional, patrimonial, and feudal elites must be considered along with the economically ambitious bourgeois of early Modernity, administrative and civil servants, or declassed intellectuals. It is far less an absolute situation on the periphery than the *status inconsistencies*, such as those between a group's traditional honor and its meager economic power, or conversely between its high wealth and its low political privilege, that set off the search for cultural autonomy and national identity among the disappointed and excluded.

Nonetheless, such excluded and disappointed elites on the periphery, or middle classes just outside the gates of power, require the support of the *masses* if they are to mount any kind of serious challenge to the metropolis, and deny its claim as voice of the encompassing collectivity – of the *Allgemeinheit*, the general trope, "the people." Attempts to create this manner of alliance between peripheral elites and the mass of the people favor a *populist* and romantic idea of national identity, one that falls back upon traditional symbols and everyday myths. In the articulation and literary substantiation of these national myths, *the intellectuals* within peripheral groups take on a special significance. They may be in command of the education of the hegemonic culture, but they are excluded from access to political power, from a share in the wealth of the metropolis, and from entry to the respectable, hegemonic elites. Out of this dissonance – between (high) culture and education on the one side, and (low) social prestige and political power on the other, there arises a self-evident compulsion to radically redefine the relation between periphery and center, and to attribute to the periphery an autonomous, original, and indeed superior culture, even while viewing the center as commanding power and wealth only through historical coincidence, and as projecting its hegemonic cultural claims without substantiation.

4) All of the considerations on "nation-becoming" sketched up to this point are located within the framework of conflict theory. Within that paradigm, collective identity and the ability to act, *agency*, are explained as arising from the unequal relationship between several *sociostructural* groups. These groups already exist – as intellectuals, middle classes, or peripheral elites – and they enrich or redefine their existence by acquiring national consciousness. This does not yet bring up the question of *why,* and through what processes, rituals, or mechanisms, the members of a group discover their commonalities, and set themselves off against third parties.

This kind of question primarily addresses the particular *institutions* that create the framework for communication, and limit or extend the range of communication. Seen from this perspective, social groups, ranks, or classes are not simply and naturally "there"; nor are they generated just by material conditions. Instead they *produce* and reproduce themselves through particular forms of *communication* – through the familiar discussion among equals that excludes "outsiders" and generates social differences as the boundaries defining familiarity and community.

The reproduction of a social group, rank, or class enters into crisis when relations of communication start to cross the boundaries of the group more than just occasionally, and do so with increasing frequency. The expansion of transportation routes and the increased density of communication networks at the dawn of the modern period, for example, resulted in increasingly frequent encounters with strangers. Once such a process is under way, it becomes increasingly rare that an elementary degree of trust in a partner, which is indispensable to interactions of trade, administration, power, or law, can be produced and assured merely by pointing out the same regional origin or membership in the same class. Interregional forms of integration, crossing class borders, must therefore be found, anchored in social consciousness through specific markings, and reinforced in daily activity through specific rituals. This sort of everyday form of integration, linking diverse regional and class communities, can very effectively be created through the idea of a nation.[18]

But it is not only the expansion of trade routes, a higher density of communications, urbanization, and a growing degree of participation in decisions within the metropolis that necessitate new foundations for community and integration. A decisive role is played by the growth in *mobility* between various social groups. If social and regional origins no longer set final limits on an individual's career or life story – offer no steady expectations; if an individual's identity is in flux, and must be determined by the individual in the course of a difficult process, then a compensatory general search for a *comprehensive community*, within which an individual can feel protected from the changing tides of modern life, becomes all the more likely.

In the process of modernization, the weakening of traditional ties and the growth of regional and horizontal mobility go hand in hand with a comprehensive process of *functional differentiation*. The diversity of particular societal sectors increases, with the individual put into an ever-more complicated network of division of labor, within which he or she has little in common with others. To counteract the alienating and disruptive effects of differentiation, particular and new forms of integration and inclusion become necessary. The nation thus forms the integrative basis for the differentiation process of modern societies.

This explanation of how nations come into being, as a result of modernization, of the intensification of communications, and of increased vertical and horizontal mobility, usually stresses the significance of *systems of education and upbringing.*[19] These are not only switchboards or selection procedures governing individual career paths, but also institutional platforms upon which the obligation of the individual to a particular encompassing identity, to the prince or nation, is established.

5) The building of a general system of upbringing and education is closely bound by the borders of a language – at the same time demanding the

standardization of that language, and dissemination of its literary traditions.[20] On this level, of shared literary traditions, of hero and origin myths, or of symbolic markings through emblems, flags, and colors, there sprout the *culturalist perspectives* of the nation. Seen this way, belonging to a nation is neither a natural fact nor a side effect of modernization. Instead it is substantiated through participation in a common symbolic culture that is both unique and inalienable, in the view of its adherents.[21] Here the rise of nations occurs through the symbolic distinguishing of a national culture, of a high literature and a classical period in the history of literature, music, and art. And here as well, in the cultural/symbolic reconstruction of national identity and history, intellectuals – literati, philosophers, historians – again take a central position. Especially wherever the nation is not yet constituted in any form as a state, intellectuals frequently become the high priests of a secularized, national ersatz religion, heralding the ultimate reconciliation of culture and politics, of state and nation, of rulers and ruled. These millenarian and chiliastic elements of nationalism can build upon Christian traditions, and serve to ease the transition from the reconstruction of a mythical past to historical action and political movement.[22]

Let us summarize. Various perspectives can serve to guide the comparative approach to nations adopted in recent decades by research in the social and historical sciences. One of these perspectives begins from the particular position of a structural group or a people, and explains the becoming of a nation through the particular situation of a defined collective, in relation to other groups, peoples, or nations. Here the nation appears as the result of efforts to substantiate, understand, and enrich one's own situation with respect to others. This perspective could be called *sociostructural* or a sociology of knowledge.

A second perspective does not consider groups, classes, or peoples who already exist in history and are struggling toward a self-awareness, but sees the nation as an *integrative countermovement* to processes of modernization, individualization, mobilization, and differentiation. In the course of these processes, traditional forms of collective identity break down, and are replaced by new patterns. Accordingly it is not the previous existence of a collective actor that leads to collective actions understood as expressions of such a real, previously existing actor. Instead, it is only through the process of collective action, through the expansion of social networks to meet the requirements of modern institutions, that national identity is created in the first place. The direction of view is thus reversed: process explains structure. Action constitutes the actor, and not vice versa.

A third perspective begins neither with the actor, nor with the determining processes of interaction, but with the pictures, ideas and myths contained in the *cultural traditions* available for use in the construction of national identity. Such a culturalist perspective has until now remained theoretically underdeveloped, and largely limited to a reconstruction of national myths and traditions. A general logic by which cultural construction of a national identity, of a mythology of the collective in a narrower sense, might operate, has not yet been proposed. The following chapter attempts to fill this vacuum, and presents a general model of construction of collective identity. This model places the cultural codes by which collective identity is constructed at center stage; but it does so without downplaying the weight of the sociostructural situation of particular carrier groups, or the significance of communications and interaction processes in the genesis of national identity. Instead, cultural code, communicative process, and sociostructural situation are linked together in a general model that does not treat them merely as some isolated "important explanatory factors," but sheds light on their internal functional relations.[23]

After establishing this general model, the main part of the book then examines the development of the national identity of the Germans between the Enlightenment in the late eighteenth century and the founding of the Wilhelmine Empire in 1871.[24] According to this thesis, the cultural identity of the Germans, carried by the educated bourgeoisie – the *Bildungsbürger* – and formulated by certain groups of intellectuals, arose within this timespan of a "long" century. The structure of this cultural national identity is reconstructed in four scenarios, each determined by a particular form of intellectual discourse: that of the Enlightenment, of early nineteenth-century German Romanticism, of the *Vormärz* (the "pre-March" period, as it was later called, between the Restoration of 1815 and the Revolution of March, 1848), and of the *Reichsgründung*, the "foundation of empire." Out of these discourses, as I shall argue here, there arose a repertoire of various codes for the national identity of the Germans, a repertoire which then remained available, to be called upon in later periods. This was especially true in the time between 1945 and 1990, during which, as in the century between 1770 and 1870, the national identity of the Germans was not substantiated in a political, single-state unity. A longer epilogue is therefore devoted to these four decades between the Second World War and German unification.

1

The construction of collective identity: proposal for a new analysis

Codes for the construction of collective identity

Classical social theory in succession to Marx and Durkheim was persistently concerned with oppositions posited between society and community, between mechanic and organic solidarity, social order and collective identity. But it treated the two sides of each of these oppositions in a completely different fashion. The issue that consistently occupied sociological analysis above all others was the constitution of social order, understood as a highly tense combination of state power and social division of labor. Both seemed like frail and historically mutable constructions, and it was thought to be only this fragility of the social order that opened the way to social transformation or revolution, posed the problem of legitimation and crisis, and made progress or history possible.

The constructed nature and fragility of social order becomes even more obvious when contrasted to the quasinatural fact of collective or individual identity. This comparison makes identity look like a nonsocial foundation, a given for social action: premodern, stable, immutable, an opposite to the historicity, flux, and alienation of modern society. Or, viewed from the reversed perspective, that of developmental theory, identity is even viewed as the ultimate reference point for history and its redemption. And this posing of opposites – in society and community, in system and lifeworld, or in social order and collective identity – is normally reinforced by drawing the analogy to individual and collectivity. Parallels are seen between individual identity and action, on the one side, and identity and history of the collectivity, on the other. Much as action expresses the individual identity of the acting subject, history aims at returning society to its unreified foundation: to communal ethos and identity of collectivity. The concentration on the tension between society and community, or historical movement and collective identity, tends to banish the problem of collective identity from sociological analysis altogether. Collective identity and communal ethos appear as the self-evident and ultimate reference point for social transformation, a reference point that in itself no longer seems to require any kind of explanation.[1]

The following theoretical sketch attempts to return once again the problem of collective identity to the realm of social transformation and history. *Collective identity itself is constructed in social processes*. Although the constructedness of collective identity obtains even in simple "band" societies, it acquires an additional and critical significance during the onset of the modern age, as a result of accelerated change and the struggles by individual and society to emancipate themselves from heteronomy. These initiate a dialectic particular to Modernity. If society is freed from tradition and divine commandment, and viewed as an empty space for the autonomous activities of individuals determining their own identities for themselves, then the classical opposition between individual and society, as a struggle between autonomy and heteronomy, revolt and repression, freedom and power, gradually collapses. Accepted everywhere, the ideas of liberation and emancipation lose their power and their pathos. They become a part of the indubitable values of Modernity, and are finally lost in daily routine. In their place arises a new and pressing need for fixed orientations in a realm of flow, transformation, and anomie. Crisis is no longer perceived in subjugation and power, but in insecurity and a lack of orientation. The elementary vacuum of individual and society summons up the problem of existential meaning, and calls forth the *Angst* at the core of the "condition moderne."[2] Beyond oppression and tradition, there stirs a new demand for an "iron cage." In counteraction and contradiction to structural differentiation and universalist values, and as a means of expanding social networks and dependencies, images of unity must be constructed and borders set up, boundaries that are impervious to the transformation of history or choice of the individual. Modern society thus "discovers" its primordial foundation, and classical social theory reflects that discovery as the tension between mechanistic and organic solidarity, between traditional lifeworld and systemic differentiation.

Classical theory thereby runs into a snare particular to the construction of collective identity: *that identity itself is socially constructed is precisely the circumstance that collective identity is designed to hide*. If the process of construction were not kept "latent," the foundation, which secures identity, would itself fall prey to the suspicion of being contingent. The outer borders of a community must therefore seem self-evident, obvious, and substantiated; the inner uniformity of the community obvious and unquestionable. And this in spite of the fact that the boundaries defining identity could always be drawn along entirely different lines, and in spite of the real variety and differences among individuals, which can hardly ever be overlooked. This "latency problem" forms the reference point for the following theoretical sketch and analysis of various codes of collective identity.

The construction of boundaries

Within the real variety of interaction processes and social relations, boundaries are what separate and divide. They mark the difference between inside and outside, strange and familiar, relatives and non-relatives, friends and enemies, culture and nature, enlightenment and barbarism. Precisely because these borders are contingent social constructions, because they could be drawn differently, they require social reinforcement and symbolic manifestation.

When borders and dividing lines are drawn within the real diversity and flow of social processes, when things receive a name, then this presupposes a "*code*," a pattern for making the differences in the flow and chaos of the world visible, for lending outlines to things.[3] Codes can be compared to maps that provide the actor on a journey with instructions about what to expect. Much as maps could never reproduce the diversity of an actual landscape, but always abstract landscape after a particular fashion, so too do codes always offer only an arbitrary simplification of *situation*. And much like maps, codes can be more or less precise, can correlate more or less accurately to reality. But just as we cannot make a purposeful motion without having an elementary map in mind, social reality cannot be perceived without codes.[4] Codes of social classification are the core element in the construction of communality and otherness, of collective identity and differentiation. No boundary would have substance without codes. In order to comprehend the logic governing the construction of communality and friendship, we are well advised to lay bare the elementary distinctions presupposed in every idea of collective identity.

The mediating realm

From a Kantian perspective, we might distinguish on the categorical level between the *spatial*, the *temporal*, and the *reflexive* dimensions of encoding. The spatial dimension is the referent for distinctions between up and down, left and right, inside and outside. The temporal dimension becomes obvious in the distinction between past and future. The reflexive dimension places the difference between subject and object at the center of concern.[5]

Within this categorical framework, reference to the world at first seems to be based upon dichotomous distinctions. But a more precise view reveals that, at least within occidental tradition (if not universally), these apparent dichotomies actually contain hidden trichotomies. Between inside and outside there is the *border*, between left and right the central point, between past and future the present. And between God and the world stands the subject. Even on a very elementary level, codes thus reveal a trichotomous structure containing a border realm that mediates and divides. *This "mediating realm" is the location of identity in perception and consciousness*: the center, the present, the subject. The "here," the "now" and the "I" are the indisputable and self-evident starting points for a view of the world, for speaking with others, for remembering the past, and for planning the future. To construct a world means to begin with a given and "unmediated" identity, and only then to stretch a construction out from this center point toward further and more remote areas: from present to past and future, from subject to God and the world.

This logic of construction, which regards the mediating realm as the source of identity, has important consequences if we assume a certain parallel between the logic of construction, on the one hand, and the evolutionary genesis of constructions on the other. There follows a certain and limited analogy between the structure of the center, the present, and the subject, on the one side, and the structure of remote areas, past and future, God and the world on the other. The projection of the structure of the known on the unknown, of the familiar on the strange, of the present on the past and future, or the idea of God in the image of man, etc., are all well-known strategies of observation and understanding. This "analogical" encoding of the world naturally does not preclude the possibility of fundamental differences between past and present, central and distant, or subject and world. Clearly we cannot change the past, the future is uncertain, the outer world by no means completely dependable, distant things cannot be perceived, etc. It is entirely obvious that analogue encoding does not only imply similarity. It also implies differences, and it is the differences that are decisive.

Original referents

The unmediated circumstance of center, present, and subject has a great impact upon the genesis of construction; but the genesis of construction has also left its traces in the meaning of the resulting structures. At this point we are well advised to abandon a strictly Kantian perspective, and to give due respect to a *pragmatist* view of the origin of meaning. The meaning of distinctions is prefabricated and predetermined by earlier experiences, and by our position within a web of interactions.[6] Fundamental and elementary social relations – our first experiences of the world – in particular shape the meaning of codes, and could be considered their "original referents." The distinctions, for example, between parents and children, men and women, the raw and the cooked; and later those between relatives and strangers, hierarchy and equality, exchange and self-sufficiency, all belong among these *original referents*. Even after a long series of evolutionary transformations, their symbolic encodings can never be entirely escaped.[7]

It is through these original distinctions that the world is made susceptible to ordering and classification. They nonetheless do not serve merely to distinguish between various *objects* in a situation; they are also applied in the creation of communality, in the establishment of similarity and equality between active *subjects*. Our concern here is the creation of a collectivity whose members can mutually identify each other. Ultimately, this collective identity can become the object and theme of a particular *reflexivity* that locates identity within the structure of an interpretation of the world. In the chapters below, these three levels – classification and construction of differences, mutual identification within a collectivity, and reflexion about collective identity – should be kept in mind separately. On all three levels, the issue is that of the difference between "we" and "they," of a demarcation arising from a narrow connection to original referents, of a division that can be manifested in completely different ways depending upon which of the original referents is used to establish and reinforce the boundaries.

Code, process, and situation

Only through the framework of codes does the great variety of social reality appear as though organized in collective identities. Assuming these symbolic prerequisites of collective identity are now apparent, we might again reverse our direction of view, and pose this question: under what social conditions does a particular code develop, or become appropriate in the first place? This in turn brings up a further elementary distinction, one presupposed in any action or observation, but of which actors or observers only become aware under extraordinary circumstances: the difference between code and situation, between language and world, theory and reality, categorical prerequisites and empirical conditions. Once again a trichotomy is concealed here behind the dichotomous distinction. Both points of reference – code and situation – arise only from the perspective of action, observation, speech, or position-taking. Sliding in between code and situation, theory and reality, language and world, is thus a further level, of practical processes: spoken actions and social interactions through which codes acquire referents to the variety of the world, and can be employed in the first place.[8] In what follows, this trichotomy, based in the theory of action, will be described as that of situation, process, and code.

"Situation" means "that which is," the "environment" of an actor, the social relations in which an actor is placed, the state of things encountered in taking action – in short, spatially, temporally, and socially determined conditions that from the actor's perspective appear as given and unalterable through any direct or immediate action. These might include the presence of persons, the history of a social relationship, equality or inequality of actors, available technical means, spatial isolation, etc. Such circumstances are constants only within a given situation. Fundamentally they can be operated upon and altered, subjected to spatial change or transformations over time, and are actually just as various and complex as the concrete and real are various and complex. Precisely because each situation is so different and particular, an actor encountering a situation can never know everything about it, can never take every detail of that situation into account. Situations are always more complex than the calculations of their actors. They can never be completely supervised from the actor's perspective, they are given and already in existence. Nor can they be completely comprehended: they are spatially, temporally and socially *specific*, while the actor commands only a *general* knowledge upon which to act, always derived from other situations. Limits on the actor's experience are what make surprises possible.

Processes, meaning sequences of action and communication, are less specific than the situations within which they occur. Communication and interaction do have social and temporal dimensions – they refer to others, they have a beginning and an end – but they can remain spatially indeterminate, at any rate such that they cannot be fixed precisely to a point in space. Demand on markets, publication of scientific research, or appeals to the orthodox, just to name a few examples, can be specified temporally and socially, but not spatially. Processes, action, or communication can obviously occur without clear spatial location, but are inconceivable without temporal determinants and social referents. As a result of these communications processes, social structures arise – institutions, boundaries between social groupings, etc. Collective identity is thus always the result of social communications processes. By no means does the process of social construction of identity always proceed in the manner imagined by the actors taking part in it. Its result is substantially influenced by the situational circumstances within which it occurs; to succeed, a process of construction needs to take these circumstances into account. Social communication must be adapted to the situation within which it is embedded. When communication does not adjust to situation, when presences are overlooked or wrongly assumed, when equality and inequality, familiarity and strangeness, or proximity and distance are mixed up, then action is misunderstood and the flow of communication flags, breaks off, or requires correction through additional procedures. Much in the same way that the biological reproduction of organisms needs to adapt to the factors of selection operating within a given environment, the processes of intentional action and social communication are also under pressure to adapt to each particular situation.

Each of the three levels – codes, processes, and the situations within which they take place – has its own form of order. Codes (or languages) are purely symbolic structures, in no way bound to a location in space or temporal limits. Processes (or speech acts) by contrast are ordered not only symbolically, but also temporally. And situations, besides having a symbolic structuring and a temporal dimension, also include a spatial location. They either persist or change, and have a limited range and a particular meaning.[9]

The situational construction of difference

In the *natural attitude* assumed in everyday action and speech, these three levels are not separate,[10] but blend into each other to the point of being indistinguishable. Names are not only signs for things of the world, but also characteristics of the things themselves. Changing a name, we also change the properties of the thing described. The manner of description selected only reinforces the publicly apparent. In the "natural attitude" of everyday action, no distinction is made between codes and the things to which they refer. The meaning of a symbolic sign initially arises in largely "indexical" fashion, meaning out of situational indications such as the parties present, what has come before, or what is. The course of communication is strongly influenced by the development of situation. People react to changes in situation, to new events. Those who have not participated, "who do not know the situation," have trouble following the discussion. To clarify, let us return to the analogy of a relation between map, journey, and landscape. In this case, of the natural attitude, of narrow coupling to situation, our traveler moves without an overarching plan, in a sense simply sauntering through the landscape. The traveler follows the impulses of situation as they arise, going first in this direction, then in that, and his or her idea of the landscape is entirely determined by the impressions so gathered. The traveler is not yet aware of employing any signs or codes in his or her experience of the landscape. Much as it is possible to speak flawlessly without being able to specify any rules of grammar, one can also classify one's opposite in interaction without being aware of the codes that are being applied. The world is experienced as simply out there, as the "obvious" sameness or difference of things. This blending of signs, speech acts, and the things of the world – of code, communications process, and situation – couples process narrowly to the situation within which it takes place. Action occurs without conscious consideration, as a spontaneous answer to situation, without any thoughts about available possibilities for taking different positions in the same situation. The flow of interaction is still narrowly bound to changes in situation. Only a change in the position of things, a new situation, can further the flow. Insofar as the operative situation does not change – as long as no new actors or unexpected events of the world requiring comment appear – then there is also no cause, from the perspective of narrow coupling, to continue communicating. (One nonetheless continues talking; see the next section.)

It is precisely this stability or variability of situation that is not at all a simple given in itself, but must be produced by the communicative process. In the *process* of speech, the world, chaotic in itself, must first be typified and normalized. Similarity and difference among the things of the world must first be generated through the practical application of codes, through action and negotiation. The truth is that the world becomes a situation to which "one can react spontaneously" only once it can be treated as "a case of," i.e. only after a process of constant repetition, mutual confirmation and assurance.[11] In everyday activity, this process of typological construction of similarity and difference is admittedly always kept latent. People act in the "natural attitude," as though the world exists without presuppositions.

All this also applies to attributions of collective identity. They occur according to codes and rules that must remain hidden from everyday activity. Otherwise the element that is supposed to serve as a secure starting point – identity – is questioned, and the interactive process goes into freefall. Although this manner of collapse is always possible, everyday activity persists precisely because it serves to keep crises latent. In the natural attitude codes – with which differences can be constructed and the social world classified – are not yet separate from the things of the world, and in the case of identity, that means they are still inseparable from the presence of a strange counterpart, of an interlocutor who is "other." The blending and narrow coupling of code, process, and situation is apparent in the way that the differences in the stranger appear as "obvious" and unquestionable: skin color, gender, and age are demonstrably not the result of practical construction, but immutable and objective properties of the opposite party. (Ethnomethodology and phenomenology have drawn attention to the construction processes of precisely these seemingly objective properties.) Every such difference, even the seemingly most objective, nevertheless contains an irreducible element of practical decision, and of contingent classification – again precisely the dimensions that must be kept hidden and latent. In everyday activity, the concealment occurs through suppression of the difference between sign and world. If otherness is seen as a property of the opposite party, i.e. effectively of the situation itself, then classification of "otherness" always remains linked to the actual presence of an "other." Only when "obvious" strangers and others appear in the situation is the question of difference even posed, with spontaneous reactions following according to the directly applicable code. In the "natural attitude," differences are thus construed as objective properties of situation.

Self-production of the collectivity

But social processes rarely stop at the mere construction of situation, at typologies of differences between the things of the world. Even after the completed construction of a situation – in fact precisely then, when the world can be presupposed as ordered – there develops an independent variation of the communication, at least for a certain period of time. This process is decoupled from situation, and no longer driven by the construction of situation, or by "objective" differences. This process no longer reacts to the "outside world,"[12] but proceeds from the past expressions of others. In contrast to the typological construction of a situation, a "decoupled" process does not work only through confirmation, but also through *negation,*[13] meaning through doubt, criticism, or questioning. One can create a difference, through such negations, from the person to whom one is responding – something to which that person can then link a further negation. In this manner, a drying-up of discussion, following the achievement of uniformity through confirmation and repetition, can be avoided. The process can thus continue, and displays its own, *temporally* ordered variations, even if the situation remains the same. But the reverse is also true: the process can remain the same even when the situation changes. This decoupling of process from situation can again be clarified through the image of the journey. As soon as a travel route superordinate to situation develops in the mind of the actor, as soon as the actor considers several possible travel routes and directs his or her movements within the concrete landscape toward a destination not bound to a particular situation, as soon as the actor can find "short cuts," the process of traveling begins to divorce itself from direct experience of landscape. It becomes possible to think about the journey without constantly keeping the concrete landscape in one's field of view.

A similar decoupling of situation from process can also occur in daily communication. Here too episodes may develop in which treatment of situation shifts to the background, in which the dynamic of discussion is decoupled from the movement of situation. Someone might remember something from the past, report on distant things, or consider hypothetical situations. This ability to distance oneself from the current situation, to alter one's attitude to situation, forms a decisive prerequisite for what we could call the beginnings of symbolic communication. It is the very stuff and basis of social reality's self-sufficiency from the natural world. It is the means for *decoupling* actional process from situational circumstance, without which processes of learning and evolution could never start.[14] Such decoupling is admittedly never complete. Memory of past experience, reports about distant things, and designs of the possible are all sooner or later interrupted by situation. They also require, for as long as they persist, an arrangement to restrain situation, to switch it off. Such restraint and indifference of situation is extraordinarily fragile, and never permanent. The "here" and "now" sooner or later break into all attempts to escape situation. If it were possible to completely disengage interactive process from situation, from local circumstance, so that it thenceforth only referred to itself (as theorists of autopoiesis seem to assume), then learning and experience would become impossible; the world would be lost from sight. Conversely, if the interaction process remained bound completely within local situation (as some ethnomethodologists seem to assume), then the reference of intentionality, or of a memory superordinate to situation, would be lost from sight. Trapped entirely within the limits of situation, the autonomy of social processes would be based only in blindness and self-deception. By contrast, the *decoupling* of situation from process allows an autonomous variation of communication. This also requires a situational and local frame, however, one that cannot be crossed by the communication process, and one in which processes may or may not "fit" well. The narrowness of this frame can vary greatly. The narrower it is, the more the variation of action process will be limited, and enclosed by situation. It is only through this opposition between variation in process and situational selection that learning and evolutionary change become possible.

To return to the process of identifying with a collectivity, it too can be decoupled from its direct situational cause, meaning *the presence of a stranger*. Even when no strange other is present, communication processes can tend toward the formation of collective identity, through mutual intensification and reinforcement. Here the issue is no longer construction of otherness – i.e. of differences between oneself and the interlocutor – but identification of the interlocutor as an equal, creation of equality and commonality. Here the focus is on mutual imitation, similarities are reinforced, differences are overlooked, communication is granted only under certain conditions, and discussion with deviants and strangers is kept limited. All of this does not occur at the command of a third party or as a planned procedure, but as a self-organizing process that remains latent; ethnomethodologists speak of *order producing activities*. Planning and heteronomy would destroy this latency, and furthermore conflict fatally with the conception of identity as the irreducible starting point of action, as its prerequisite, and not its result. The genesis of a collectivity must remain latent. By no means does that preclude specific, planned rituals for reinforcing and assuring such processes of creating uniformity in a collectivity. The decisive point is that the functioning of the rituals must be kept latent among the participants.

Out of the great variety of differences among individuals there thus arise, at first gradually and then ever more rapidly, similarities and uniformities; unity and identity from diversity and chaos. The actual, physical presence of otherness, meaning the defining situation in the processes by which collective identity organizes itself, begins to play ever less of a role in them as they go on. Otherness disappears behind a horizon of activity oriented entirely around interactive mutuality. In fact, otherness is even kept at a distance, through spatial or social exclusion. In contrast to the situational construction of otherness, which is set off by the interlocution of someone who is other, the *exclusion* of otherness from the process of identity construction poses a different question: how is it that border crossings are sanctioned, and/or controlled, in spite of (or is it because of?) the distance maintained between the collectivity and its outsiders? Regulating border crossings (such as initiation in a collectivity) is thus just as central to the construction of a social collectivity as symbolizing unity and uniformity. These border crossings – involving the acceptance of a new member, or expulsion of a member from the collectivity – are controlled by rituals. The difficult passage is held on exceptional occasions or particular days, in special or secluded spaces, in the presence of the community or its representatives. Once again decisive is that the actual presence of otherness must be barred from the ritual of inclusion or exclusion. Purification rituals, recantings, renamings, and exorcisms of demons are intended to effect an exclusion of otherness, protect the collectivity's homogeneity against the corrupting influences of the outside world. Special situational arrangements are nonetheless required to facilitate the decoupling of ritual collective self-production from the outside world. Any analysis of a collectivity's ritual self-production must take these situational preconditions, of isolation and intensification, into account.

Reflexion on collective identity

Even after the communication process driven by negation has been decoupled from situation – in the case of collective identity, meaning from the presence of otherness – the levels of code and of process remain closely linked to each other. A variation of code, independent from process, has not yet entered the picture. Such a decoupling of code from process, or of language from speech acts, is nonetheless entirely conceivable. Codes or languages always contain more possibilities than can ever be actualized through spoken action. Returning again to our metaphor of the journey, a decoupling of code from process would mean that aside from concrete traveling plans and specific travel experiences, our traveler also has resort to *maps:* abstractions away from specific journeys, capable of being used for a large number of possible journeys. Once available, maps can furthermore be improved and varied, and their correction or revision does not always require a new journey. The logic governing mapped depictions tends to reveal mistaken information and make new travel routes visible. Such a separation of map from journey – or more generally, the decoupling of code from process – allows low-energy creation of various symbolic codes, *and* does so without requiring a direct implementation of new code elements into corresponding actions. By contrast, when there is close coupling of code to process, action processes bind and limit potential variations on symbolic encoding. Individual and collective interests, and dynamics of conflict and cooperation, set narrow limits on the free and unbound construction of new codes. In that case there are only travel plans, recommendations and reports, but no full-fledged maps. Knowledge and interpretations of the world then still retain strongly particular, ideological, or dogmatic features, and their ability to build bridges over social borders and collective differences is limited. New knowledge is necessarily viewed with suspicion and mistrust, for it could channel the flow of communication in a new direction, and erase the clearly drawn borders between social groups. Magic and totemic encodings of the world, much like religious dogmas and party ideologies, are examples of such close couplings of code to process. Furthermore, narrow coupling does not just mean that variations in code are limited by process, but also that a new code variant, should it actually come into existence, must be implemented into fact without delay.

Extraordinary developments in communication situations can advance the decoupling of code from process. The elimination of a direct and present interlocutor, to whom communication is personally directed, plays a decisive role. This kind of elimination of the interlocutor is required above all when writing and reading texts (see also p. 46).[15] With text, communicative action is no longer directed at classifying an object in a situation, or at creating sameness to a personally present interlocutor, but addresses all possible interlocutors (within a particular frame), and all possible objects of the world. Once the personally present interlocutor is eliminated, and if the situation can also be ignored, the speaker enters into a reflexive dialogue in which personal and particular matters lose significance. In this solitary dialogue with oneself, or at any rate with a faceless and anonymous other, mere negation can no longer place restraints on process, while actually present things – the situation – also offer no cause for discussion.

Such conditions favor a new form of process, in which the difference between code and situation, between language and things in themselves, becomes visible – whereby encoding is recognized as contingent, and the connection between sign and signified as fragile at best. Then codes are viewed as variables, and thus become issues in themselves; and in the place of the "natural attitude" of everyday activity, there arises *the critical perspective*. We call this particular form of monologue *reflexion* or *reflexivity*. Reflexion about codes cannot operate without presupposing the existence of (other) codes, however. In reflexion, codes are applied to codes. Codes are expanded, supplemented, and systematically ordered. Independent and additional variations are produced, in a span of time during which situation and process are, in a sense, switched off. This is the case when monks devote themselves to the interpretation of a holy manuscript, or scientists translate their observations into theories, or writers muse about literary ideals, or law scholars reorder and review laws according to new criteria. In these cases it is not the situation that is being constructed, or the proposition of the interlocutor that is being negated; instead, codes are reflected upon in a *monologue*. The person of the actor and his or her opposite, the particular history of the interaction, the local circumstances – all withdraw behind a diffuse and anonymous form of address. One speaks without temporal or spatial limitation, and addresses all subjects endowed with reason. Monologic reflexion tends to be *universalist*, and only allows *symbolic* creations of order. In monologic reflexion, gestures of indication and turn-taking rules are supplanted by new and peculiar rules of association – logic, theory, method, in short: metacodes. These open up new associative possibilities to universalist reflexion. Contradictions can be solved, conclusions drawn, presuppositions revealed, generalizations made, differentiations extended.[16]

The decoupling of code from process does not just open up possibilities for an autonomous variation of the symbolic plane, however, but also allows an easier transposition and reproduction of codes. Codes arising from universalist reflexion have in effect dissolved their links to particular processes or special circumstances, and can easily be applied – in a free-floating manner – to all possible conditions or events. They claim relevance to everything; their range is barely limited by anything.

Turning again to the problem of collective identity, analogous scenarios are also conceivable there, in which reflexion about code is released from both the process of mutual identification, and the situation of an immanent otherness. This manner of independent reflexion about collective identity has as its goal the reinforcement of the substantiations for communality – that is, it obtains once communality no longer arises self-evidently from the encounter with otherness, or from communication among equals. Deeper and more lasting foundations, autonomous and beyond local impulses or specific action by a community, are therefore sought. Identity, no longer self-evidently arising from situation and social process, is reinforced instead through an expansion of the symbolic code, a metalevel of encoding.[17] Thus theology compensates for the erosion of practical religiosity; a national metaphysics makes up for the decay of regional ties; and the philosophy of gender difference for the social leveling of that distinction. Such reflexions on creed, nation, and constitution, or gender, attempt to forge the difficult connection between the particularism of a collective identity and the universalism of reflexion. In this way even those who are no longer so sure of their faith – or who no longer experience the encounter with the unknown as disconcerting, or for whom the experience of the other gender loses its sharp contours – are supposed to be convinced, through *general* reasons, of the importance of *particular* boundaries. As will be shown in the next section, this can be accomplished with "universalist" codes far more easily than with "primordial" ones, but fails altogether with "traditional" codes. Universal codes, strengthened through universalist substantiations, can be pressed in the service of missionary expansion. Primordial codes can also achieve this universalist level, through a process of "naturalization": the particularity of a collective identity is given its basis in "nature," which after all also assigns a place and an identity to those excluded from the identity. By contrast, traditional codes lose their particular logic once it becomes explicit, and is substantiated as a planned procedure. In that process, they tend to be "universalized" (see p. 33).

For all that it must be kept in mind, however, that reflexion about codes of collective identity is only made possible and propelled by particular situational framework conditions. Constructivist analysis sets out to discern precisely those situational conditions, which are suppressed or switched off during reflexion. The portrayal, in the next three sections, of the logics governing three codes of collective identity presupposes a connection between the distinction "We"/"Others" and the "original distinctions" described above (p. 14).[18] This connection will be examined below, with respect to its role in the construction of differences and boundaries, and in the identification of a collectivity; and with respect to its reflexive form of collective identity. Finally, the three logics by which codes of collective identity can operate, as described in the following three sections, should be understood as ideal types. Concrete historical encodings of collective identity usually blend together elements taken from several ideal-type codes, in regard to which, however, it should be noted that as a rule, only one type dominates.

Primordial codes

If collective identity is based and constructed as gender and descent, kinship and region, ethnicity and race, then the constitutive distinction of the code is related to primordial differences, like man and woman, or parents and children. *Primordial codes* refer to properties which are exempted from communication and exchange. They are tied to the factual order of things which seem to be unalterable by voluntary action, but have to be considered as given. The occidental concept for this realm of the world is "nature."

Encountering others

In situations of direct encounter with others, primordial codes direct our behavior in a way similar to how the rules of language pattern our speech acts: depending on the color of the skin, or gender and age, a person is assigned his or her location within a network of signs, without taking account of or reflecting about the rules of assignment, or even knowing them at all. The *alter* is classified according to seemingly "self-evident" and "obvious" properties, and by this very objectification the process of typification and construction can be kept latent. But this natural classification also results from social processes of construction. Whenever codes are applied to the unstructured world, practical decisions have to be made – and these decisions could also be assessed in a different way; uncertainty, arbitrariness and contingency have to be kept latent and undiscovered by the actors. In carrying forth this everyday classification of the other, we face differences of familiarity: some objects are similar to us or at least can be considered to become similar under certain circumstances, while others are experienced as unvaryingly strange and different from us, as puzzling or difficult to understand. This strangeness or otherness which we cannot assimilate has a disquieting and threatening appearance, it excites and fascinates. Narratives and symbolic representations present primordial otherness as hostile, strange, barbaric or exotic, and juxtapose it to the demonic and the creatural. The uncertainty released by otherness is an uncertainty of classification: the other is neither an object, nor a subject similar to us, or susceptible to our understanding. Otherness stimulates, provokes and endangers; it has an almost erotic attraction and hints thereby at its origin in the fundamental distinction between man and woman.[19] This alluring and endangering otherness cannot be assimilated and connected, or adapted and educated; the others are not guilty of having opted for the wrong direction; they cannot be developed and included, they cannot even be understood; they are merely and unalterably different, and this difference conveys excitement and danger at the same time.

Primordial communities

When the demarcation between the familiar and the unfamiliar is blurred and loses its inclusiveness, and when the boundaries are disputed and the others conceal their nature, then particular occasions, localities and modes of communication are required in order to disclose the core of the community, to indicate and emphasize membership in primordial communities, and to produce and reinforce the unity of the collectivity.[20] This is the case for example when differences between nations cannot be assessed unequivocally, but have to be marked as being particularly important among other memberships. A special home dialect therefore is not merely spoken, but cultivated on particular occasions, much like regional or national dress and costume are kept alive by special efforts and presented on special occasions. Flags and colors, feasts and celebrations can be used to support and strengthen primordial communities: here, the process is not so much one of demarcation of differences as one of *ritual construction of unity*; it is less a matter of classification than of uniformity: everybody sports the same colors, costumes and flags, sings the same anthems and speaks the same solemn words. Even more important for primordial communities are rituals of purification, by which the traces of the polluted outside world in the members of the community are extinguished: rituals of silence and isolation "purify" the members and ensure the homogeneity of the community. After purification, the participants identify each other as alikes and thereby produce the collectivity. Strangers and outsiders are strictly excluded, they disturb the presentation of uniformity and identity, they could question the unity or challenge the boundary. Therefore it is better to keep them at a distance. *Spatial distance* guarantees the external boundaries and the internal unity. The community has to be kept "pure" and the soil of the homeland is not to be touched by strangers. Here, boundaries are still constructed in the original sense of the term: as the demarcation of a territory and as the isolation of an internal space against intruding enemies. This very mode of keeping a distance also hints at the fact that the boundaries are not natural barriers which could dispense with social reinforcements.[21]

However, although every participant is well aware of the fact that these boundary constructions emphasize the obvious in a special, additional, and not self-evident way, the justification of the unity cannot yet be challenged, and the explication of the criteria of membership cannot be asked for. Happy to be united under a symbol, nobody wants to risk this unity through doubting.

Primordial boundaries cannot be moved socially, and passing them is extremely difficult. Every passage of a boundary blurs the distinctions and calls the boundary into question. Sometimes, however, such a *passage* cannot be avoided, be it in order to expel members in case of internal crises, be it in order to gain new members from outside. However, even in primordial communities these unavoidable passages are never achieved only by biological processes like birth and death, generation and killing; instead, elaborated *social rituals* control these passings of the boundary: baptism and funeral, marriage and consecration, conversion and expulsion.[22] These rituals do not ignore the boundaries, or leave them to natural processes; instead they construct and confirm the boundaries in a *social* way; thus, primordiality emerges not from natural givenness, but is constituted by a fragile social construction, which is contingent on social actions and has to be confirmed by and grounded in these actions. This can be illustrated by the constitution of *corporation*. Here a seemingly changeable boundary is contained with elaborated procedures of constructing an institutional distance to the impact of societal structures: membership in a status group is dependent on birth and descent, but the ranking structure of these collectivities is constituted by the principles of societal hierarchy.

Naturalization

When the territorial and ritual distance to outsiders is increasingly dissolved, when encounters with strangers cannot be avoided any more and belong to common everyday experience, when communities request exclusive commitments from an individual, or when social and regional mobility demands a change in orientation, then collectivities too lose their once clearly demarcated contours.[23] Society appears to be dissolved into a multitude of individuals, who try to determine their identity by themselves, and become members of *organizations* by their own voluntary decision. However, modern organizations with varying members and shifting attachments render the emergence of collective identity difficult. If collective identity is furthermore to provide a stable frame of reference which is exempted from the change and flux of modern social relations, then primordialities are required. But criteria need to be elaborated, types must be standardized, and the unity in question has to be grounded in deep foundations, if the contingency of construction is not to be laid bare and open in the "confusion" of modern discourse. This problem of latency is solved by special and additional *symbolic constructions* put forward by intellectual specialists. They range from poets collecting and inventing tales and myths of origin, to philosophers explicating national identity, to biologists defining the anatomical standards of races. Primordial codes, which control everyday behavior in an unconscious way, can only be confirmed and pushed forward by collective rituals, but they can also become the subject of particular reflexions. In contrast to spatial constructions of distance, the boundary construction is here achieved only by a *symbolic* order, by particular loops of reflexion and the metaphysical formulation of differences.

This symbolic construction of primordial identity may be called *naturalization*.[24] By naturalization identity is linked to biological attributes like gender, descent or race. The existence of such differences and boundaries can neither be denied nor altered: they are beyond the range of practical action and deeper than societal change. The foundation of community being non-social, the constitutive property cannot be imitated, changed or achieved; even communication will not provide access to it. Understanding is finally impossible. You have it or you don't have it, an external access remains impossible, and every general attempt to define identity in a discursive way is bound to failure. Every effort to educate and instruct outsiders will fail, because they simply lack the natural capability of understanding. The particular mode of constructing primordial properties prevents any attempt to copy them. (In this way the aristocracy of the eighteenth century could mock at the bourgeois' efforts to imitate noble behavior. Even if the bourgeois' imitations of aristocratic life-style were carried out to perfection, they could never hide their "superficial" pretension.) These socially constructed barriers to imitation grant a special importance to primordial codes in modern societies; in a world of change, fluidification and mobility, they define seemingly immovable boundaries.

Quite unlike the everyday construction of borders or production of a collectivity, the *intellectual* substantiation of a collectivity through "naturalization" is a relatively recent development, with many historical prerequisites. As the product of explicit reflexion, naturalization can only succeed if nature can be posed as a realm of immutable structures and objective, eternal natural laws, in opposition to the realm of willed activity, reason, and history. The so-called primitive mind's analogue encoding of the world also posited the construction of the same order in culture as in nature, but this was not yet a special intellectual reflexion. In fact, the "savage mind" could do little else than regard nature and culture as identically structured, separate areas. By contrast naturalization, as an intellectual fortification of primordial identities, is dependent upon the specific modern distinction between nature and history, a distinction that frees the field of history and society for the progress and change that could, for example, be pursued by the idea of a nation.

A further problem thus arises. Naturalization, intended to do away with any doubts about the security and irreducibility of primordial borders, simultaneously points out the contradiction between history's disquiet and confusion and nature's supposedly immutable order. This gives rise to a *redemption motif* for historical action: when history finally adapts to nature, then the natural communities concealed – shaken, and denied over the course of history – will finally be returned to their self-evident right. Only when society is finally brought back to its communal foundation, its "natural home," will the miseries and alienations of socialization be healed and overcome. Only then will history reach peace and be reconciled with nature. Since the nineteenth century, the idea of natural community has thus become the guiding principle of political action in various shadings, as *Volk* or nation, as family, or as an idea of ecological community at peace with nature.

Traditional codes

In contrast to primordial codes, a second type of encoding relates the constitutive distinction between us and them to the difference between the *routine* and the *extraordinary*. Here the inside is considered as the realm of familiarity and stability whereas the outside is associated with unexpected variation. The boundaries of the community are defined by traditions and routines that are taken for granted. This code of constructing collective identity by assuming and defending a particular continuity between past, present and future may be called traditional. *Traditional codes* do not consider collective identity to mirror an external reference, e.g. nature or the sacred; instead the internal routines of everyday action, the particular rules of a local lifeworld and local traditions and arrangements, are regarded as the core of collective identity. Other collectivities may have other identities, and other codes are entirely conceivable and legitimate. But right here and now, this particular criterion of membership applies for this particular group. Therefore traditional codes are linked to a particular locality and differences between local sites are the core matrix of traditional constructions of collective identity.[25]

Local lifeworlds

First of all, these routines and rules cannot be separated from the praxis of activity and participation in day-to-day life. Every attempt to call them into question, to ask for instructions about proper behavior, or even just to justify them and mark the boundary, indicates the outsider. The insider is simply familiar with the *rules of a lifeworld*, even if he or she is only seldom able to call them by name, or explain them. Because the validity of these rules of a lifeworld is nowhere explicitly challenged, they cannot be questioned or criticized. Thus the core of the community is kept away from argumentation and intentional change. The rules are followed because they are the rules, and every doubt challenges the boundaries of collective identity, even risks confusion and crisis. Whoever starts a conversation without some kind of greeting will face rejection, whoever changes the rules of language will risk misunderstanding, whoever disrespects the local traditions will be treated as a stranger.

On the level of everyday acting, these implicit rules are reproduced by continuous repetition. Speaking a language reproduces its rules, and everyday interaction reproduces the rules of the lifeworld: imitation, repetition, reinforcement and confirmation are the mechanisms producing the order of everyday life.

The outsider in this case is a *stranger*, who is simply seen as other and "unusual," without assignment of charismatic or demonic properties.[26] The stranger is neither seductive nor threatening, nor in need of education or help. The group accepts this otherness with indifference, but also desires to be left undisturbed. Because the stranger's actions are difficult to understand and his behavior is unpredictable, the logic of interaction itself demands a certain caution and distance, clearly differing from the loose and relaxed behavior allowed with acquaintances. Should proximity to the stranger become unavoidable, his or her behavior is carefully monitored, and attempts are made to figure out his intentions.

Commemorative rituals

With attempts to understand strangers or to repair misunderstandings, it occurs that rules which were up to then implicit occasionally become the object of interaction, or the basis of agreement. This can lead to special procedures and occasions for reiterating and reinforcing the rules in an explicit way: parliamentary sessions are formally opened, anniversaries commemorated, calendary events are celebrated, etc. In all these cases, the participants are well aware of the existence of special rules which have to be observed on this particular occasion in order to maintain the meaning of this interaction; violation of rules can be observed, challenged and debated. The correct observance of the rules is frequently controlled by a respected person, a master of ceremonies or referee. Although different rules are conceivable and do indeed apply at other places and on other occasions, the validity of the rules is not questioned in a given case. The game need not be football; other rules can be invented for a ballgame. But the rules of a football game are never subjected to criticism from the players during the game. Anyone who criticizes them, or demands additional justifications, will only summon incomprehension among the football players. The doubter assumes a position outside the group's borders. Distance and boundaries are here constructed by the rule not to discuss the rules. These *ritual rules* do not require additional reasons; their continuing existence is reason enough.

Temporal continuity being the central mode of reproduction in these communities, the celebration of traditions and commemoration of past events becomes the core issue for rituals. At special places and on special dates, the tradition of the community is constructed and reconstructed by elaborated rituals, by public celebrations as well as by private parties. Commemorative rituals represent the past of the community, founding myths recall the beginning of its history, special commensural rituals unite the members, and special classicist forms show its continuity on the level of aesthetics.

In contrast to these rituals of commemoration, the inclusion of new members mostly happens without special rituals of initiation or confession to indicate the passage of the boundary. Instead of a clearly demarcated boundary, there is only a diffuse and undefined frontier. The only chance to be accepted as a member of traditional community and to partake in its collective identity is to participate in the local practices, and slowly adapt to local customs and routines. Time, patience, and a certain level of caution to avoid anything extraordinary are indispensable to this endeavor.[27] Breaking the rules, or challenging the existing practice in the name of universal reason, are as incompatible with this code as is missionary expansion. Considering the implicitness of most of the rules and routines, any special instruction and education will ultimately fail. Traditional codes of collective identity usually maintain the boundary by not mentioning it.

But even if the rules are well known and available in a written form, they do not invite adoption and strict respect. On the contrary: in order to keep outsiders at a distance and establish social barriers, the rules are complicated, and combined with special additional routines and usages, which are nowhere mentioned. Knowledge of these additional rules is what displays true belonging.

Traditionalization

Occasionally even these rules are challenged by doubts and criticism. Defenders of the tradition sometimes address these situations as crisis and revolution; the community in question seems to fall apart into its components, and collective identity seems to dissolve into a multitude of individuals.

Such challenge to collective identity tends to provoke particular intellectual efforts in order to support the endangered routines by assigning to them additional values and to keep traditions alive by pointing to general ideas. Subsidies are asked for, morale is appealed to, the tradition is transformed into a constitution, the constitution is revered by special civic rituals and praised by local poets, outsiders are invited to participate by citing all sorts of arguments. If routines thus need reflexive argumentation, if pedagogical efforts are required and rules are simplified in order to facilitate their acceptance, then the traditional code has lost its self-assured vitality. It is the very effort to stop the decay of traditional communities which sometimes causes their decay: lifeworlds can hardly be inspired and revitalized by blueprints and plans.

By contrast, truly traditional codes of collective identity are structurally self-sufficient. There is no invitation to participate, no claim to universal validity. The individual conviction of the participants is concealed, as is the overarching substantiation. Local traditions substantiate collective identity through competent participation and nothing more. But whoever wants to participate must heed the rules.

With the gradual dissolution of local lifeworlds in the course of modernization, the self-evident basis of traditional codes also fades away. It is replaced by explicit efforts to revive traditions, to proclaim a classical heritage, to revere the remnants of the past, to invent past history. Museums and archives are established, specialized disciplines take over the administration of the past, and particular places of memory attract the pious attention of the collectivity. Thus traditionalization compensates for the drying out of local lifeworlds and the modern orientation towards the future. Institutional constructions of traditions and the fading away of local memory are both part of the same process of modernization.

The core of this process of modernization is, however, carried by new rules: money and power, the modern media of interaction. Media-directed interaction has very similar effects to ritualized convention. Both establish a comparability of action through abstraction, live only from the process itself, are not exclusive in inviting participation, and bind membership to nothing more than competent participation. However, as meaningful as media of interaction may be for the constitution of modern social relations, they are hardly suited to the construction of stable borders for collectivities. On the contrary, they fray those borders, keep them constantly in motion, and are systematically blind to the personal characteristics of the participant. Thanks to modern media of interaction, the circle of participants opens up; but this does not yet allow reflexion about conventions. If social life is entirely shifted to abstract interaction media like money and power, then the problem of collective identity rapidly evaporates in the process of market and politics, or seeks old and seemingly obsolete solutions: it becomes predictable that primordial qualities like gender and lineage receive renewed attention.

Universalist codes

A third type of code differs from traditional codes in that the constitutive difference between us and them is not bound to self-evident, practical routines, but involves instead a specific relationship to the sacred.[28] At stake here is not so much the simple classification of an other or creation of sameness, homogeneity, and collectivity, but the interpretation of an invisible and inaccessible world – a stand on all the possibilities and uncertainties that the world contains. The distinction between the sacred and the demonic locates an "interpretative axis" within this invisible area, and proves useful indeed to the construction of social collectives. Such *universalist codes* construct borders by connecting to the immutable and eternal realm of the sacred and the sublime – quite apart from whether this is defined as God or Reason, progress or rationality.

Emblems

In the beginning, such connection to the supernatural, sacred, and sublime is the self-evident secret of those who possess it. Invisible, it therefore requires specific, if rarely conspicuous, everyday symbolizations, so as to indicate membership to other adherents. Allowing the detection of a universalist culture's difference in daily life cannot be accomplished through the kind of obvious properties that are employed in primordial or traditional encodings. The sacred is simply not something present in everyday routine. It is a nontemporal and extraordinary authority that cannot be encountered without great strain. The sacred is an invisible world, at first the secret custody of the adepts, and participation is prohibited to outsiders. Nevertheless, some means must be chosen to display membership in the community, to show that one shares in the secret of the sacred. Allegiance to a universal community is displayed to the knowing and the benighted alike by wearing *emblems* of community – coats of arms, articles of clothing, hairstyles, other accessories. Modes of behavior, turns of speech, and nutritional habits all also function as visible emblems: one shows one's knowledge of the secret, and displays communal membership to strangers, but without giving the sacred itself away. Emblems symbolize the borders of universal community in everyday life, but do not automatically invite border crossings. By the very emblematic demarcation of community, outsiders become strangers in fact, and it is only with respect to these excluded but present others that the display of emblematic signs makes sense.

Missionary expansion and stratification

In secluded places and on special occasions, however, the secret connection to the sublime is directly laid bare and communicated among insiders. The sacred words are solemnly repeated by all, the holy writings are read aloud, and the images of the sacred are revealed. By the common reverence of the sacred, by the simultaneous ritual repetition of prescribed texts and anthems, the members recognize their sameness: the cultural unity is collectively constructed and reconstructed. These particular ritual gatherings are the more important as cultural differences are not clearly exhibited in everyday life; the fact that the ties to the sacred are not based on natural order, but dependent on the uncertainties of revelation, or of a personal conviction, requires a compensatory protection of the secret. Spatial seclusion in temples and cloisters, and temporal particularities like holidays or special hours, are supposed to create the distance, emphasize what is extraordinary in the sacred. An important occasion for gatherings of initiates is offered by rites of initiation to the secret for new members of the universalist community. The border crossing, the conversion, may only be embarked upon with substantial ceremonial effort, under supervision of community members, and with outsiders strictly excluded. Such ritual conversions first demand the recantation of the old, mistaken faith, a purification from past errors, and the newcomer's explicit profession of allegiance to the community's faith. Another important ritual of universalist communities focuses on the critical connection between the particular community and the realm of the sacred. Rituals of sacrifice are meant to show that the commitment of insiders to the sacred cause is not mere lip-service. These sacrifices have to be absurd from the mundane point of view: the more they are useless and non-functional, the stronger the bond to the sacred which they establish. The rituals are carried out as temporally marked, solemn events, open foremost to true believers and the core of community members. Sometimes the universalist culture's secret is thus kept at first within the borders of kinship and personal acquaintance.

But here too, growth of the community and the encounter with otherness can result in a confusing situation. Communality and trust are then less and less able to depend on personal acquaintance. At times it becomes necessary to open the border, to take in those to whom one is not yet bound through acquaintance or kinship. A different strategy, in monotheistic religions, might involve intolerance and the great God's command to conquer: "You shall have no other gods before me." "Fill the earth and subdue it." Such *expansions* of universalist cultural communities change the logic of universal encoding in far-reaching fashion. Expansion opens borders to the practice of conquest, mission, and pedagogy. The codes are reoriented to substantiate collective identity as all-encompassing, as responsible for everything. Doubts about the fragility and particularity of the drawn borders can thus be eliminated, kept latent. Insecurities about a specific border are converted into demands for expanding the borders and turning the still-limited and particular identity of today into the all-encompassing collectivity of tomorrow. This universalist reorientation is normally carried by *intellectual specialists* who systematize, substantiate, design, and make it communicable; and who administrate the communication of the doctrines they have designed to outsiders, who oversee the instruction and conversion of otherness. In the hands of intellectuals, the invisible secret is turned into fixed writings.

The missionary zeal of universally constructed communities does not just open the borders to include outsiders, but insists on overcoming all borders and differences. Those who resist the universalist mission are not only different and inferior, but also misled and *mistaken*.[29] Unaware of their own true identity, they must if necessary be converted *against* their wills. Outsiders are viewed here as empty "natural" objects that first achieve identity and subjectivity through the appropriate cultural education. The construction of the border is accomplished much less through spatial distancing than through devaluation by the look from above. Outsiders are inferior, must be conquered and converted. In the "great chain of being," they are somewhere between humans and animals. In any first dealings with them, the question might legitimately arise as to whether they are saleable goods or baptizable souls. And even after their subjugation is moderated by a bit of civilization, and they are allowed entry to society through proselytization and pedagogy, the center's devaluation of the periphery continues.

Clearly, the image of the other is blurred in the process. Quite unlike a description through primordial codes, here the alien outsider remains remarkably faceless. The other has nothing that threatens, that causes flight or necessitates a declaration of war. In this sense, the missionary expansion of universalist communities occurs as though running into an empty space, and only stops when all have become equals.

The universalist opening and missionary expansion create new risks in the problem of latency. Collective identity is based on the construction of cultural borders, but in principle anyone is capable, and called upon, to overcome his or her inferiority and backwardness through conversion to the right faith, through assumption of the superior culture. Anyone is capable of crossing the border.

But when the broad cover of a universalist cultural identity offers a place to everyone, the drawing of borders itself tends to be endangered. Universalism and pedagogy open up the borders between nature and culture, savages and saints, superstition and reason. The very fact that cultural attributes can easily be reproduced and communicated provokes special barriers to communication and special taboos protecting the sacred from profanization. The most important institutional mechanism to protect the sacred center is *cultural stratification*. Here, the universalistic openness of the boundaries is compensated by a stratified and layered access to the center. Boundaries are thereby leveled and multiplied at the same time. Complex rituals of initiation and education, the burdens and toils of learning and instruction, have to be accepted in order to approach the center of a universalist community; only the select few, the virtuosi who have endured all hardships and have devoted themselves entirely and without reservation to the service of the sacred and sublime, are finally allowed to enter the central core, and to see the secrets of the sacred revealed. An *internal* boundary is established between the virtuosi who are trusted with the secrets of the sacred core and are its gatekeepers, and the uneducated lay persons at the periphery. The expansive movement on the periphery is thus counteracted by a defensive "blockade" of the center, and the combination of both movements can engender a complicated stratification and ranking structure of the universal community.

The invention of the novel

As soon as the expansive movement of the cultural mission prevails against the defensive and conservative tendencies of stratification, then the secret of the center is communicated by education and instruction up to the periphery. Stratification itself does not suffice to break the inclusive movement of cultural communities and to stabilize the constitutive tension between the sacred center and the profane outside. In this case, the position of the center is sometimes supported by a new pattern: mediated and constructed by the virtuosi, ever-*new* interpretations and imaginations of the sacred are invented and elaborated in the center.[30]

The center then becomes the *source of innovation*; these innovations arrive in attenuated movements from the center to the periphery, only to become trivialized and to be finally replaced by a new idea of the sacred, which again is generated in the center. Thus the tension between the sacred center and the profane periphery is temporalized, and transformed into a lag between the avant-garde in the center and the backward masses of the periphery. A pulsating and alternating rhythm of innovation and trivialization arises which – in combination with the conflicts between several expanding centers – determines the dynamics of stratified societies.

The pressure for innovation also gives rise to surprising new perspectives on the sacred for the guardians of the sacred. The sacred is detraditionalized, and becomes the subject of autonomous discourses which focus on variation and consistency, and contrast the mundane order of this world to the eternal, otherworldly order of the sacred. The opposition between this world and the world beyond, between the sacred and the profane, is now conceived as a matter of divergent principles and *methods of reflexion*, and not viewed as an antagonism between persons or a rivalry of norms: inside

Table 1 *Type categorization of communications processes according to code and situation*

Code / Situation	Primordial	Traditional	Universal
Face to face with a stranger	Natural classification	Classification according to life-worldly familiarity	Classification according to cultural emblems
Face to face among equals	Self-reproduction of primordial communities through purification commandments and rituals	Self-production of community though inclusion in rituals	Self-production of community through proselytization and pedagogy
Mediated communication with an invisible audience	Naturalizing reflexions	Reflexion on "constitution"	Invention of the novel through reflexion on identity

the walls of the monastery, a new interest in theory is born, which finally reflects even on its own cultural movement, the invention of the novel, and the progress of knowledge with respect to a universal ideal of reason. In the end, the philosophy of history arises as the reflexion of a missionary movement, giving rise to an explanatory motif of the Enlightenment that proved very difficult for Modernity to escape.

Sociostructural networks and collective identity

Primordial, traditional, and universal codes describe various possible patterns in the construction of collective identity. Depending upon whether it is employed in the "natural attitude," on special social occasions, or in critical reflexion, the same pattern might facilitate differing constructions of collective identity. In the preceding sections, we (implicitly) examined nine types of encoding that may arise (see table 1 for an overview).

At several points so far it has been obvious that the power of these codes to confer meaning is embedded within particular situational conditions, within which a specific encoding can prove more or less adequate. Simple lifeworldly rules, for example, no longer allow satisfying constructions of boundaries once the encounter with strange interlocutors becomes a daily experience. Rules can come under substantiation pressures if new groups feel excluded from participation. Such ambiguous and new situations, in which new and expanded interactive relations demand acknowledgment, exert pressure both for shifting the borders and for fortifying them, or at least defining them more precisely. New groups must be taken into the community. As its consequence expansion demands an emphasis of the barrier against those who remain excluded, or are to be excluded. The most important situational condition for the construction of collective identity is thus the dynamic of social networks drawn up through other codes – money, law, creed, or political power – codes in turn dependent upon the functioning of communication paths and the level of technology.[31] Only in borderline cases are such social networks isolated or mutually exclusive units. As a rule, several networks exist simultaneously, at least partially overlapping. For example persons who are bound together by the money code are to some extent also linked through a network of political power, or of common religious practice. Inside the networks, the exact combinations between single positions vary according to the frequency or duration of interactive contact, or the similarity or dissimilarity among the partners interacting. Equality and inequality, frequency and duration, and unified or multiple encodings of interaction serve to help in setting up a large variety of networks, to which codes of collective identity may react in more than or less than appropriate fashion. Of central importance here are those areas where networks thin out because of low interaction density, dissimilarity, or the lack of superordinate codes. Here borders of collective identity can obviously be constructed more easily than in dense areas, where drawing borders slows and blocks the flow of social interaction. Of course, even at the frayed edges of interaction networks there are still isolated relations that cross borders, and therefore subject them to doubt: luxury goods and slaves were also traded beyond the borders of the traditional empires; administration and taxation bridged over the deep gaps between castes and ranks; religious affiliations spread over and beyond the borders of states and ethnic boundaries, etc. To a certain extent, the encoding of collective identity will thus always be inappropriate and arbitrary. But there are differences in arbitrariness, and these are decisive.

The following considerations concern the special position of intellectuals, and their forms of communication. Although these are expressed in a general fashion, it cannot be overlooked that we are considering *occidental* history, and in particular the situation of intellectuals in the modern age. This manner of narrowing the focus in a developmental history is justified because the historical process treated in the main part of the book involves the rise of the national identity of the Germans; but it also has its more systemic reasons. Although other great civilizations also brought forth significant groups of intellectuals, intellectuals occupy a unique position within the European tradition, as a critical "reflexion elite" in highly tense opposition to the political elite.

Intellectuals and politicians

Since the construction of collective identity always needs to overlook the fact of diversity and difference, it occurs self-evidently and spontaneously only in borderline cases. Otherwise exceptional efforts, procedures, and substantiations are required to suppress the arbitrariness of the code, to overcome doubt. This work of persuasion and substantiation succeeds more readily if obvious diversity and undeniable border crossings can be portrayed as *superficial,* in contrast to the *essential*, hidden identity of the collectivity; if the confusion of the visibly apparent is contrasted to the certainty of deeper knowledge; if the order of the actual and essential is shown to follow principles other than the rapid shifting of appearances. The distinction among two levels of reality – a fundamental and invisible order, as opposed to apparent and direct experience – signifies a far-reaching transposition of the axis of the world.[32] One no longer distinguishes between the familiar "inner area" and the unsettling, strange and demonic "outer area" – a place built curiously like our familiar world, and separated from it only by diffuse spatial and social boundaries. Instead, the boundaries are transposed *into society itself*, which then *simultaneously* represents both: the deep, eternal, and invisible order as well as superficial and rapid change. Horizontally arranged *areas* thus become "vertically" arranged *levels* of reality, no longer separated and distinguished by a spatial border, but defined by their fundamentally divergent forms of order. This "transposition of the world's axis" gives rise to a need for new forms of demarcating, substantiating, or bridging the fundamental boundaries. Whereas the crossing of boundaries between the familiar home area and the demonic, unknown, outside was still an act of courage and conquest that found highest expression in hero and *warrior* cults, the discovery of the two different levels of reality becomes the concern of intellectuals who know how to interpret (or design: *auslegen*) the secret. As R. Michels argued, intellectuals are "people whose judgment [is achieved] less directly, or not merely, from sensual perception, and in any case never entirely lacks a learned reflexion gained from knowledge."[33] Mannheim sees the task of the intellectuals in the interpretation of the world; Lipset views them as those who create and spread the symbolic world; Shils understands them as the administrators of the sacred, alienated from worldly things.[34] The "sacred" remains hidden and withdrawn from everyday activity. In contrast to the obvious and directly accessible, intellectuals construct the otherworldly, whose principles of order can only be comprehended through exceptional effort and special training. A simple transference of the order of the known onto the unknown misses entirely what is exceptional and peculiar about the otherworldly order. In fact, the invisible can come into conflict and tension with the visible world; and as Weber showed, there are various different ways of resolving that tension.[35]

Intellectuals do not merely command the key to the otherworldly, to the "sacred," to the source of identity. They also attempt to acquire a *monopoly* in the resolution of all such tensions.[36] Such interpretative monopolies are precarious and require safeguarding. For one thing, new designs of the order of the world can never be prevented, at least not *within* the walls of the monastery. Indeed, intellectual discourse necessarily forces variations of its own themes. On the other hand, competition and alternatives do more damage to interpretations of the world than to any other good. In contrast to material goods, which do not lose their use-value even when alternatives arise, the value of an interpretation of the world is solely based on its being held true by everyone, its serving as the background for general understanding. Of course, this interpretative monopoly of the intellectuals might also be grounded in superior and highly sophisticated argumentative arts, into which any reasonable subject can gain insight. However, external guarantees through force and privilege are by far the better wager.

If the power of intellectuals is based on the external safeguarding of an interpretative monopoly, then their relations to political elites and counter-elites gain a critical significance. This is all the more so in the construction of collective identity, for the political center attempts to substantiate itself precisely by protecting and administrating collective identity. The power of intellectuals can thus always be observed in their relation to elites.[37] This has exceptional impact upon the sociostructural position of intellectuals, i.e. upon their relations to other social groups.[38] But here as well, ambivalence is unavoidable. A close connection to the political elite may assure intellectuals of an interpretative monopoly against heretics, but this dependence in turn endangers the tension established between the "this-worldly" and political, as opposed to the "other-worldly" – i.e., the very tension which made the rise and power of the intellectuals as a group possible in the first place.[39] An overly obvious alliance between political and intellectual elites blurs the separation between the "here" and the "other-worldly," and tends to disengage intellectuals from the very problem whose solution they want to monopolize. Conversely, radical dissidence or opposition between politicians and intellectuals favors that separation, that opposition, that acting in the name of a higher order that assures identity. But in that case the interpretation of this identity-assuring "other-worldly" order can end up looking rather arbitrary in the face of the large number of interpretative possibilities thus let loose.

Admittedly, both radical dissidence and complete convergence must be seen as extremes. Usually the simple circumstance that a political elite is never entirely homogeneous, and cannot prevent power conflicts permanently, facilitates various and limited coalitions between intellectuals and fractions of the political elite.[40] In favorable cases, intellectuals can end up in the position of a mediating third party, whose judgment is made in the name of God, Reason, or Progress, and determines whether particular claims to power can be substantiated.

Such a position is constantly endangered, however, through the internal formation of (political) fractions and (intellectual) schools, opening possibilities for "criticized" power elites to legitimate themselves after all. Ultimately the possibility must be considered of retreat from political engagement altogether, of withdrawal to apolitical and purely cultural reflexions. In that case it becomes possible to view not only existing politics, the current situation, as unworthy of intellectuals, but also to define the this-worldly business of politics as a whole as being beneath their contempt.[41]

Intellectuals and their public

Of similarly critical importance for the status of intellectuals is their public: that part of society who read, discuss, and take up the intellectuals' interpretations of the world. This public can be great or small, but to intellectuals themselves it appears as an anonymous, faceless, indifferent third party, to whom intellectual communication is in fact directed. In each case, the relation of intellectuals to their public tends towards a fundamental asymmetry. Only when intellectuals – and be it only for a moment – maintain an interpretative head start, a standpoint superior to their public's, can the typical distinction between intellectuals and their public be generated. Should this interpretative advantage be lacking, then the interpretation of the intellectuals remains a mere proposition, surrounded by other expressions of equal weight, all equally worth hearing. But should the interpretative advantage lead to the complete isolation of the intellectuals, then the special role of intellectual communication is endangered. In short, intellectuals must communicate to their potential public something that this public does not yet know, but could possibly take up. They are especially subject to the contradiction which was described above as a specific dynamic of universal codes: between a missionary urge for expansion as against cultural stratification, between universalist opening as against particularist enclosure.

A typical ambivalence arises from this position. Intellectuals bewail the lack of understanding from a public that is unaware, insufficiently aware, or even hostile to their interpretations.[42] On the other hand, precisely this rejection by the public typically creates the tension that can be understood as the interpretative head start of the intellectual avant-garde. In his or her complaint about the public, the intellectual initially constructs the basic structure within which he or she can gain exceptionality as an intellectual. Conversely, the adoption of intellectual interpretations by a wider public always poses a danger to the distinction of an intellectual.

This is especially true when, as is hardly avoidable, the adoption of interpretations is associated with trivialization. Trivialization causes reflexion to lose its variety and multiplicity of levels: the pressure to introduce new levels, to find new distinctions, ebbs away; the finesse of argumentation is sanded down. Simple, easily reproduced rituals replace reflexion. The self-evident supplants doubt and criticism. This sort of trivialization devalues intellectuals' cultural capital. They are forced, precisely in the case of public success, to distance themselves from trivialization, and insist upon the refinement of their reflexion.

The compulsion to cultural distinction gives rise to new forms of social distancing. It might at first precipitate in a categorization and stratification of groups among the public. The innermost circle is the group of other intellectuals, who as competitors and colleagues also have an intimate knowledge of the problems. Then come the critical public, who identify emphatically with their intellectual heroes, and invest much time and trouble in their own education and in achieving an understanding of intellectuals' work, but who are nonetheless treated by intellectuals with a hidden contempt. They may be glowing admirers and followers, but in the end merely an audience, and not intellectuals. Influential "propagandists" play a special role within this critical public. Although not directly involved in the discourse among intellectuals, this group (which might include pastors and teachers, as well as publishers or journalists) often has a greater influence upon the reception of intellectual work than do the intellectuals themselves. Finally, there is the great mass of the public, held entirely distant and in contempt, whose first reaction to original and innovative ideas is a lack of understanding; but who, after a time, and largely through the influence of the critical public, begin to adopt the trivializations of these ideas. As a rule, this manner of trivialization leads (often thanks to a generational change among intellectuals) to a new form of intellectual discourse, carried forth by a new group of intellectuals. For the successor intellectuals, this helps in creating their own cultural distinction from a public that remains content with the trivialized, but long-obsolete, interpretations of the predecessor intellectuals. Here as well, the cycle of esoteric reflexion, alternating with trivialization, repeats itself, and propels the history of intellectual discourse further forward.

Intellectual discourse rituals

A sociology of intellectuals does not grasp the whole if it limits itself, in the tradition of Marx or Gramsci, to the relationship of intellectuals to other social groups. Karl Mannheim, by contrast, directed attention to a large number of institutional conditions defining the genesis of intellectual knowledge, and the social formation of intellectuals themselves. If intellectuals are not just to be randomly distinguished and differentiated from other sociostructural groups on a case-by-case basis, but are to reproduce themselves as sociostructural units, and persist over the long run, then specific institutional mechanisms are necessary.[43] Most important among these are surely the distinct and differentiated processes of upbringing, schooling, and internal debate. These serve to set up obstacles on the way into the intellectual camp; and because of the investment in time and personal involvement, they make leaving that camp difficult. But that by no means exhausts their functions. Through their specific forms of communication, ruled exclusively by intellectuals, these institutions also protect and safeguard the unity and exceptionality of intellectual understandings of the world. The differentiation of an independent *educational system* thus contributes decisively to intellectuals' self-distinction as a sociostructural group – and to holding their mobility beyond the borders of this group in relative restraint. An intellectual attitude to the world cannot be changed like a shirt or a consumer brand. The relative stability of intellectual attitudes results primarily from the circumstance that readiness to adopt an interpretation of the world abates greatly over the course of an individual's lifetime. Only during a certain "educational phase," normally after puberty and after leaving the family, does a chance arise to adopt radically new attitudes to the world, and take up traditions not received from the parental generation – and only in the rarest of cases are these later replaced again by fundamentally different schemes. This lends exceptional weight to the formation of intellectual generations, i.e. to the opening of same-age groups to new interpretations of the world at the same time.

But it is not just the succession of generations that forms and sets off groups of intellectuals. Additional institutional barriers exist. Complicated initiation rituals and highly involved training procedures serve less to convey knowledge or secrets than to fortify sociostructural borders. Intellectuals are thus able to distinguish themselves as a social group with long-lasting, indeed lifelong membership – even though one does not join through birth, but through effort of education. Intellectuals thus form a *non-ascriptive corporative body* (*nicht-askriptive Korporation*): membership among them is proven through competent participation in particular forms of communication. The communication rituals specific to intellectuals facilitate reproduction of intellectuals as a sociostructural unit: bridging individual differences and combining a variety of opinions, establishing unity of internal process and the peculiarity of the intellectual form of life. By way of these rituals there arise – mostly without conscious intention, and in a manner shaped by the specific logic of the intellectual community – the ideas of the "general," the *Allgemeinheit*, the encompassing collectivity that lies in the other-worldly order, i.e. the very ideas that define codes of collective identity. A constructivist macrosociology, one adopting Mannheim's line of questioning and focusing upon the embedding of symbolic codes within sociostructural positions, as well as the reproduction of such positions through communication, therefore must focus attention upon these rituals.

Viewed from a macrosociological perspective, not only are the great differences in social position among intellectuals immediately conspicuous, but so too are the differences in their *forms of communication*. Academic disputations and journalistic commentaries, literary correspondence and encyclopedic classification, salon conversation and the construction of philosophical systems, a monastic organization of sacred texts and public polemic – each follows entirely different rituals of intellectual communication, and each favors rather different ideas of collective identity. In each case sociostructural position, discourse rituals, and the codes employed exist in a "symbiotic" relationship.[44] Particular sociostructural situations favor the definition of particular discourses, and make particular codes plausible; but sociostructural position is itself only reproduced through discourses, and discourses are informed by particular codes. Given the forms and processes of communication among intellectuals, one evolutionary threshold seems especially significant: the transition from oral to written communication. This is not only a matter of the fundamental availability of writing – in the absence of which it becomes difficult to speak of intellectuals at all – but also, and primarily, of the jump in the speed of reproduction that came with the transition from manuscript to the *printing press.*[45] As long as the dissemination of written information was bound to the costly and time-consuming process of manual copying, access to books remained a precious privilege of a few places and persons, and was nothing upon which the normal discourse of intellectuals could be built. The reproduction and spreading of knowledge was accomplished primarily in oral teachings, in lectures and disputations. Rhetoric was more important than logic or source verification. But as soon as texts could be reproduced and disseminated, without the relatively great effort of manuscript, communication structures also readjusted. Many persons could simultaneously have direct contact to the same text. The texts themselves took over the position of a personal interlocutor whom one could engage in dispute with rhetorical refinement. The standardization of knowledge and the shift in communication, from orality among physically present parties, to what below is called "the dialogue with an invisible interlocutor," facilitated the rise of the critical perspective towards texts, with which intellectuals were able to dissolve their ties to "sacred texts." When there are no great technical obstacles to the reproduction of a text, then the faithful repetition of the text no longer needs to be advanced as an intellectual virtue. The printing press opened up a field where criticism could overcome tradition, where the critical subjectivity of the intellectual could be cultivated.

The dialogue with an invisible interlocutor

At this point a microsociological focus on the situation of the individual intellectual may prove helpful in illuminating a special characteristic of intellectual criticism – at any rate, one that arose after direct oral communication was replaced by the printing press as the key process of reproduction, and intellectuals could assume a critical distance from the text.

Under these conditions, intellectuals no longer address a physically present interlocutor, but an invisible and faceless third party, an anonymous and confusingly diffuse public. In the guise of an impersonal, encompassing collectivity, this public accompanies and influences the considerations and pronouncements of the intellectual to a far greater degree than with other social groups. The situation of *solitary dialogue* with an invisible interlocutor, with a "generalized other"[46] – whether under the title of God, History, Reason, or the Public – forces intellectuals to place the course and continuation of communication under new rules, entirely different from those governing exchange in a conversation between several actual persons: rules of speech and counterspeech, question and answer, claim and confirmation.[47] Recall that the commutation and negotiation of social order, and of assurances of security, are facilitated in the first place by the actual presence of an interlocutor, allowing indication and orientation to a "significant other." In the absence of an interlocutor, the reflexion of the intellectual leads to a vacuum of orientation. This must be filled with imagination, patched into an impersonal order through special processes.[48] *But in these processes text and the writing of one's own thoughts replace the presence of a partner in communication.*[49] The text becomes an interlocutor who can be questioned, repeated, doubted, confirmed, or set forth. The objectification of one's own thought in text creates the distance that first allows one to think about thinking. The *temporal sequence of the discussion* is dissolved, however, and supplanted by the *simultaneous coexistence of signs*, and by the possibility of quickly recalling and remaining aware of a high number of signs, claims, and pronouncements during the act of reading. If sequence is in this way marginalized as a working and structuring principle of consciousness, even as the number of symbolic contents present in awareness grows, and if ultimately even the directly accessible and sensorially perceivable environment thus ceases to make a difference, then the principles of order that are favored tend to be independent of time, abstracted from the senses, and socially indeterminate. The intellectual converses with his or her text; the text objectifies an abstract order of the world that can be interpreted or designed in *multiple* fashions. This form of perceiving texts – the discursive exchange with the text as interlocutor – leads to the construction of a supersocial, invisible, and timeless world, ordered according to exceptional principles.[50] Subjectivity and objectivity, individuality and the encompassing collectivity thus enter into a new and highly tense relationship. The secluded intellectual writer finally stands facing an impersonal and general order, with which no communication and no negotiation is possible. The interlocutor is incomprehensible, inaccessible, and no longer conceivable as the reflexion of one's own thinking.

In exemplary fashion, the situation of reflexive monologue (or: dialogue with an invisible interlocutor) leads to a decoupling of process from code. In the monastic cell, at the scholar's desk or the library, etc., monotony and quiet rule. The flow of outside events is screened out, kept quiet. Even if others are present at the library, discussion with them is prohibited, or limited to the unavoidable. Only when situation and communication are screened out through such special institutional arrangements,[51] through voluntary isolation or coincidental solitude, can a code itself become the object of consideration, and be rearranged into independent variations. Certainly the shutting down of situation and communication is only possible for a limited time, and requires exceptional practice and effort. It is also certain that discussion among intellectuals is not without meaning to their form of life. But the indispensable foundation of this form of life is always the specific and socially marked moment and place of monologic reflexion.[52] In the simplest case, this is the time of quiet reading and writing. Elaborated rituals of silence, concentration techniques, procedures of notating and objectifying results, all ultimately help in forging chains of reflexions on constantly higher levels, infinite in principle. The situational frame in which the rituals arise is forgotten and suppressed, or at the very least retained only in latent form. Hence it is not at all the existence of intellectuals that "floats freely." It is their thoughts, the results of their reflexions and codes, that are liberated from all social relations. So do the codes created in monologic reflexion wipe out the trail of their own creation, and become available as elements for many situations, in an unbound symbolic universe. This decoupling of symbolic codes can admittedly occur through other means than just the reflexive monologue of intellectuals. But only through that monologue can it be pursued systematically, or result in the transcendental duplication of reality.

Even beyond the reflexive monologue, there are also aspects that favor the decoupling of code from process in the *discourse* between various intellectuals. Intellectual discourse is, as already mentioned, freed from the burden of action. It sets its own rule of not acknowledging particular interests of social groups or individuals as any kind of guidance. While interests may well provide the motivation for participants in a discourse, they cannot be substantiated, or withstand criticism. This manner of decoupling discourse from particular interests supports statements and efforts oriented to general principles, which attempt to mutually outdo themselves in their affirmations of the encompassing collectivity; and which work towards a complex determination of the general. This lifting of practical interests is described by Karl Mannheim as a lack of social location, a deficit in social identity. But according to Mannheim, this lack of location also summons the intellectuals to assume the political leadership of society.[53] A further circumstance supporting orientation to the encompassing collectivity is that while formulating interpretations of the world, intellectuals are relieved not only of action, but also of responsibility. And even otherwise, they only seldom command a direct experience of that which they interpret. Because one does not hold responsibility for the specific, one seeks responsibility for the whole.[54] In this situation, the encompassing collectivity is discursively constructed as the actual, deeper level of reality. Much as they may differ, disputations at medieval universities, the philosophical salons of the Enlightenment, cliques of Romantic poets, and conflicts among social critics all follow this pattern of a discursive construction, freed from action, of the encompassing collectivity in each case.

Their positions do differ, however. Therefore the specific *forms of isolation,* within which intellectuals no longer construct the world dialogically, but must conceive and invent it in solitude, need to be sketched both historically and typologically, and viewed with respect to the other-worldly encompassing collectivity to which each form gives rise.[55]

The construction of the encompassing collectivity in the reflexion of the intellectual was not the kind of invention that, once created, proved impossible to recall. Nor did it unforeseeably and irrevocably change the history that followed, banishing any chance to return to the concrete. On the contrary, it was capable of being forgotten again, and was repeated in various different historical connections, with various different historical carrier groups. The historical processes of constructing the encompassing collectivity can be termed "axial ages."[56] The universalism of the great world religions, the idea of a constantly uniform nature, the Enlightenment conception of natural law and universal reason, and the ideas of history and progress were all such "axial breakthroughs," each occurring in a different historical period and propelled by a different social group. Each of these axial breakthroughs had its own problem history, and it is surely too much of a simplification to speak of *one* Axial Age in world history, or the single axial age in the development of a particular society. A more sophisticated perspective associates axial phases or paradigmatic changes with specific "problem histories" and "discourses" carried by specific groups of intellectuals, and influencing their internal communication.

Within these discourses, the question of a collectivity's means of assuring identity can often rise to a special rank. The construction of a comprehensive collective identity appears to be a problem that gets discourse moving among intellectuals, and has caused axial changes of code at different historical times. It hardly need be emphasized that intellectuals are by no means the only possible carriers of collective identity. A large number of collective identity codes arise without any intellectual reflexion whatsoever. Only in relatively recent times, and then specifically in the course of occidental development, did intellectuals step up as a separate social group, with specific modes of reproduction. Nonetheless, sophisticated discourses reflecting on collective identity are usually first brought into play by intellectual carrier groups.

Certainly discourses about collective identity and constructions of new codes of identity do not occur in a cultural vacuum. On the contrary, they are incorporated within a comprehensive cultural fabric, and show a large number of horizontal connections to other discourses and their underlying codes. In the age of religious wars, for example, the construction of national identity was narrowly coupled with confessional codes, manifested in a discourse oriented around religious disputes. Towards the end of the eighteenth century, the rise of the bourgeoisie to a dominant political subject in turn placed the construction of national identity within the context of doctrines of bourgeois virtue, and the self-determination of a state citizen. Only in the nineteenth century did the discourse on national identity itself achieve the rank of an ultimate reference point, around which all other discourses and codes had to be oriented. In the following chapters, we will attempt to sketch these diverse relations of intellectual reflexion on collective identity. Our attention will be directed especially to the typologies of isolation and uprootedness among intellectuals that initially propel reflexive monologue to formulate new constructions of an encompassing collectivity. According to our thesis, the discourse rituals of intellectuals lead to axial breakthroughs in the context of a specific problem history only when they are associated with specific forms of communicative isolation – and not just with social, but also individual seclusion. In short, only if the discourse gets nowhere, and finds no answer, will it focus upon the general, the *Allgemeinheit*, the encompassing collectivity. An attempt will now be made to set forth and reformulate Karl Mannheim's epistemological sociology of intellectuals. If they are ever to arrive at their descriptions of an encompassing societal collectivity, intellectuals must decouple themselves – not only from other social groups, but also from the this-worldly requirements of situation – and thus generate their "free-floating" position themselves.

2

Prelude: the encounter with otherness

Otherness at the edge of the world: classifying the unknown

Otherness places our own security in doubt. Our first reaction to the "nameless fear" that otherness inspires is a spoken observation. We give a name to otherness. It receives a place in the network of signs by which we make distinctions, order the world, and lend outlines to things. By specifying a border, oral descriptions of otherness construct identities, commonalities, and communities. We cannot avoid the necessity of ascertaining the world through language. But this does not yet make clear why some things appear in our perception as "environment," while others require description as "other." Nor is it clear how the exclusion of otherness is actually carried out. The border between self and other, between the familiar and the uncanny, is drawn somewhere on a continuum that runs between the "absolute" object and the self-conscious subject. In between lie many levels and subtleties in the way otherness is experienced.

The description and significance assigned to otherness are defined by the circumstances of the *situation* in which otherness is discovered and perceived. Potentials for communication and solidarity are in one sense always denied within the situation of experiencing otherness: if such obstacles to understanding were entirely lacking, then the border would be overcome, and otherness would soon become familiar. The restrictions of situation that block understanding and solidarity, and support exclusion, also have their spatial and social correlates.

a) Otherness arises from the *distance* between one's own location and that of the other. Distancing can sometimes be done in a self-evident, elementary way thanks to the *spatial situation* itself. In that case otherness arises directly from the accustomed absence of the other, from the other's lack of participation in shared praxis. Otherness simply appears, suddenly, in a situation, and we are unprepared, inexperienced in dealing with it, disturbed or unsettled: otherness appears by surprise in an *open situation*.

This type of surprise encounter, resistant to ordering through social experiences or expectations, occurred in the sixteenth century between the people of the "New World" and the European seafarers and *conquistadores.* Neither the Indians nor the Europeans possessed any experience of their respective interlocutors. There was no accessible common language; the strangers hardly corresponded to any familiar conceptions. The sailing ships with which the Portuguese and Spaniards approached the coasts, their iron armor, and above all their horses and firearms made them appear entirely alien to the residents of the New World, something like superpowerful beings. Upon landing, these beings often displayed friendly gestures, "threw some trinkets at them, which they took and observed with a smile, and they trustingly came on board."[1]

In a situation of "speechless" terror, the friendly gesture becomes an occasion to view the strangers as benign *gods*. An encounter with the gods crosses over the frontiers of the familiar, of experience, indeed of spoken communication altogether. But one may presumably reckon with their benignancy. The far-reaching and lasting effects of these first encounters, within an entirely *presocietal situation,* are demonstrated by the contrasting, infrequent case of an aggressive first encounter. Magellan, during his attempted circumnavigation of the world, the Spaniard Váez de Torres, landing on the coast of New Guinea, and the English Captain John Smith, along the coast of Virginia, were all reported to have treated friendly natives in a bloodthirsty manner. As a rule, this resulted in the flight of the natives inland. Subsequent seafarers would discover, sometimes even decades later, that they could no longer restock their provisions, or get any information about the lie of the coast from the now-elusive natives.[2]

But when the terrifying otherness and overpowering strength of the aliens was accompanied by the giving of gifts – to which they were by no means obligated – then a formulation, among the Indians, of a concept of equality and reciprocity between Europeans and Indians was still precluded; but the demonization of the strangers was also prevented. They were thus seen as gods, whom one could approach with deference, but full of trust.

b) The natives' naive confidence in the alien gods in turn reinforced the feeling of superiority among the European seafarers. Their own friendliness sprang entirely from strategic considerations. For all their circumspection, their manner leaves no doubt as to their plans for conquest and subjugation. They acted on orders from the Spanish or Portuguese crown, paid respect to celebratory rituals of laying claim like the Spanish *reque-*

rimiento, set foot on the foreign ground with military escorts while firing gun salutes, and engaged scribes and chroniclers to record the moment of taking possession – to bear witness to their rights as discoverers. Obviously this ceremony could not be addressed to the clueless and uncomprehending natives. It was intended instead to secure a claim of possession against absent competitors, other conquerors and other crowns. In reality, the Indians were not partners, but the mere object of a contract.[3]

The asymmetry, and extremely hierarchical nature, of the relationship to the Indians was also obvious to the Europeans, albeit from the reversed perspective. To the Europeans the aliens were not infinitely superior, but quite the opposite. They were considered obviously inferior, even to simple sailors and soldiers. (And in any case the Indians' view of the intruders as gods would have been considered a blasphemy, subject to prosecution by the Inquisition.) Thus were the strangers placed at the bottom of the "great chain of being."[4] In contrast to the known peoples of the Old World, they did not even require subjugation. To the Europeans, the Indians obviously did not put up the kind of resistance to conquest that bespoke a sovereign subjectivity, a demand for equality. They were neither gods nor opponents, but rather things that one could find, take possession of, use or sell.[5] Communication with them was as difficult as with animals, and an elementary caution against their unpredictability was called for. In the first travel reports from the fifteenth century, the occupants of the New World are described as bizarre beings whose strangeness did not require comprehension, and was anyway impervious to it. They were mere window-dressing to adventure, or else future subjects of a European prince.

In handling the unknown, the chroniclers of discovery resorted to the central axis of their own (Christian) understanding of the world. The lost (spatial) distance was reconstructed in the social dimension through hierarchization, and the hierarchy was given cultural validity by means of missionary doctrine. Nevertheless, most of the chroniclers of the discovery of the New World were very well aware that the natives were people with dormant subjectivity – that they could fundamentally overcome their misfortune, of having been born heathens, through conversion and baptism.

Subjugation in exchange for the offer of baptism thus became the official doctrine of the Spanish colonizers. The idea of mission was bound seamlessly with the hierarchical code of early modern Europe. If the circumstance of nameless otherness was to be overcome, the alien required an assignment of rank in the order of existence. To be raised above the status of a mere thing, the alien had to be baptized.

c) Over the subsequent course of events, the association of the two codes, of the "great chain of being" and Christian universalism, proved to be extremely precarious and unstable. It presented one of the great issues for Catholic intellectuals in the sixteenth century, and was of concern not only within cloisters, but also among special committees appointed by the royal colonial administration. The *situation of these intellectuals* was quite different from that of the earlier, seafaring chroniclers. The *Conquista* was successfully completed, colonial administration already established, economic interests carved up. In short, the situation was no longer an open one. The issue was no longer how to deal with absolute otherness, but instead how to reconcile theological doctrine with the administrative concerns of the new colonies. The position of Las Casas's followers, who stood up for the missionary universalism of Christianity and against the enslavement of the Indians, was also closely interwoven with the colonial interests of the Spanish crown. Long-term interests of proselytization and rule were set against those of short-term exploitation, and the cleverness of pedagogy was to replace the terror of chains.

These premodern and modern modes of handling otherness clash in the famous debate between Las Casas and his adversary, Sepúlveda. The premodern attitude depends upon social distancing from those who spatially (and socially) have come too near, while the modern attitude demands inclusion of precisely those who are distant. From a distance, the other appears to be someone like the observer.

The debates between Sepúlveda and Las Casas show the two-faced nature of the missionary universalism that established itself world-historically at the threshold to modernity. Cortés and Sepúlveda emphasized the inferiority and otherness of the Indians, but were still capable, from their position of distance, of highly accurate observations of their "objects." By contrast, Las Casas lacked this key ability of perceiving that which was inherent and alien in the Indians. Las Casas is an intellectual in the modern sense. In the name of a general and comprehensive morality, he is obligated to overlook particularities and differences as merely factual, as coincidental matters. The interest in moral socialization – the quest for sameness in otherness – misses out on the particular and "inalienable" part of the alien subject, whereas an interest in the subjugation and objectification of aliens favors the ascertainment of differences. Classification, meaning the observation of the outside world, and identification, the construction of the inner world, are in contradiction.

Nevertheless, Sepúlveda and Las Casas are alike in one respect. Neither makes an adequate distinction between the contrafactual universalism of morality and the empirical diversity of nature and culture. For Sepúlveda, natural differences justify a claim to rule. In Las Casas, moral equality conceals cultural differences.[6] The chroniclers of the first encounter saw otherness merely as a rationalization for the journey. Out of practical necessity, they paid little attention to the wonders of the New World.[7] But when the Las Casists showed no interest in the particularities of the alien, this was for *intellectual* reasons.

d) By contrast there arose, already starting early in the sixteenth century, a European literature of travel. This portrayed the curiosities and wonders of foreign worlds – first those of the Turks and the Orient, then of the continent to the west. The readers of this literature were very interested in the particularities of foreign peoples. In their case, the spatial and social distance, out of which otherness initially seems interesting and seductive, was a given. Neither the public nor the authors of these travel reports were subjected to the direct impressions of an encounter with the distant aliens. Nor did they have to solve any practical problems of how to treat otherness. The first travel reports are largely based on misunderstandings of native informants, while in later periods literary form was given higher priority than the requirements of accurate reporting.

In any case, it was precisely this distance from direct encounters that gave rise to enhanced sensitivity for the particularities of alien worlds. It largely obviated the need for any *social* reconstruction of distance through hierarchization. In fact, from this distance, an abstract sympathy for otherness could arise, ultimately even turning into a yearning for the exotic. Otherness was no longer just terrifying and threatening. It could also be a distant paradise, the long-lost home. In the early modern period, a premodern curiosity about the exotic and monstrous aspects of aliens still inspired descriptions of fabulous creatures and monsters, i.e. a banishing of the alien from the realm of the human through symbolic classification. Following Montaigne, the alien instead became associated with the modern urge to include the figure of the noble savage, who embodies natural morality and virtue in a pure and uncorrupted form. Operating at a spatial distance, intellectuals like Montaigne and Defoe constructed moral proximity and familiarity out of the seemingly savage and alien.[8]

e) In the "Old World," first encounters between natives and aliens did not always lead to subjugation under the heel of foreign conquerors. Assuming an initially open situation of encounter between the seafarers and the native holders of power, it was possible to develop nearly equal relations. Fragile relations, involving mutual exchanges of gifts, did occasionally lead to trade relations of longer duration, in which both sides, natives and aliens, had something to gain. This was often the case on the west African coasts, for example. The interest in commercial relations over a longer term, counteracted intentions of betrayal, requiring in turn the construction of social obligations. In these almost balanced relations between alien and native, those who were familiar to both sides – mediators, mixed offspring, *frontier crossers* – held far greater weight than was the case in the extremely imbalanced and unequal relations between masters and slaves, conquerors and indigenes. Such oral mediators were not yet available for cases of first encounter, where communication was instead accomplished – with astonishing ease – by using universal gestures. Later, however, hostages, slaves, mixed offspring, and the veterans of earlier journeys could assume such middle positions, gaining in relative prominence and influence as frontier crossers between the different cultures. Later still, the mediating role was no longer left to individual coincidence, but institutionalized in specific offices: missions, colonial functionaries, the European-educated aristocracy of Asia, Jesuit missionaries in South America.

f) Unlike balanced trade relations, and unlike the encounter between European seafarers and the residents of the New World, the arrival of Europeans in the Orient was usually accompanied by a feeling of superiority on the part of the native elite. This inequality between alien and native was impressively emphasized through ritual effort. When the strangers arrived to pay court to local eminences, to offer gifts and entreat goodwill and protection, the latter would stress their superior position with corresponding pomp and humiliating court ceremony. The reception given European travelers at the courts of Beijing and Edo, or the early encounters of the English with Indian Nabobs, display this attitude as clearly as the treatment received by non-European delegations at the French and Spanish royal courts of the early modern period. Here otherness, no longer at a spatial distance – in fact come disturbingly near – is handled through the social construction of distance. Horizontal distance, in space, is transformed into vertical, social distance, in a hierarchy. Long before legal rules construct such social distance, or substantiate the obligations involved, the situation of otherness is handled through culture-crossing gestures: obeisance, exchange of gifts, arrival without arms, feasts, and the showing of pictures or objects from one's country of origin. It need hardly be emphasized that such visits and encounters still carry the risk of misunderstandings and tensions that can end in hostilities or flight. In particular, if both sides intentionally attempt to guide an undefined relation of otherness toward one of socially defined subordination, then hostile distancing becomes unavoidable: the aliens are treated as invaders, killed or set to flight.

Others within society: discrimination and inclusion

The chroniclers of first encounters, much like the Spanish intellectuals of the sixteenth century, and even the later authors of travel literature, all had the task of assigning to the alien a name and place in the order of the world. The aliens themselves had no voice in the debate over their classification. The distance of speechlessness lay between the aliens and the seafarers, entirely precluding alien participation in public debates or societal conflicts. (Only through marriages between Indian women and Spaniards did it finally become possible, generations later, for the Indian population to gain access to arenas of political conflict.)[9]

Obviously different from this situation of classifying the unknown, the new, the alien, is the situation of otherness *within* the societies of the Old World. Strangers were not surprising or unexpected manifestations in the ancient empires and city-states, or even in the medieval world. Above all economic traffic, but also slavery and religious pilgrimage, meant that foreigners, barbarians, or metics could settle alongside the local population, or come into contact with natives while passing through as *peregrini* – as traveling or seminomadic peoples. Especially under the legal conventions of the ancient empires, but also in the late Middle Ages, *travel traffic* was intensive, involving a substantial part of the whole population. Insofar as these migratory currents brought together several groups of different derivation, there arose a particular internal climate, to which we shall return below.

By its nature, contact between the strangers traveling through and the local residents was *temporally* limited, and bound to *practical* matters. It called only for an exchange of the necessary; otherwise social distance was maintained. Hospitality to strangers was always praised as a virtue, but this virtue can only be practiced for as long as strangers appear rarely and for short durations, allowing a temporal form of distancing. Once strangers begin to appear regularly, taking care of them is usually left to special institutions such as cloisters, princely courts, guest-houses, and inns, where experiences in dealings with strangers accumulate.

Hospitality to a stranger traveling through is made easier when the stranger can present the proof of a specific association or obligation between himself and the natives – a princely letter of protection, the recommendation of an acquaintance, a credible religious concern. This establishes the level of trust that cannot initially be provided by social proximity or experience, kinship or personal acquaintance. Locals and strangers are thus bound through a mutual relation to a mediating third party such as God, the prince, or the shared acquaintance. In the absence of mediation through a *third party*, the situation opens up in a dangerous manner, and everything becomes possible: robbery or theft, killing or enslavement. But even when the moderating influence of the third party is decisive, relations between strangers passing through and natives are still asymmetrical and unstable. Strangers are tolerated because their presence is of short duration, because they enjoy the protection of a third party, or because the abilities they command are useful for a time. The relationship is quickly reversed if the strangers appear instead as plundering soldiers or splendid lordships – here as well, distance and caution remain the appropriate and self-evident behaviors.

Of course the position of *strangers residing locally*, of "*denizens*," is very different. They are not completely foreign beings; nor are they temporally infrequent or spatially distant manifestations. To an extent the locals are accustomed to their presence, and a certain social obligation cannot be denied. Denizens often have resort to protective treaties with princes or city authorities, who profit from their particular economic or manual skills. And they command the native language, although they often maintain their own everyday culture, clothing, or religion. Here a social construction of distance can only be built upon various forms of hierarchization, imposed on the obvious social ties between strangers and natives. Precisely because the presence of strangers cannot be overlooked or denied in this case, precisely because they can communicate easily and command useful skills, mistrust and the construction of communal borders are called for. The larger the group of resident strangers becomes, the easier their access to the language, culture, and education of the natives, then all the more powerful become the tendencies to summon forth other, "deeper" and inimitable foundations for communality – and to restrict rights of power, of public speech or land ownership, according to provenance or lineage. The strangers who can no longer be kept at a distance in space, or limited to fleeting encounters, are thus legally put at a distance, and discriminated against.

Traffic becomes all the more inevitable as the institutions of a society increase in sophistication and complexity. Primordial borders are endangered, and must be reconstituted in a political and legal fashion.[10] The Greek city-states of classical antiquity show this quite clearly. Much like in Sparta, full citizenship in Periclean Athens was granted only after proof of Athenian ancestry, through both parents. Certain parts of the city were kept off-limits to foreigners. Foreigners had no right to buy land, had to pay special charges, and were kept excluded from public speaking or military service. Defensive reactions against settlements of newly arrived strangers are the historical rule – from the Jews in late medieval Europe to the immigrants of nineteenth-century America. Such reactions can in no way be neutralized by the readiness of locally residing strangers to integrate institutionally, or even to assimilate culturally. The readiness on the part of denizens to respect the rules, to work or take part in politics, is in fact viewed by the natives as a further threatening intrusion.

There is a graduated middle area on the spectrum between strangers traveling through and full native citizens, where distance is created through a complicated system of privileges, even as it is moderated and bridged by economic exchange and the formation of multiply layered borders between inside and out.[11]

The specific skills of strangers, as well as the fact that tasks of upbringing and education are mostly assigned to persons of low rank – often meaning foreign tutors – are reasons for the unusual influence exercised by denizens in these matters. Europeans at the Chinese court, Greeks in the Roman Empire, or Christians in the Islamic empires thus gain access to the discourse of the natives through activities of education and entertainment that are barely given social regard (at first). As educated discourse gains in importance, however, so that situations arise where only words count and the authority of the speaker becomes unassailable, the position of denizen (or minority) teachers also rises accordingly, and they can no longer be excluded from participation in this discourse. Finally, the form and course of the borders are displaced to the horizons, although never are they lifted altogether.

Both the relations between the discoverers and natives in the New World, and those between established populations and newcomers in the Old World, are asymmetrical and unstable. The groups are not only separated by differences of appearance and dress, or by barriers to communication or trust; the border is also felt by the two sides as the difference between powerlessness and superiority. Uncertainty and mistrust beyond it explode the situation, create a tension that discharges in violence and flight. In such asymmetrical relations, hostile attacks by the natives on the foreign intruders, and correspondingly violent reactions, are therefore endemically predetermined.

Others in a strange country: the discovery of national peculiarity

The situation changes entirely when the advantages and superiorities of being native or resident are lacking, and the possibilities of flight or violence are precluded; when strangers encounter strangers on strange ground, and the tension between them cannot be solved through simple distancing. Here a simple primordial code, differentiating inside from outside, is hardly adequate to the situation. To encompass the difference, new and symmetrical encodings are required that treat it as a difference among equals.

Such a situation occurs when, in the course of migrations, several groups foreign to each other are gathered together for a limited time and for the same purpose: commercial seafarers in the harbors of antiquity, medieval pilgrims on the way to Santiago de Compostela, crusaders on the island of Malta, bishops attending late medieval councils, students at the great premodern universities. The members of these groups could hardly refer to previous experiences with their respective foreigners in each case. Spoken communication was possible, but difficult, and the recognition of a higher authority only weakly formed. Such a situation is unsettling, but flight or an escalating use of violence would be dangerous, and could bring no stable advantage. The disconcerting aspects of the strange host country and the hostility of its natives can be better tolerated in combination with other strangers. Viewed against the backdrop of the foreign country, the other strangers appear similar and of equal rank. Thus the disquieting part of the other stranger cannot be handled through either subordination or distancing.

In such a situation, of an unavoidable encounter with the alien other who is also other, pressures arise for specific kinds of codes, to deal with the difference and equal rank of the groups. Hierarchical encodings, such as distinction according to social status, hardly apply. In this case the stranger is just as equally a crusader, student, Christian pilgrim, or whatever. Missionary and pedagogical distinctions, like those between believers and unbelievers, teachers and children, or educated and uneducated persons, also fail to cover this particular situation of otherness. This sort of encounter in fact often results from a common cultural orientation, and the different heritages and lineages of the others cannot be bridged by pedagogical effort. The distinction between different *nationes*, however, is thoroughly adequate to this situation. It allows the classification of strangers who can no longer be avoided through spatial, temporal, or social distancing. It describes the differences between others as inalienable and equivalent. Certainly an elementary ethnocentrism of perspective remains, for example when communicating within one's own group about the curious qualities of the strangers, perhaps employing caricature and wit to secure relief from the highly tense encounters. But if the common goal – the pilgrimage, the crusade, the course of study – is to be attained, then equal treatment and a readiness to communicate must rule in the unavoidable negotiations among these mutually alien *nationes*. Of course rivalries, conflicts, and violent encounters between various national groups are by no means precluded, but the situation of involuntary and unavoidable proximity, combined with equal status, does not only create tension: it also exerts pressure for compromise and negotiated moderation of conflict. Although strife and conflict are especially difficult to avoid among equals, any disruptive consequences arising from them must be avoided when in the common isolation and rootlessness of a strange country. Here the strangeness of others is to be taken as inalienable, and handled through national codes. Thus do international encounter and experience discover, and reinforce, national differences.

These can be seen first of all in the social and spatial separation between the hotels, camps, inns, or hostels of the different nations in the strange country. At first the foreigners are kept all together, without being differentiated in the guest rooms of the temple, the court, or the cloister. If their numbers increase and their prestige and power grow, however, chances arise for the differences to be differentiated and stabilized. The foreigners distinguish among themselves according to provenance and language, and seek to preserve these qualities within particular spaces. Examples of these kinds of institutionalized "national free spaces" within third countries can be seen in the separate hotels for French, German, and Spanish knights on Malta, the various "houses of the nations" in Papal Rome, and the usual grouping of students into residences by nation. Within these spaces, strangers can feel at home in the strange land, speak their familiar language, presume a self-evident shared knowledge, forget the insecurity of otherness, and relax for the duration. Here there are also opportunities to recall common memories, or achieve relief from the difficult encounter with otherness through jokes. Here too, others do not appear as threatening demons or children in need of upbringing, as an exploitable different species, or as parasitic guests. They are spatially near and unavoidable, curious neighbors with whom one needs to reach an arrangement, whose appearance and customs can be *banalized* in caricature. In this banalization, the other receives a name. It becomes graspable and bearable, its threat is defused and socially distanced. This social distancing of the other nonetheless remains informal and private. On the serious level of communication, the equality of others cannot be denied. They experience us in a way similar to how we experience them, and both sides know why. The nation code thus discovers the equality of nations who are other to each other, and who find themselves in the midst of otherness.[12]

3

The nation as invisible public: the patriotic code

The modernization of social relations brings the stranger into one's own society. The unknown stranger no longer merely surfaces at the edge of society as an unusual manifestation among the members of elites who are specially equipped to handle this encounter, but becomes an everyday, unexceptional interlocutor who must always be taken into account in modern action processes.[1] By the beginning of modern times – certainly no later, after an interruption by the wars of religion, than the eighteenth century – transport routes and trading relations in central Europe had multiplied; merchants, officials, scientists and churchmen traveled more, the Grand Tour passed out of the cultural hegemony of the aristocracy, and the exchange of persons, goods and knowledge beyond the borders of the principality lost its exceptional character, including for the bourgeoisie. Goods were exported abroad, foreign writers were read, and travels undertaken for business or pleasure. Not only this growing regional and horizontal mobility, but also the gradual dissolution of corporative and feudal structures contributed to a loosening of the ties to what was familiar and known. If the century after the Thirty Years War was still characterized by a revival of corporative associations, in the second half of the eighteenth century an orientation around individuality, self-reliance and functionally assessed achievement gained ground in its stead. Social relations of lifelong validity were submerged by casual encounters between mutual strangers; social positions lost the ligatures of a legible feudalism and became mobile. Individual life histories and achievements took on crucial importance: just as the journey individualizes and temporalizes the spatial location of the individual, so too was the social situation individualized and temporalized in a society that had become more mobile and restless.

This movement was triggered off and encouraged by the rise of the modern functional systems – of impersonal science and a money-oriented economy, but above all by the territorial state of modern times. The expansion of monarchical rule during early modern times represented not only the centralization of political and military power, but also that of taxes and duties, administration and jurisdiction. Ever more areas of life were detraditionalized and subjected to centrally enacted law and central administration. The exercise of state rule through a specially educated corps could thus no longer be implemented by control of the interlocutor through the personal charisma of the ruler or his superior power, but depended on abstract orientations between mutually unknown and absent parties. Whoever rules has to take into account the agency of manifold unknown parties, and whoever is ruled has to take his orientation from stable rules applicable across all situations, i.e. the law. Precisely as in mercantile activity and scientific dispute, the actions of the state administration must cease to *consider* a personal, known other, and relate to manifold unknown and invisible others. This relation is functional and impersonal: money, truth and law.

Nonetheless, special risks and uncertainties emerge during the course of such abstract interactions involving large numbers of participants: contrary to the case of stable, personal acquaintances, one cannot strike back if one is cheated, since the cheat does not depend on further personal co-operation, and can submerge himself in the sea of a manifold anonymity.[2] Markets no less than scientific debates, legal contracts and state administrations therefore demand greater trust and sociality. These non-contractual foundations of the contract are constructed in modern societies by means of special codes of sociality, which, though they include a large number of unknown persons and strangers, must conversely also exclude a large number of others – the real strangers, "those who cannot be trusted"; for inclusion and sociality can only be achieved by such a delimitation, i.e. at the price of exclusion. Such a demarcation must include the interactive networks created by travel and social mobility, markets and administration, and may therefore not be predicated on feudal–corporative or regional encodings. If the customary codes of collective identity – class, region and religion – were clearly too restrictive for that, then the radical universalism of the Enlightenment was clearly too all-embracing to permit the construction of this trust-securing limit under its guidance. Differences between individual cultures, trading communities and states disappear from the universalist–cosmopolitan perspective. No one is excluded any longer, and no one enjoys a higher privilege of trust; belonging to the human species is the only requirement. The patriotism of the eighteenth century lies between these two levels, and incorporates elements of both. It proffers an appropriate symbolic encoding for the socialization of the unknown other.

This chapter is concerned with the sociostructural situation within which patriotism emerged; and with the communication processes through which it emerged, and in which it could appear as the appropriate expression of a comprehensive social identity. The perspective is limited to the German case. As also in the succeeding historical scenarios, the focus is no longer upon a generalizable paradigm for the encoding of national identity, but the particular historical and social conditions that led to the construction of the identity of the Germans as a cultural nation. Restriction of the investigation to the German case, here specifically the period between 1770 and 1870, does not merely arise from special research interests, but can be systematically justified. Unlike the nation–states of western Europe, above all France and England, the Germans proved unable, during this century, to found their national identity on political–state unity and could found it only on the uniqueness of their culture. The carriers of cultural identity, especially the intellectuals, who formulated this cultural identity in their discourses on behalf of others, therefore assume a social role of central importance in the German case. As in all "axial-age" situations, they mediate between the provisionality and limitation of the given, and the world beyond, with its securing of unity and identity. In the following chapters we shall reconstruct four historical scenarios, in which the cultural identity of the Germans was in each case encoded differently, by different groups, and with the support of different forms of discourse: Enlightenment, Romanticism, *Vormärz*, and the period before the founding of the German Empire in 1871. The axial-age tensions, between culture-based national identity and the limitations of the political here-and-now, subsided with the creation of the *Reich*. The cultural nation had become a nation–state, and the national theme migrated from intellectual discourse into practical politics. However, the foundation stone for the "special road" that the "delayed" nation–state of the Germans was later to take was laid within the framework of these four scenarios.[3]

Bildungsbürgertum

In contrast to England, the Netherlands, or even France, the carrier of the modernization process in the German states of the eighteenth century was not the traditional feudal bourgeoisie, the patriciate, the stratum of merchants and guildsmen of the towns, but an ascendant new group: the *Bildungsbürgertum* [class of educated bourgeois].[4] The important role played in the France of the Ancien Régime by the "noblesse de robe" and the educated salons should not deceive one as to its far closer ties with the urban patriciate and the landed bourgeoisie than was the case in the German territories: the "noblesse de robe" obtained its positions by purchase or through service, and the intellectuals of the salons were taken under the wing of bourgeois as well as aristocratic patrons, in cases when they could not themselves secure their livelihood through property, office or business. The decisive antithesis in the France of the Ancien Régime was not between *Bildungsbürgertum* and *Besitzbürgertum* [landed bourgeoisie], between intellectuals and merchants, but that between the Enlightenment and tradition, between the salons of the intellectuals, on the one hand, and the church and the Ancien Régime on the other.[5] In England, by contrast, the members of the "natural-scientific movement," who gathered at the Royal Society, were as a rule affluent private individuals or aristocrats who did not depend on public office.[6]

The depopulation of Germany, especially of central and southern Germany after the Thirty Years War, had weakened the traditional commoner estate or *Bürgertum* demographically and economically. Even in the towns, which had suffered less from the war, the population had shrunk by a third. The great bankruptcies of the sixteenth century had led to a long-term weakening of the leading position of the southern German banking houses, and the upturn in the fortunes of sea trade had diminished the importance of the land route between northern Europe and Italy. The leading role that the German towns had played in Europe during the fourteenth and fifteenth centuries had been passed on to the Netherlands and to France. Amsterdam, Antwerp, Paris and London took the places of Augsburg and Nuremberg, Cologne and Leipzig. The traditional *Bürgertum* increasingly sealed itself off through guilds and tradesmen's orders: it enacted a ritual securing of privileges, stressed a "secure livelihood" and a "fair wage" instead of backing individual achievement and market growth.[7] The corporative regulation of commercial life was initially supported by the sovereigns of principalities, for it enabled prices and duties to be controlled centrally. Soon however it led to a weakening of the craft and trade guilds (*Zünfte* and *Gilden*) in favor of the central state administration. The latter extended its domain of rule and control through an increasing legislation of commercial life, though it also encouraged new forms of manufacturing industry in its efforts to create new sources of income, seeking within the framework of a mercantile economic policy to bring about a supplementing of domestic production through new industries.

In the process, the absolutist small states of Germany could have only very limited recourse to the traditional *Bürgertum* of the small towns, to manual workers and innkeepers, small shopkeepers and small traders, who were not at all favorably disposed to innovation.[8] Their commercial mentality was concerned more with meeting local demand than conquering new markets.

Partly in order to compensate for the demographic retrogression – especially in Brandenburg-Prussia, Hesse-Kassel and Ansbach – Protestant *immigrants* from France, though also from the Netherlands, were brought into the country, and with their technical, economic and administrative skills the absolutist principality initiated a first modernization process.[9] At times in Berlin during the eighteenth century, for example, a third of the total population were immigrants; tensions between the old, established *Bürgertum* and the *Bürger* who had newly settled by royal decree could hardly be avoided. The latter (enjoying special royal privilege) were frequently subject to special courts, and exempted from taxation and military service.[10] Not least from this group of immigrants, there emerged the numerically small but economically significant group of the new *bourgeoisie*, composed of traveling merchants, bankers, manufacturing entrepreneurs and publishers, who no longer oriented their economic activity by the traditional ideas of "subsistence" and "a living appropriate to one's estate," but by the *market*. Not only linguistic, economic and legal differences, but also differences in cultural convictions and the logic of professional activity separated the old and the new *Bürgertum* of the towns. Whoever backed technical progress and Enlightenment, and became rich through new modes of production not bound to the guilds, could not win the approval of the old estate of townsmen, the traditional *Bürgertum*.

But it was not only the new bourgeoisie of the large merchants and privileged entrepreneurs that contributed to the emergence of a new urban *Bürgertum*. The attempt at a legislative regulation of religious conflicts and of disputes over jurisdiction between sovereigns and the organs of empire, between feudal classes and the towns; the constitutional "monstrosity" of the Holy Roman Empire; above all, however, the large number of territorial entities, all of which built up central administrations: all these led in Germany (by comparison with France or England) to an especially dense network of *public administrations.*[11] The construction of the absolutist state, the administration of the royal domains, the judiciary and the police, mines and roads, required ever-increasing numbers of officials whose posts were assigned to them not on the basis of privilege or birth, but of their specialist knowledge and individual achievements. New state-controlled examinations took the place of class or regional provenance, and education and specialist knowledge increasingly replaced an aristocratic upbringing or purchase of office as the keys to an official post.[12]

According to a decree of the *Preußisches Generaldirektorium* [Prussian Directorate-General] in 1722:

They must however be as safe a pair of hands as can be found far and wide, of evangelical-reformed and Lutheran religion, loyal and honest, open-minded, understanding the economy and having themselves engaged in it, possessing good information regarding commerce, manufacture and other relevant things, while also literate, above all our born subjects . . . thus they must be such people as are capable of anything that we might require of them.[13]

Thus it was precisely the special significance of the absolutist state to the modernization process in the German territories that gave rise to a new, statist *Bürgertum* that owed its position above all to its special abilities, its education and its specialist knowledge.[14] This *Bildungsbürgertum* comprised engineers and lawyers, professors and pastors, administrative officials and teachers. It was committed to the project of enlightened absolutism, and could never achieve that distance from the monarchy so typical of the French Enlightenment and of the "despotic" monarchy of France.[15] The professional practice of these officials and professors was not predicated on the particularism of the mercantile profit motive, but on the universalism of law and science, public spirit and universal utility. (It is for this reason that Hegel was able to say, with an eye on the Prussian situation, that officialdom was concerned with the common interest.) It is impossible to overlook the beginnings of a contempt for the merely mercantile, above all indeed for entrenched class attitudes – no matter whether in the interests of the aristocracy or of the *Bürger*.[16]

As a rule, pastors and professors, regional administrators and customs officials were not posted where they had grown up, within social networks of which they had long formed a part, but by royal decree to places where such a position was available to be taken up.[17] The old, entrenched, craftsmen *Bürger* of the small provincial towns, in which feudal rules were more strictly followed than in England or France, usually closed ranks against the new arrivals. Social intercourse between the two groups remained scarce. Contemporary reports refer to this greater social distance between businessmen and the educated, by comparison with England or France.[18]

Madame de Staël noted that "the scholars and the businessmen . . . are too divorced from each other for a common spirit to manifest itself."[19] C. Garve distinguishes clearly between the "common *Bürger*" and the "higher classes of . . . *Bürger* educated by extensive trading or by contemplation and science," of whom one might even ask oneself whether they were not closer to the aristocracy than to the guild master and the small merchants.[20] The Hamburg teacher Johann Wolfgang Büsch noted in 1765:

that intercourse between scholars and the unlettered [i.e. merchants] is almost as unnatural and forced as intercourse between Christians and Jews, commonly lacking entirely in instruction as well as entertainment, and that they are only suitable companions at the gaming table and at feasts.[21]

The new educated class was thus in several respects "uprooted" and individualized: not only was its professional situation independent of origin and privilege, but private life was also largely disengaged from local ties. One remained a stranger to the local townsmen, even if one was not a Huguenot immigrant. The local provincial world directly present to the senses did not fill out the *Bildungsbürger's* horizons of Enlightenment and reason. The mistrust of the locals was answered with contempt.

If the expansion of the absolutist principality was the motor for the emergence of the new *Bürgertum*, its reproduction took place through the new and fast-growing system of *higher education*. Apart from the clergy, whose oath of celibacy always compelled it to rely on recruitment through special educational institutes, and from the aristocracy, which provided its heirs with a special upbringing, socialization until early modernity was not yet subject to planning, and did not have recourse to separate institutional spaces. The idea of a special upbringing and education by specialist pedagogues only came into its own among the *Bürger* class during the course of the seventeenth century. One was educated outside home, one traveled and reserved a special time in one's life for education, the home library grew, etc. Breeding and education now no longer served merely religious, but also and above all worldly and bourgeois purposes.

Thus in the German states, besides the traditional educational institutes controlled by the churches, there emerged a dense network of universities, *Gymnasien* [grammar schools] and academies, which – set up by the state and controlled by state examinations – took over the training of administrative officials, judges, teachers, engineers and physicians, whom the expanding principality required.[22] This training was at once demanding and practically orientated. The model was initially the University of Halle (under pietist influence), where cameralistics (public administration and accounting), economics and policing were taught starting in 1727. Towards 1750, the political sciences at the new university of Göttingen took over this paradigmatic role. In marked contrast to England and France, the natural-scientific subjects hardly played any notable part until the beginning of the nineteenth century. Stress was laid here on administrative and legal sciences on the one hand, and philosophy on the other. Nevertheless, the respect and authority accorded to the philosophical faculty during the eighteenth century was still very low. It served above all to train people for entry into the clergy: its students derived from the petty *Bürgertum*, and the salaries of its professors were markedly lower than those in the more respected legal and political science faculties. Just as in England, Holland and France, practical craftsmanship exercised an influence on the development of the natural sciences,[23] so the practice of state administration and of the educational institutions in Germany during the eighteenth century provided an engine for the political and administrative sciences.[24]

In their efforts to create educational institutions specific to their particular territory, the mutual competition between the numerous German states led to the founding of a large number of universities, which individually had very few professors and students, but whose overall significance surpassed that of the corresponding institutions in England or France. Around 1770, there were forty scientific institutes of higher learning, compared with twenty-three in France and only two in England.[25] One ought nonetheless to bear in mind that scientific research in England and France was not based at the universities, but was institutionalized in the French academies and the English "Royal Society." The weight of a socially differentiated *Bildungsbürgertum* was far greater in Germany than in France or England. More markedly than in France, where the purchasing of official posts was still widespread, the educational system in Germany disengaged the reproduction of the social structure from birth and origins, property and money, opening channels for an ascent whose principal parameters were the knowledge and capabilities of the individual. Official posts in the administrative and juridical institutions were reserved for such persons as possessed the appropriate educational qualifications. The number of applicants was larger than that of the available posts, and the examination result assumed the selection function.

The established aristocracy initially resisted this new recruitment procedure for the civil service. But the fact that only part of the aristocracy disposed of extensive properties or court positions, while another part was pauperized and dependent on careers in the service of the state, led to the requirement that the aristocracy also satisfy the new educational criteria and examination regulations. Even the privileging of the aristocracy for officer ranks under Frederick II, the increasing significance of the *Ritterakademien* (courtly academies) for the upbringing of the aristocracy, and the general criticism of the traditional university system had not the slightest impact on the decisive role of education and specialist competence for a career in the service of the state. The aristocracy still composed a considerable proportion of the students at the legal faculties of the universities of the eighteenth century.[26] Its associated integration – especially of the Prussian aristocracy – into the civil service is in marked contrast to the corresponding situation of the French aristocracy.

It was precisely this officialization of parts of the aristocracy that led in Germany to the emergence, right across the traditional feudal social structure, of a modernizing elite, which reproduced itself through education and specialist competence, and oriented itself toward supralocal Enlightenment horizons. Minor, above all unpropertied aristocracy was represented there no less than the scions of *bürgerlich* families. This heterogeneous provenance[27] – cutting across the feudal structure no less than the professional practice of the officials – favored a perspective assuming the mediating standpoint of a third party in both the opposition between *Bürgertum* and aristocracy, as well as local differences. It was only with the decoupling of particular feudal and local ties that the space was created out of which society in general, common utility, virtue and the reasonable will of the state could become visible.

Associations, morality, public life

This new, sociostructural stratum of heterogeneous origin could no longer organize its internal communication within the feudal–corporative framework – through craft and trade guilds, for example. It required forms that ignored the origins of the individual and depended only on individual, self-made characteristics to which the self alone was answerable. Membership had to be open and voluntary, and the discourse was to orient itself not by prescribed hierarchies but by the ideal of impersonal reason and Enlightenment. The distance of the *Bildungsbürgertum* from the particular interests of feudal groups established the goals of the organization as the cultivation of the common good. In conversation and in the activities of the association, a virtuous cast of mind and commitment to the common good and to reason had to be proved. At the same time, the proximity to state and administration demanded a certain formal organization of its members, in order to justify the serious claim of the *Bildungsbürgertum*. This form of organization was provided by the new institution of individuals freely associating in a *Verein* [association or club].[28]

By the first half of the eighteenth century, *Vereine* were being founded here and there, and from 1760 they were founded in a wave that swept through all the larger towns of Germany, and had no correlate in the western European states: language societies, patriotic associations, learned societies, musical societies, Masonic lodges and – increasingly significant – reading societies. Their goals are distinct, their memberships vary in size, but they share a common orientation around the new stratum of officials and professors, civil servants and immigrants. The German *Bildungs-*

bürgertum of the eighteenth century found its new, particular kind of sociability in the *Verein*.

The *Verein* is entirely distinct from informal sociability as it was cultivated, for example, within noble courts. Unlike the latter, the *Verein* does not permit just any theme of discussion; it does not live by the variation of themes, but directs its communication towards particular, stable purposes. Yet it distinguishes itself in this not only from "pure" informal sociability, but also from the *traditional fraternal body or corporation.* In contrast to corporative–feudal forms of organization, it does not embrace the individual in all his attitudes towards life, but only in one specific respect. Unlike traditional corporations, to which particular and socially bound interests of diffuse content can be ascribed, but no general social goals of specific content, that is precisely what characterizes the *Verein*. It ignores the peculiarities of its members and directs its attention to generally valid goals with a specific content: the cultivation of language, art, science and music, general economic and technical concerns, patriotic or national ethos.

Disengagement from particular sociostructural foundations opens the organizational type of the *Verein*, in principle, to the idea of *functional differentiation*. The person as a whole no longer counts as relevant, but only particular areas of his (or her) life; no longer the whole lifetime, but only certain occasions. For equality within the *Verein* is simply not constituted by an impregnable equality of origin and birth, but rather by a labile equality of convictions that relate not to the past but the future. Therefore, it demands additional safeguards and ever-renewed assurances of this common basis. Criticism and doubts as to the purpose of the association are therefore excluded from the *Verein*'s framework of communication. Whoever harbors such doubts is welcome to leave, unlike the case of the traditional corporation. Communication within the *Verein* is effected through a reciprocal encouragement to augment one's contribution, and by surpassing the previous speaker with respect to the apodictic, fundamental and general goal of the *Verein*.[29] Communication is therefore restricted neither by consequences nor by any considerations of brevity. Disengaged from external pressure to act and from practical restrictions, conversation is directed towards the emphatic confirmation of the common good. The risk of failure by making radical claims is considerably less than that of inciting the disapproval of the others by one's reserve and doubts. This leads to a communicative spiral of reciprocal amplification and outbidding. Outside the *Verein*, within a context of different objectives and in other situations, the threatening manifold of possible orientations in the world of free individuals demands consideration. It must be excluded and ignored within the *Verein*. Precisely *because* other purposes are equally thinkable, communication must exclude them. The *Verein* is held together neither by the stable foundation of equal birth, nor by the reciprocal personal sympathy of those present, but only by the assumption of equality and a consensus as to a generally valid, reasonable objective. Hence this consensus must, on the one hand, be continually reproduced and reinforced, and kept so generally valid that every reasonable individual can agree with it. On the other hand, anyone who breaks with this consensus must be excluded from the communication as an "unreasonable person." The price to be paid for the autonomization and individualization of membership in the *Verein* is thus the compulsion to manufacture internal sameness. Internal differentiation is only possible along the time axis, i.e. permitted if it has the character of progress over time as regards the prescribed objectives. Inasmuch as the free association of individuals in the *Verein* serves as a model for modern socialization, this form of communication also fosters the idea of history as progress through free and reasonable action.

The special dynamic and the equality of the participants directed communication within the *Verein* to a great extent towards morality and rules – an orientation that still characterized the literature around the middle of the century.[30] Before the *Sturm und Drang* movement, literary work was still tightly bound to the canon of classical rules.

From the perspective of rules and morals, the merely factual aspects, the actual differences between individuals, the inevitable consequences, the scarcity of means, all lose their significance as motives for reconsideration or reflexion. On the contrary: the moral attitude gains its emphasis only by the contrast to the merely factual and given. The moral perspective distances itself from the complexity and numerousness of the facts, and can neglect and ignore the difficulties of the concrete individual case from this distance. It is only such a simplifying distance that permits a clear demarcation line to be drawn between those who share this moral view of things, and those who have placed themselves beyond this region through their doubts, contradictions, or indifference. Conversely, this neglect of detail is justified by the great purpose that applies to everyone: the common good, the future, history, the divine mission, the fatherland.

This towering purpose also disengages moral communication from the local, given, or physically present. As distinct from sociable discourse among those present – which generates the necessary variation in the conversation by changes of theme and contradiction, and whose boundary is drawn by the simple presence in the here and now of individuals – moral communication extends in principle beyond those present. In fact it especially refers to those not present, who can be counted in or excluded. Above all, those who are not present are best suited for exclusion, for if one excludes those present, one risks a general collapse of the conversation. It is only by reference to excluded outsiders that moral communication can determine its circle of participants, and only by the counterfactual assumption of the identity of the participants that moral discourse can construct a labile boundary between inside and outside, irrespective of literal presence. *De facto* heterogeneity and moral identity stand here in a compensatory relation: the more differentiated and heterogeneous the society, the more insistent the demand for identity. It is precisely in complex societies that sociality and integration can no longer be based on the primordial identity of the members, but must have recourse to a *counterfactual identity of moral convictions*.[31] Thus, through morality, communication can disengage itself from the circumscribed locality and individual heterogeneity of the participants, and assert the unity of the social whole.

The moral perspective thereby clears the way for communication throughout a society of mutually absent persons. It was precisely this that began to develop dramatically, during the last third of the eighteenth century, in what Schlegel dubbed the "reading revolution." In all the larger towns, but occasionally also in the country, reading societies were founded, whose members did not only share the use of books and periodicals, but were frequently able to exchange comments and discuss what they had read.[32] At least 370 such reading associations were founded between 1780 and 1800 alone, in which members of various classes united as equals in respect of education and reason. The *Bildungsbürgertum* in particular was seized by a "reading addiction," which rendered the weekly arrival of the newly published newspapers and books an impatiently awaited event, and caused a fundamental revision of reading habits. One no longer repeatedly read "canonized" texts, but was hungry for what was new, unknown, and extraordinary.[33] The reading matter was commented on and discussed among equals: a discursive public came into being.

Around 1770, some 15 per cent of the population of Germany could read, but probably no more than 200,000 people, i.e. less than 1 per cent of the total population, belonged to the more restricted circle of the educated public to whom most of the newly founded periodicals and newly published books addressed themselves.[34] The annual number of new books published in the German language increased constantly during the last third of the century, reaching 3,560 in 1790; by contrast, the proportion of Latin publications dwindled to 4 per cent by the end of the century. By far the larger part of the publications were dedicated to philosophical themes and – towards the end of the century – also to poetry. These supplanted theological works and works of traditional scholarship.[35] They were usually relatively small editions, with print runs of 3,000 to 4,000 being accounted comparatively successful. Similarly for the plethoric political, literary or philosophical periodicals, which appeared among the enlightened public of Germany after 1760. Few of them achieved circulations into the thousands: Schlözer's *Staats Anzeigen* [State Reporter] 4,000, Wieland's *Teutscher Merkur* [German Mercury] 2,000, Nicolai's critical review *Allgemeine deutsche Bibliothek* [German General Library] 2,500. The "moral weeklies," which appeared during the first half of the eighteenth century and took their cue from English models, had even lower circulations. (One exception was provided by the Hamburg *Patriot*, which at times had a circulation above 4,000 copies.) Yet periodicals, newspapers and book publications were very effective in reaching the enlightened public of the new educated class: the latter was not very large in number, and every copy of a periodical or book was read by several persons.

The expanding reading public gave the *Bildungsbürgertum* a communicative space extending beyond the boundaries of locale and class, one that could hardly be restricted even by censorship measures. Unlike France, where the linguistic community coincided with the territorial state, in the numerous German territories it was possible to evade censorship by switching to the other side of the border, and thereby write for a large public beyond the reach of local censorship. Censorship at the border was a rare occurrence. Thus a relatively liberal climate could emerge, filling German Enlightenment society with pride and distancing it from "despotic" France.

The disengagement of public communication from the restrictive horizons of locale, class and territorial state favored an orientation towards universal reason, Enlightenment, and the common good, and thus had a particular influence on the needs of the new educated class, which in its uprooted situation was anyway at cross-purposes with the traditional classes.

In public communication, Enlightenment society constituted itself as a structure that escaped the confines of class, religion, dynasties and regions.[36] A written communication of this socially universal kind could no longer have recourse to personal acquaintance, or to the potentially activated presence of an interlocutor. Even representative conjurations of persons of supreme power – the Christian God or the figure of the sovereign – were no longer available within the framework of Enlightenment communication: all participants were equally endowed with reason, and encountered one another only as abstract, faceless (and not infrequently also nameless) individuals. Public communication could only succeed if the given situation, the perceptible differences which required special consideration, were screened out on principle. One addressed oneself to an invisible and innumerable public of equals: "We are writing into the blue beyond, for all people and for our dear successors – and thus for nobody," Wieland stated as early as 1776, and Herder addressed his works to "an unlimited audience," an "invisible intercourse of spirits and hearts."[37] Even the positions of author and reader were not yet clearly socially differentiated: a large proportion of the readers of the "ink-spilling saeculum" were occasional authors, people encountered one another as equals under the sign of discourse, and this demanded an interchangeability of perspectives. Not to be overestimated, moreover, is the fact that German was for the first time considered a literary language, spoken by author and public alike.[38] All these circumstances contributed to the fact that among the *Bildungsbürgertum* of the Enlightenment intellectuals were not yet systematically and permanently counterposed against their public, and internal communication between intellectuals was not yet distinct from communication with a larger public.

Patriotism and the moral construction of collective identity

The disengagement of public communication from personal presence, but also from traditional local and social differentiations, necessitated a new encoding of sociality that could underpin the free movement of communication with trust, and construct the idea of an invisible public.[39]

The code by whose means the *Bildungsbürgertum* could represent to itself this invisible and impersonal public was *patriotism.*[40]

Hardly any form of self-categorization or address is so frequently to be found in the periodicals and journals of the eighteenth century as that of "patriot."[41] The patriotic code permitted a construction of community that disengaged local and class ties, all the same still remaining below the threshold of the universalist cosmopolitanism of the Enlightenment, which included all peoples and was therefore of no use, for political and practical purposes, for the organization of the social entity.[42]

The combination, precarious for all universal codes of collective identity, of universalist openness with particularist closure, was successfully effected in the case of patriotism, above all by its assumption of the available codes of collective identity – the class code of the bourgeoisie, the cosmopolitan code of the Enlightenment, the religious codes of pietism,[43] and the rulership code of absolutism – and its successful transformation of the contradictions contained therein. Here too, a symbolically constructed unity of multiplicity and contradictions gives rise to collective identity.[44]

One was a patriot not on the basis of primordial characteristics, through origins or birth, but through virtue and cultural conviction.[45] Insofar as the patriotism of the Germans was still characterized by local and regional ties, a distinction was made between "stupid," narrow, and rowdy "Germanness," which was conceived of as crude and natural, and reasonable and enlightened patriotism, which was based on education and enlightenment and also entertained the possibility of other fatherlands.[46] Stratificatory metaphors cannot therefore be entirely avoided: the low, crude, dark patriotism was excelled by the higher, educated and enlightened patriotism.

A third form, based upon shared social relationships and interests, is sometimes intercalated between crude, natural patriotism and culturally produced, reasonable patriotism.[47] This was located at the juncture between bourgeois practices and the collective identity of society as a whole. In patriotism, the ethically molded self-interest of the bourgeoisie, its professional industry and individual business sense, are translated into the general virtues of the patriot, and bourgeois society is constructed as a realization of bourgeois virtue.[48] Self-interest and the common good, the individual and society, bourgeois and state no longer appear as antithetical, but as a harmonious conjugation of two perspectives. The *Bürger* [a word that covers both "citizen" and "bourgeois" – Translator's note] is a good patriot precisely if he pursues his own self-interest, thereby fostering the common good. Conversely, state and government are reasonable precisely if they serve the common good and enable the *Bürger* to achieve worldly bliss. In order to achieve this, every *Bürger* must do his duty. The collective identity of the society is thereby disengaged both from transcendental guarantees and from the person of the ruler,[49] and integrated into the utilitarian class ethic of the bourgeoisie, which is made out to be reason pure and simple, to which everyone has access. By appealing to this utilitarian patriotism, every possible situation can be provided with social significance. If one characterizes oneself and one's public as patriots, thus rendering this specific attribute universal, one can command widespread attention in the fields of agriculture or accounting, education or forestry alike. This is successful above all if the patriotic encoding is heavily stressed. In the process, the moral emphasis of the patriotic encoding subsumes the practical, limited character of the theme.

The sophisticated patriotism of the *Bildungsbürger* also has recourse to existing codes: above all, the cosmopolitanism of the Enlightenment is used here to refine the patriotic encoding of collective identity. And even this educated and reasonable patriotism is predicated on the bridging of an apparent contradiction. Cosmopolitanism demands the dissolution of all special ties to a country, while patriotism on the contrary stresses the differences, and affirms the uniqueness of the fatherland. In enlightened, "cosmopolitan" patriotism, integration into a community is praised as a *universal* virtue which is also valid in other fatherlands, and can encourage a reciprocal understanding for particular ties. Above all, however, the enlightened cosmopolitan can and may only have patriotic ties to a community that itself realizes the ideals of Enlightenment, reason and tolerance. Thus patriotism produces the bond with a particular community that is indispensable for political action in the light of enlightened universalist ideals, and is a prerequisite for political realization of the Enlightenment.[50] This combination of uniqueness and universalism in the patriotic code can thrive in public, impersonal communication. Here too, apparent contradictions – individuality and anonymity, equality and freedom – are combined in a special way. Moreover, the range of public communication gives an additional foothold to the patriotic encoding of collective identity. The patriotic appeal goes one step beyond the narrow confines of the locality and of the power relations of the principality, without getting lost in the endless seas of the generally human.

Just as it bridged the contradiction with Enlightenment cosmopolitanism, patriotism occasionally linked up with pietist ideas and could thus build on Protestant religious codes of collective identity. The pietist orientation towards inwardness and personal faith seems at first to be in contradiction with the virtue of the outward-looking patriot as celebrated in the *Verein*. Yet it was possible to manufacture links between patriotic virtue and pietist devotion, through the concept of duty and the idea of the emphatic surrender of the individual to a higher destiny. The fatherland is seen as a "spirit that descends, as it were, from above . . ., sinking itself into the hearts of men."[51] One can hardly miss the influence of these pietist ideas on Herder's concept of the spirit of the people, and on Moser's idea of the national spirit, situated outside the individual's range of intentional actions. Protestant thinking facilitates such conceptions, since it leaves the position of a personal mediator between God and the single individual unfilled. The fatherland represents this position in an impersonal yet comprehensible way. It gives the pietist need for duty and sacrifice a particular point of reference, and can be anchored to an emphatic discourse.

Nonetheless, it can hardly be overlooked that patriotism of the pietist stripe is difficult to bring into line with utilitarian–eudaemonistic patriotism: "bliss on earth" or even only "reasonable contentment" are far removed from the inwardness and devotion of the pietist. Here at last it becomes clear that patriotism permits of very different shades, and that patriotic virtue remains largely undetermined. The patriot can be pious or self-interested, cosmopolitan or national, republican or monarchist – what is decisive is less the particular virtue to which patriotism has recourse than the moral emphasis with which this happens. The patriotic encoding constructs collective identity through moral emphasis, and in the process forgets the heterogeneity of that which is emphatically superelevated and united.

Unlike absolutist monarchy, which derived its overarching unity from the visible person of the monarch, of whom images were to be encountered everywhere, the social community thus created through a manifold of individuals remains impersonal and invisible. This abstractness and invisibility requires additional communicative safeguards to shore up its existence: that which is no longer unquestionably given and perceptible must be strengthened by an unconditional morality and emphatic reinforcement. Here, society becomes a communication community in a double sense: not only does the extensive network of communication among the class of *Bildungsbürger* make appropriate encodings necessary, but these codes also exclude anyone who submits them to doubt from further communication. The moral emphasis of patriotism puts sociality on a new historical–developmental foundation: society is no longer conceived as composite, made up of different and unequal groups of people, and held together by its orientation toward a personal center – the king, the emperor, God; rather, society arises through the moral consensus of equal individuals. The development of individuality and the achievement of equality are predicated on this moral consensus; morality can only lay its claim to integration with reference to the society of individuals who enjoy this abstract equality. This integration of abstract individuality and abstract morality is precarious, demanding special rigor and strictness in order to delimit the collective identity. Skeptics and the unorthodox must be expelled from the communication community. Concrete threats and falls from grace must be made public, scandals uncovered and crusades staged in order to render perceptible and effective the invisible boundary between the morally pure and the sinners.

Looking at France: enthusiasm and disappointment

It is not surprising that the *Bildungsbürgertum*, as carrier of the moral codification of national identity, reacted with alacrity to the great French Revolution of 1789. Here, indeed, the patriotic idea of a society without class distinctions, oriented only towards virtue and reason, seems to have become political reality to a far greater degree than in the Prussia of Frederick II. The enthusiasm of the German *Bildungsbürgertum* for the French revolutionary project is well known. People traveled to Paris and founded Jacobin clubs, and the traces left by the revolution in the works of the great intellectuals cannot be missed.

With virtue's reign of terror, however, it became clear that the strict moral encoding of national identity had a dark side. Besides the descent of the Enlightenment into the bloodbaths of Revolution, there was also the irritating circumstance that the Revolution, after an initial cosmopolitan openness, soon took an imperial–expansionist turn. As a German in Paris, one was still a foreigner and under suspicion. Germany itself finally ceased to appear as a patriotic people of equal rank to be liberated, and instead became the object of French conquest. In this situation, the enthusiasm of the German patriots soon turned into disappointment and hatred for the French.[52] A new generation of *Bildungsbürger* stepped onto the stage.

4

The nation as Holy Grail of the intellectuals: the transcendental code of Romanticism

The uprooting of the intellectuals

The enlightened public of the eighteenth century did not as yet distinguish sharply between the intellectuals and their audience. The perspectives of writers and readers were interchangeable, with a large proportion of the readership also trying their hand at writing from time to time. It would be difficult to discern any interests exclusive to the intellectuals. While quite a few intellectuals were already able to make a living from their literary activity, it was not until the last two decades of the century that men of letters achieved a special social situation distinguishing them from the ordinary public. They increasingly complained of the poor taste of this public, and treated their own literary activity as a vocation granted only to a few elect, because of their "original genius." The *Sturm und Drang* generation shored up the fragile divide between the intellectuals and their public by tracing the socially created difference to birth and talent, things unalterable and inalienable.

Other developments also point to a social and institutional differentiation of the literary industry. The public's adulation of the great literary heroes increased, critical reviews were established, and a large number of quality periodicals were founded that ostentatiously despised the tastes of the wider public. The circulation figures for the popular periodicals and for trivial, low-brow literature both continued to rise. The literary market's expansion[1] permitted an internal distinction to be drawn between quality literature for the literati and the production of disposable literature for an "uneducated" public.[2] In the case of quality literature, the perspectives of author and reader (who was conceived of as another author) remained interchangeable, while this was no longer true of trivial literature. The latter was produced in utter contempt for the public, which was restricted to the role of consumer.

Towards the end of the century one may assume a total of nearly 10,000 writers in Germany, of whom about a third sought to make a living as professional, independent writers.[3] These literary people were of heterogeneous origins – most of them derived, it is true, from the *Bildungsbürgertum*, from the families of pastors, officials and professors, but some had their origins in the industrial or commercial bourgeoisie, or in the aristocracy.[4]

Young writers near the end of the century had less in common with respect to origins than in certain biographical traits, and in a shared social situation that contributed to the social particularity and distinctiveness of this group.

Over the previous decades, the university education system had produced a large number of students for whom civil service positions were not available in the appropriate numbers. Graduates of the universities and of institutes of higher education were confronted with dashed career prospects and long-term economic insecurity. Contemporaries were already worried by the logjam in careers and the lack of available academic posts, leading to a crisis in demand for university education around the turn of the century.[5] It seemed hardly feasible to take up mercantile or trade pursuits. This escape route was forbidden not only by the lack of requisite abilities, but also by the ambition and pride of this educational stratum. An increase in educational achievements seemed more conceivable; one wanted to be not merely educated, but *an educator oneself*; to excel and surpass what already existed; to be an author rather than a reader; to herald things new, unprecedented and of genius to the world. From this perspective, mere commerce, but also conventional literature, could hardly suffice. Success among the wider public seemed tempting, on the one hand, but nonetheless despicable. This increasing distance from the literary market culminates in Brentano, who was so ashamed of the commercialization and commodification of literature that he refused to trade in the "free and spiritual goods . . . of heaven."[6]

The new generation of literati thereby repeated on its own behalf the process of *distancing* from received social structures that had earlier enabled the *Bildungsbürgertum* to distance itself from traditional feudal society. The literati, however, assumed distance from the *Bildungsbürgertum* itself, whose lifestyle was felt to be as limited as its tastes were vulgar. The new generation of writers sought distance through *superior education*. It, too, enhanced its self-respect by imagining its viewpoint to be of an elevation from which the base considerations of ordinary life might be viewed with indifference. The "poetic existence" became a new ideal. The poets no longer conceived of themselves only as "bards of the nation" (Wieland) but as "Brahmins – a higher caste ennobled not by birth but through free self-initiation" or a "patriciate of the political nobility" (F. v. Schlegel). Novalis demanded that poets and priests should again be one, and Campe indeed considered them "guardians and councilors of humanity."[7]

The great ambition of the new nation of writers came up against well-nigh insuperable obstacles. The literary heroes of German Classicism, above all Goethe and Schiller, blocked the prospect of literary fame and success in the market. "Goethe shall and must be excelled," wrote Novalis, and Kleist declared: "I shall tear the laurel wreath from his [Goethe's] brow."[8] The "addiction to originality evinced by our poets" (Goethe) characterized the literary industry in Germany after the *Sturm und Drang* movement. Such originality, however, was increasingly difficult to achieve, not only in the face of the generational conflict with the larger-than-life figures of German Classicism, but also because of the inexorably growing competition.

> The whole misfortune stems from the fact that poetic culture has become so widespread in Germany that nobody writes bad verses any more. The young poets who submit their works are not inferior to their predecessors, and do not understand why their works are not also lauded, since the latter are so highly praised. And yet one ought to do nothing to encourage them, precisely because there are hundreds of such talents, and one ought not to encourage the superfluous.

Thus Goethe.[9]

This generational conflict, increasing competition, and the foreclosure of careers in the civil service and in the universities forced many ambitious young writers into employment by no means commensurate with their self-esteem or ambitions. With few exceptions, the young writers lived in perpetual financial difficulties; a large number took up posts, at least temporarily, as *Hofmeister* (tutors) and private teachers in aristocratic or bourgeois households.[10] Even writers who were later to become celebrated, such as Kant and Fichte, Hölderlin and Schelling, had to seek a living temporarily as home tutors or *Hofmeister*. The few desirable posts as companions and *Hofmeister* to young noblemen were more than outweighed by a large number of ill-paid tutorships in bourgeois homes. Young theologians in particular would retain these posts, which were considered *déclassé*, for considerable periods, thus finding no place in the traditional economy of the "whole house." Hölderlin, for example, lamented:

> Do you know the root of my ills? I would like to live for art, and have to labor among people, often to the point of tiring of life. And why so? Because art assuredly feeds its masters, but not its pupils . . . More than a few have gone under who were born to be poets. We do not live in a poetic climate.[11]

Materially dependent on a bourgeoisie that not infrequently despised them, at times humiliated by their charges, in provincial backwaters that hardly offered a stimulus or opportunity for direct encounters with kindred spirits, and without any genuine prospects of improving their social and economic situation, but full of disdain for the role of domestic that was forced on them – in short, in an extremely isolated situation – the only road open to them led into subjective *inwardness*:[12] the faculty for perceiving feelings was enhanced, and life was displaced into the internal space of sensibility. Self-observation and diary-writing came into fashion, susceptibility to nervous and pulmonary diseases became widespread, and new medical ideas, magnetism, oxygen treatment etc., drew attention to the sufferers.

Corresponding to that, there was a form of sociability predicated on the direct encounter between subjects, breaking through the conventions of bourgeois life and distancing itself from the world of normal commercial life, from the banality of the obvious, reasonable and given.[13] Actual, real life was shifted to the place where one happened not to be, from the present to the future or the distant past. A yearning that extended beyond the finite and limited became the basic motif of the literary epoch; travels were undertaken without ever really arriving, and the isolation was the more powerfully felt in alien surroundings. This is especially true of journeys abroad, to wit Paris, which was felt to be the modern Babylon, reigniting the flames of yearning for one's own, invisible fatherland.

The present did not at any rate constitute a suitable goal for the ambitions of the intellectuals. They sought out the silent margins, peace and idle hours in which to direct their gaze at an invisible and as yet undetermined world, disengaged from the excitements of bourgeois life. A petty-bourgeois, provincial and constrained situation by no means proved an obstacle to that. On the contrary, it provided no distractions whatsoever, and thereby compelled one to set one's sights on this invisible world.

Driven out of feudal society and out of the *Bildungsbürgertum*, unlike their French counterparts and the aristocratic-court culture with which they associated, the intellectuals could only find their identity in the distancing process itself. The further the Enlightenment spread among the bourgeoisie, the fewer the chances it presented for intellectual distinction. And the greater the distance that the intellectuals took from the bourgeoisie, the more emphatic and deranged was bound to become their attempt to discover the universal. The Romantic intellectuals not only repeated and intensified the distancing trope of the *Bildungsbürgertum*, but also the emphasis it laid on individualization.

Of course, individualization no longer meant merely a sundering of one's career from class ties, but also an inclination to put the family and conventional gender relations into question. A considerable number of intellectuals lived alone, and few founded families according to received models. One was no longer prepared to found relations between the sexes on the basis of law and business sense, but reserved this domain for erotic attraction alone, as one reserved sensibility for a feeling surpassing the finite. Romantic love was realized as an exclusive encounter between two subjects who reciprocally augmented one another's individuality, each considering the other to be unique and irreplaceable. This was all the more true the more isolated and alone the lovers felt, and the more common the experience of misunderstanding and inadequacy was in any lifeworld.[14] Love was then felt to be supernatural, a sudden miracle, that sustained the lovers' excited passion.[15] Obviously, these erotic relationships disconnected from law and convention were particularly susceptible to complications and turbulence. (The Schlegels' relationships or Hardenberg's love for Sophie Kühn are classic examples.) Not only can individuality be emphatically enhanced through romantic love, but also one's distance from reality and convention can be increased. This new love is boundless and unreasonable. It overcomes all class barriers as well as every other social measure, being inaccessible to argument and rationality, and deranging the vision of those who fall victim to it. "Love is the final end of world history – the oneness of the universe."[16] It is not infrequently intensified by unrealizability, the death of the beloved. Here too, the banality of the achievable stands in an unbridgeable antithesis to the yearning for the infinite. Only death makes that realm accessible. Consequently suicide is discussed a great deal, and sometimes chosen as a way out.[17]

In the extreme case, as described by Schlegel in "Lucinde," love lacks even an object:

> A love without an object burned within him and convulsed him inwardly. The slightest occasion caused the flames of passion to burst forth; but soon these seemed to disdain their object out of pride or selfishness, and turned back with redoubled violence upon themselves and on him, in order to tear at the marrow of his heart. His spirit was in a perpetual ferment; at every moment he expected to meet with something extraordinary.[18]

The abysses of feeling that open to romantic love cry out for a compensatory support. To this we shall return.

Esotericism, cliques and irony

Driven out of the established *Bildungsbürgertum* and intent upon keeping their distance from the common public, the new intellectuals communicated with one another in a special way that was inaccessible to outsiders. *Esoteric periodical projects* were founded as a counterweight to the journalism of the *Bildungsbürgertum,* addressing aesthetic and philosophical issues under the eye of a small circle of initiates and highly educated persons. Their circulations were low, and as a rule they were short-lived.[19] *Athenäum*, published by Schlegel, is exemplary for the ambition and short lifespans of these esoteric and high-toned periodicals. They rarely appeared for more than two or three years, some, like *Nemesis*, *Memnon*, or *Kynosarges*, not outliving their first year of publication. Many took the form of literary–philosophical manifestoes that appeared to herald a cultural or literary revolution.

In spite of being addressed in principle to the wider public, these periodicals were not concerned with widespread dissemination, but with a journalistic demonstration of the extraordinary character of an esoteric group of literati. Whoever read them and did not belong could not and was not intended to understand them. The intention was not to educate a real public but to reveal one's genius to an ideal public. The actual public was excluded, and *romantic sociability* could only develop at a distance from it.[20]

This form of sociability became the vehicle for the Romantic intellectuals. It consisted of intense personal and profoundly subjective relationships in small groups, whose composition could change owing to biographical circumstance – or as a result of personal conflicts. Quite unlike sociability in the *Verein*, it did not develop by ignoring personal differences in the cause of an indisputable common good. It expressly refused to direct itself toward stable purposes communicable to everyone in simple slogans. But a "superficial" directedness toward courtesy, or a mutual desire to please in the salons could not serve as the foundation for this form of sociability. Most writers lacked such "courtesy"; nor did they want to bow to its rules. Beyond mere conventions and formal purposes, Romantic sociability was supposed to arise from the pure encounter between subjects, out of an enhanced sensibility for feelings and individuality. It is directed toward that which is ultimately unspeakable and infinite, only ever capable of fragmentary treatment, and of which there is no entirely adequate concept.

The structure of this sociability is that of the *clique*. Cliques are informal networks predicated on personal sympathy, which can only develop in contradiction to, and at a distance from, formal organizations.[21] They do not result from an unconditional socialization of free individuals "in their natural state," but from a communication between persons who can only achieve their individuality in the shadow of a supreme institution, under the exclusion of a "normal" environment. The distance taken from this institution is not expressed in terms of critique, revolt, or political strategy. Such action would risk playing by the rules of the institution, thereby losing one's distinction and distance. From the perspective of the clique, it seems neither possible nor of particular urgency to change the framework institution. Individuality and subjectivity can only be determined negatively with respect to it. Unlike moral communication in the *Verein*, which is addressed to a third party, to an invisible public, the clique demarcates itself with regard to this invisible third party. It is predicated on presence, direct interaction, and personal acquaintance, and can thereby sustain its unifying foundation without putting it into words: people feel comfortable with one another and no longer need to reinforce their relations with others by recourse to general reasons. What is at stake is individuality and a personal, implicit knowledge, not abstract rules.

Irony is an excellent means of achieving distance from the background situation, from the outsiders. Reality may be complex and unalterable, but it is also without importance – and this is no more up for discussion than the moral claim was apt to be doubted by patriots. Whoever does not join in adopting this ironic distance from reality moves outside the clique, and can only be perceived as the carrier of social roles, not as an individual subject. Through irony, precisely those ties are shaken off in which the *Bildungsbürgertum*, from the perspective of the Romantics, had become enmeshed. Irony does not only distance one from the conventionalism of the *Bildungsbürgertum*, but also from the German literary classics.[22]

Significantly, this distance is no longer sought through critical argument or moral emphasis, by whose means the Enlightenment achieved its distance from things as they were. Irony is far more effective – it permits no counterargument and cannot be disarmed. A reality without coherence is no longer approached through emphatic assertions and the conjuration of a unified meaning, but henceforth only at an ironic distance. The visible and experienced world is unimportant and should not be taken seriously. It is evaded by developing various possibilities and seeking an ironic distance. It is only at this distance, and not by identifying with what is actual or reasonable, that persons achieve individuality and subjectivity. Irony facilitates a state of "floating above the antitheses," of which Romantics such as Novalis, Adam Müller or Bettina von Arnim speak. Cut adrift from a particular place in society, the Romantic intellectuals seek a "higher point of indifference,"[23] whence new and surprising perspectives are supposed to arise. Jean Paul's "Ballonfahrer" (balloonist) or Hoffmann's "Kater Murr" (tomcat Murr) are examples of such eccentric perspectives, disconnected from the normal and earthbound, and seeking the truth from the margins. Knowledge is no longer promised by illumination, Enlightenment, or reason, but rather by darkness, irresponsibility, derangement, madness. True life is only possible outside what is generally true; and truth as asserted and uttered, being general, is always false from the outset.

"The Word is finite and wants to become infinite" (Schlegel).[24] This eccentricity of Romanticism of course evades any attempts to establish and pacify it. Romantic communication is therefore dependent on forever conceiving the possibilities inaccessible to the normal world-view, simultaneously adopting several perspectives, leaving contradictions unresolved and fragments fragmentary. As a merely banal surface, the visible conceals what is substantial and essential, but any attempt to define that only brings forth fragments. "Even the greatest system is after all only a fragment."[25] From the Romantic perspective, the fragment and the contradiction cannot be surpassed: the deeper reality, ultimately incomprehensible and unutterable, can only be approached allusively, from an oblique, sidelong perspective, in decreasing spirals. This "romanticization of the world" was programmatically demanded by Novalis:

> The world must be romanticized. In that way one recovers its original meaning. Romanticization is no more than a qualitative potentiation. In this operation, the lower self is identified with a better self . . . By giving the commonplace a high meaning, the usual a mysterious appearance, the known the dignity of the unknown, the finite a luster of the infinite, I romanticize it – the converse operation is carried out on the higher, unknown, mystical, infinite – the identification converts this into its logarithm – it is given colloquial expression.[26]

The communication of the Romantics thereby entirely dissolved the ties to the obvious and given aspects of a situation. Far removed from the earthbound of the old world, but also from firm belief in the Enlightenment, reason or morality, Romantic communication appears to be an ethereal dance that can only be initiated by itself. One can easily suppose the existence of hidden meanings, discover mysteries and contradictions, and intuit past greatness from fragments, provided that this does not lead to the compulsion to integrate the disconnected fragments into a unity, uncover the mystery, or resolve the contradiction. Such a communication, unconstrained by considerations of completeness or groundedness, easily slides off into the infinite, into a yearning without a name. Although doubtless originating from some specific situation, that soon disappears from view; the uprooted Romantic intellectuals then lose themselves in a pure communication without any situational cover.

Transcendence, individuality and the Romantic nation code

The uncoupling of Romantic communication from situational guarantees directs one's gaze into a world beyond the public and uncontroversial, the routinely comprehensible or directly perceptible. The world superficially available to experience is seen as lacking context, splintered, fragmentary and without innate meaning. Beyond this superficial world without foundations, however, communication requires extraordinary metaphysical attitudes and ligatures if it is to continue "hovering" and not collapse into a superficial subjectivity. Such "metaphysical" or transcendent substantiations maintain the feeling of superiority even if the movement of the conversation itself threatens to become blocked, or spread disheartening insights into one's own situation. The more limited and hopeless this world – one's own professional and economic situation – turns out to be, the stronger, more infinite and impalpable the other world – which is brought into antithesis with this world of money and conventions – must appear. It is in this transcendent sphere, too, that everything visible and available to experience is founded, but it is difficult of entry, which can be achieved only through special efforts of reflexion and only to those who have recognized the superficiality and fleeting character of this world and of the present. The moment in which this transcendent sphere is revealed fills the individual with speechless awe; it is overpowering and explodes every measure of custom. This idea of the sublimity of the infinite determines the Romantic experience of the world. What is at stake is incomprehensible, unspeakable, impossible to represent – and yet *art and literature* must make precisely that effort. They are the cultural spheres that can open themselves in principle to that which is entirely other, to the sublime, infinite and untamed, without of course ever being able to grasp and name it. Politics and law, economy and sociability, even a moderate, no longer fanatical, religion and classical art with its goal of "beauty," all make themselves at home in the provisional, limited and finite perspectives that cannot do justice to the sublimity of the transcendent sphere. Both spheres, the infinite and the finite, all-encompassing unity and fragment, absolute and relative, distant and near, stand in a contradiction rife with tension that can be pointed up and overcome by art. Art sees the infinite in the finite, the extraordinary in the everyday, shows the totality through the fragmentary, thereby pointing to the all-embracing and incomprehensible unity of the whole.

In the process, these new ideas of the Romantics were able to build upon Kant's transcendental idealism – especially on his epistemology and his aesthetics of the sublime – but they radically took their leave from the universalism and rationalism of the Enlightenment: Fichte's idea of the self-positing subject or Schelling's philosophy of nature, Schleiermacher's pantheist mysticism or F. v. Schlegel's theory of universal poetry give up Kant's reflexive and critical concept of cognition in favor of a speculative one, and exchange the universalism of the Enlightenment for the particularity of the subject. Unlike Kant, the Romantics did not consider the absolute to be comprehensible through universal reason. The sublime and infinite entirely eludes the finite perspective; all phenomena are finite forms, fragments, instants. Just as in Kant's criticism of empiricism the "thing in itself" is no longer available to experience, so the absolute and transcendent ideas are no longer directly accessible to understanding or imagination in the Romantic idealist conception. "Even the greatest system is after all only a fragment."[27]

Only traces in the individual subject, in the will and in the feeling directed towards the absolute, are available to consciousness. Not only the empirical things but also the representations of the absolute are ultimately no more than the creations of consciousness, of the imaginative power of the subject – for Schleiermacher, God becomes a differentiation of consciousness. With that, Romanticism finds the origin of thinking and of experience in the sphere of the individual consciousness, the will, in fantasy and in the feeling of subjectivity, in the ego. The rational individualism of the Enlightenment is ultimately replaced, in Novalis, by a magical subjectivism.

In the process of this orientation toward subjectivity and feeling, Romanticism is able to key into existing codes. Pietism and the eudaemonism of the Enlightenment had already turned the gaze inwards and created a tradition of self-observation. Romanticism, however, reinterprets the new world in a special way. It is no longer a question of reason and morality, but of "feeling" and beauty; no longer a matter of order, but of something ungraspable.

Once again, art offers privileged access toward an understanding of individual consciousness. After Schelling, the imagination becomes self-conscious for the first time in art.[28] For F. v. Schlegel, the artist becomes conscious of his individuality in the act of artistic creation, and simultaneously discovers the divine in himself. Artistic creativity is the process in which the ultimate individualization of consciousness takes place; the merely rule-based and repeatable character of the activity of communication and of social life is thus overcome. Art breaks through the barriers of society and becomes the paradigm of self-realization.

To the extent, however, to which consciousness approaches individuality and thus the absolute, the problem upon which the transcendental philosophy of the Enlightenment was shipwrecked repeats itself. Just like the sublime and infinite, the ultimate and absolute individuality is no longer graspable or communicable. The radical individuality of the subject eludes communication. It is only known and conscious to the subject itself, in dialogue with itself. This individuality communicates itself to outsiders only in their perceiving something alien, in not being able to understand.

What escape routes were still available to Romantic thinking, if it had to accept this intersubjective speechlessness concerning the individual, yet did not want to dispense with the communication constituted through individuality? One solution – of far-reaching consequences for art – pursued the estrangement of the known as a distinguishing mark of individuality. Exposure of the abyssal and uncanny in the apparently ordered and everyday pointed to the incommunicable, without needing or indeed being able to name it. A further possibility consisted in translating the idea of individuality to *collectives*, in particular that of the nation. In this way, the nation appeared as a collective subject of inimitable individuality, and *within this subject* communication could take place with reference to this identity and individuality. Thus individuality and communication could be brought together via the collective identity of the nation. Just as the personal subject could become cognizant of his individuality in the internal dialogue of his consciousness, so communication within a nation was also grounded in its collective subjectivity, and could become cognizant of its national individuality through art and poetry.

The Romantic concept of the nation was thereby able to conjoin three central code elements: 1. the idea of a transcendent world, inaccessible to vulgar communication; 2. the idea of individuality as the core of reality and starting point for experience of the world; 3. the emphasis on an aesthetic access to individuality and thus to the absolute. All three code elements are founded on structural distinctions within the patriotic code, but give them a radical reinterpretation appropriate to the special situation of uprooted intellectuals. In the following section, it will be attempted to articulate this special conjunction of transcendentalism and aesthetic individualism in the Romantic nation code.

The transcendent identity of the nation

In the discourse of the Romantic intellectuals, the collective identity of Germany was constructed in a new way that was to have far-reaching consequences. The identity of the nation was brought into an antithesis, rife with tension, to the visible and limited present of the German territories with their political impotence. There is an extraordinary parallel to be drawn here between the social situation of the intellectuals and the situation of Germany. The parallelism between the individual and collective identity was by no means coincidental, but very present to consciousness. Friedrich von Schlegel turns the interconnection between community and identity into a method of achieving self-knowledge: “In order to understand oneself, one must first understand one’s companions.”[29] In both cases, superficial reality did not correspond to the deeper essential significance. Culture and politics collided as two spheres with entirely different ordering principles. Distinguishing the splintered, impotent situation of the German states from the actual, atemporal identity of the German nation simultaneously meant salvaging one's own identity as an artist from the oppressive and constrained biographical situation. Moreover, the celebrated heroes of German Classicism had assigned little weight to the German nation, valuing cosmopolitan humanism far more highly. Identifying oneself with German culture thus also promised to delimit one from the overpowering generation of classical authors.

Such a tension – between an overarching cultural identity and the constrained, particular reality of the many German states – had already been at the heart of the patriotism of the Enlightenment. The Romantic concept of the people was able to link up with this tradition. But superficial (from the point of view of the Romantics) patriotism was hardly appropriate to the situation of the intellectuals. Patriotism urged the conversion of the better, reasonable order into the deed – if not today, then tomorrow. It believed that it had found a name for the order beyond in reason and morality. It gave a collective identity to precisely that bourgeois practice from which the Romantic intellectuals attempted to dissociate themselves.

Unlike the patriotism of the Enlightenment, the Romantic encoding of the nation insisted upon a radical tension between culture and politics. Ultimately this construction of an essential tension – between the identity-securing sphere of culture and the sphere of the quotidian and worldly present – resorted to philosophical tools. The identity of the nation was of the beyond, infinite and sublime. The present world of the state, on the contrary, was of this world, finite and contingent. Fichte makes this clear:

> . . . People (*Volk*) and fatherland in this signification, as carrier and guarantor of earthly eternity, as that which can be eternal on this base earth, lie far beyond the State in the customary sense of the word – beyond the social order as apprehended merely by the clear phrase, and built up and maintained as the phrase directs. The latter wants certain right, inner peace, and for everyone to find his sustenance and the passage of his sensory existence, for as long as God grants it to him, through industry. But this is all only a means, a condition and framework, for what the fatherland actually wants: the blossoming of the eternal and divine in the world, ever purer, more perfect and complete, in unceasing progress.[30]

State and nation, society and community henceforth stood in a contradiction that reserved history for one, identity for the other. Thus in Germany the "nation" became a depoliticized, permeable concept, which could be filled with contradictory and manifold contents.

The attempt to resituate the identity of the nation in an invisible beyond, outside the everyday and the present, first led to the scrutiny of history.

Remembering the "*Translatio Imperii*," it had always been possible to connect Germany with the Roman Empire, but when Novalis claimed that "Germany is Rome," he was no longer referring to the German nation's putative legal succession to the Roman Empire, but to a far deeper stratum – to national characteristics.[31]

Yet the tie between Germany and Greece became more important than the reference to Rome. This is the more true since it appeared that France had actually inherited the Roman legacy. The fall of ancient Rome consequently also allowed one to expect an end to French supremacy. Here too, the German classics, Herder and Winckelman above all, had prepared the ground. Germany and Greece were seen as nations whose identity was not to be found in the fields of state and politics, but in the sphere of culture and art.[32] To F. v. Schlegel – but above all to Hölderlin – ancient Greece seemed a shining example that could lead German culture to inimitable heights: "A quite new and incomparably higher stage of Greek study has been initiated by Germans, and it will remain their exclusive possession for perhaps a considerable period."[33]

While this particular relationship between Germany and ancient Greece had already been brought up by the Classicist authors, the discovery of the German Middle Ages was an achievement of the Romantic intellectuals. Onto the stage formerly occupied by Antiquity, Tieck and Wackenroder, Novalis and Schlegel dragged out the darkly luminous Middle Ages alluded to by cathedrals and ruins. But here too, the German Enlightenment had already led the way: Justus Möser had already demanded that national unity become a principle for the shaping of historiography, and traced it back to early modern times.

In another respect, however, the look back at the past underwent a basic change during the period between the Enlightenment and Romanticism. Whereas the Enlightenment posited the past in a continuous relation to the present, in Romanticism the past is "dehistoricized." It was not conceived of as a stream of change and transformation leading into the present and giving rise to it, but as a sphere entirely distinct from the present, no longer subject to transformation or change – a stable point of reference for the observation of transformation and decline. This past is timeless, unchangeable, eternal. History is at a standstill within it, and for precisely that reason, it can secure national identity. In the present, this mythical identity of the Germans is strewn about, hidden, and henceforth only fragmentary, present in ruins. This becomes particularly clear in the laments of E.M. Arndt on the disappearance of the old German strength of character, and in his retrospective look at the great Germans of early modern times. Reformers like Luther and Zwingli, scientists like Kepler and Leibniz, artists like Dürer and Rembrandt, musicians like Händel and Mozart, embody the genius of the Germans and show the way forward to a down-trodden people. It is noteworthy here (as also in other contemporary retro-spectives) that Dutchmen like Rembrandt are also counted among the great Germans. It is less the language, certainly not state citizenship, but rather an idea of German genius, unrooted in place or time, that delimits this circle.

The true identity of the Germans can by no means be established with reference to the everyday present, to delimited, special or mutable things, and certainly not to the sum of citizens. It is an encompassing essence that surpasses any specific boundaries. Novalis makes this clear: "There are Germans everywhere. The German essence is as little restricted to a specific state as that of Rome, Greece or Britain . . ."[34]

National identity is constructed here within the framework of a transcendent code: a timeless and unsituated identity is distinguished from single individuals and changes of history. But in order to be able to describe the general identity, one must once again have recourse to the particular. This particular – the German Middle Ages, the old Teutons, ancient Greece – is then dehistoricized and mythologized: a timeless period.

Even when texts rather than ruins are treated as fragments of national identity, this mythic basic structure becomes clear. The Grimms' collection of fairy tales, Brentano's songs, and Schlegel's version of the Song of the Nibelungen approach texts whose origins are unconnected by any clear, continuous line with the present. They point to a quite different world, one that cannot be precisely determined by means of the coordinates of today. This world is not the dependable product of everyday activity, but its omnipresent background – and for precisely that reason, the identity of the nation is to be sought therein.

The Romantic concept of nature offered a further possibility for constructing the identity of the nation within the framework of a transcendent code. Here, *nature* is not understood as the object of scientific experience or of technical manipulation, as the analytically distinguishable componentry of the material world, but as the unifying ground of matter, out of which distinctions emerge and individual things are determined only through the action of the mind – or more accurately spirit, the *Geist*. Romantic nature is undetermined, unconscious and infinite. It is the background and horizon of historical action, comparable, in psychoanalysis, to the unconscious.[35] This Romantic idea of nature is not *empirical* but *transcendent with respect to experience* – and for precisely that reason it is suitable for the construction of national identity. Just as nature is something general that cannot be named and grasped through individual scientific experiences, the nation must also be presupposed as an undetermined, and indeterminable, identity that historical action and the form of statehood must address, without ever being able to exhaustively apprehend or realize. The nation is organic, living and infinite nature – an "exalted affair" that can never be grasped through "dead concepts."[36] "What is the art of diplomacy compared to the tremendous natural force that is daily further unleashed in peoples? . . . The nation has an urge towards unity, and this urge is like the growth of a tree, the blowing of the wind . . ."[37]

The Germany of the Romantics is no longer composed of individual persons, as the fatherland was still imagined by the Enlightenment, but is an organized whole, no longer reducible to the individual advantages of a country, or even the special characteristics of its citizens.

> What gathers details, piles them up into masses, composes these into a unity, forever assembles these into greater ones, unites into solar systems and worlds, until together they all form the great Universe – in the highest and greatest and most comprehensive human society, in the people, this power of unification cannot be named anything other than – Volkstum [peoplehood]. It is the common substrate of the people, its indwelling nature, its rain and life, its regenerative force, its reproductive capacity.[38]

This supraindividual whole is seen above all in the German language. Language can indeed not be reduced to its individual speakers, or even to its individual speech acts. Instead it facilitates an infinite quantity of speech acts. German Classicism – and in this respect Herder above all – had pointed to linguistic consciousness as the basis of national unity.[39] From the Romantic point of view, however, the German language is given a naturalist reinterpretation. In Fichte's famous formulation, it is no longer the ligature of a patriotic public, but the property of an *Ur-Volk*, which "speaks a language that is alive down to its first emanation from natural force, while the other Germanic tribes speak a language that only twitches at its surface, but is dead at the root."[40]

When national identity is thus bound to a Romantic concept of nature, we are clearly no longer dealing with the empirical differences of climate and soil that were also discussed in the German Enlightenment, in the wake of the latter's reception of Montesquieu and his theories of national difference. Although here as well Romanticism can build on available encodings, it radically reinterprets the corresponding differences: the empirical concept of nature, concerned with differences and explanation, was replaced by a transcendent concept of nature, directed toward unity and etiology. Like all universalist codes, the Romantic, transcendent concept of nature also constructed collective identity via a special tension between universalist openness and particularist closure. Through the transcendent grounding of the nation, one gained access to the universalist ideas of Enlightenment philosophy, which the Romantics did not simply reject, but whose limitations they overcame; and on whose insights they hoped to build.

The incommunicability of the national

Nature and experience, nation and history, identity and action, are kept apart through the same tension and the same antithesis. This arises from the indivisibility and incomparability of the transcendent sphere, on the one hand, and from the comparability and finitude of empirical action, on the other. The keyword is individuality.

Unlike the empirical, spatially fixed individuality of Enlightenment philosophy, Romantic individuality is a characteristic of the non-empirical, transcendent sphere. It eludes the operations of comparison and generalization, which describe empirical conditions. It cannot be deliberately produced, cannot be imitated or reproduced. It eludes dismantling by understanding. With the concept of the individual, the elementary in the transcendent sphere – that which is resistant to conceptualization – is circumscribed, but not grasped. That which is constitutive of individuality is incommunicable; "dead concepts" fail to convey it. Therefore, Romanticism takes as its task the "representation of the unrepresentable,"[41] the description of the actual, which can no longer be apprehended discursively. It discovers in itself the extraordinary, incomprehensible, and strange, reveals the uncanny behind the surface of the everyday, and indirectly points thus to individuality. Precisely by hunting for something indescribable, which refuses access to operations of understanding or of comprehension, the Romantics can be certain that they are entering new terrain on the far side of the Enlightenment – terrain which cannot, *by definition*, be reclaimed by enlightenment. Romanticism confirms this communicative inapproachability of the individual not only in the case of persons, but also among nations. Here too, the transference is supported by parallels between the situation of the intellectual and of the nation. Inaccessible to outsiders, the uniqueness of artistic genius and of national character point to one another – in either case, individuality and inimitability are augmented to the limit. Thus the Romantic code not only gives a reason for the distance between intellectuals and society, but also overcomes this antithesis. One distances oneself from bourgeois society and finds unity and identity in the nation.

Here too, the new code can assimilate extant traditions, German Classicism in particular. One can find emphatic pleas for the principle of individuality and variety with respect to regional and national characteristics going back to Herder and Möser. In Humboldt, the nation becomes the highest form of individuality and a prerequisite for giving rise to the individuality of the single person. But only in Romanticism is this idea of the individuality of the national tied in with the *sublime*, and therefore ungraspable and incomprehensible. The eighteenth century was still interested in the *empirical* differences between the nations. It wanted *explanations* for these individual peculiarities, and found them in climate and soil. Romanticism, by contrast, saw the individuality of the nation as mysterious, and considered the love of one's own people inexplicable. The reasons for love of one's own *Volk* are therefore not to be named, on principle. One does not love Germany for its special qualities,

> for Rome and the Egyptian Delta are far more blessed with fruits and beautiful works of art, and with all things great and magnificent, than Germany. All the same, if your son's destiny demanded that he live there, he would feel sad, and never love it as he now loves Germany.[42]

In clear antithesis to the patriotism of the Enlightenment, which on principle kept its borders open for communication, the Romantic concept of the nation closes the borders to outsiders. Here membership in a nation approaches a primordial significance. It is predicated on distinctions difficult of linguistic access, on incommunicable and thus also inalienable certainties, less on the words of the language than on gesture and articulation. One either has it or one does not. Every attempt to learn a national characteristic systematically, or pass it on in missionary fashion, is predestined to failure. National peculiarity refuses to admit of practical pedagogy and theoretical description. It can be addressed in anecdotes and contrasts, in details and scurrilous ventings; it has a name but no principle, and is based on a prejudice that one cannot assert with good reason, or defend against doubters. Whoever disputes it can, conversely, always adduce good empirical reasons, but that is precisely what is not relevant. The collective identity of the nation may be primordial and natural, but it is not empirically available to experience and criticism. The Romantic concept of nature is targeted at the totality of the organic and living, and not at specific aspects – blood and race, for example.

This primordial, natural nation offers a non-linguistic foundation in a society becoming ever more linguistically mobile. After the Enlightenment, traditional and personal rule, the customary safeguards of communication, must fail. The formerly sacred core of communal solidarity is now open to revision, doubt and criticism. Here too, Romanticism proceeds from the situation created by the Enlightenment. But impersonal morality and reason, the codes of the Enlightenment, can no longer be a valid, solid ground for linguistic understanding, for they too can clearly be discursively surpassed. Only a terrain that refuses to admit of description, not for socio-normative but *communicative* reasons, which can be named but not imparted, mediated, or passed on, was suitable to protect this core of communal solidarity from discursive dissolution.

Thus the Romantic code of the nation also gives rise to a fundamental reorientation of society. While the Enlightenment comprehended the unity and identity of society to be ultimately universal, it is now precisely identity that is taken out of the universalist sphere of money and law, and reattributed to what is individual and incommunicable. The Romantic nation code thereby solves a new problem. It constructs limits to communication in a world whose structure has just been made volatile by the dissemination of communication. It compensates for the dissolution of reality fomented by Romantic irony. It offers security and familiarity in a world that had become abyssal and uncanny precisely because of the Romantic perspective. Romanticism does not only thereby offer the nation code in order to deal with the general instability, differentiation, and mobility of modern relations, but can also deploy it to solve *the specific problems that it has itself created.* In sharp antithesis to the Enlightenment and to Classicism, which had still attempted to assimilate what was alien, to construct an encompassing unity, Romanticism discovers the alien and puzzling in trusted, everyday things. It thereby opens a groundless, dark space of inner demons, Edens from which nobody can be safe. The version of the alien other that appears with Romanticism can in principle not be understood, enlightened, or assimilated. It remains "unconscious." Conversely, strong safeguards become necessary that remain inalienable, inexplicable, and incomprehensible, yet are taken for granted. For Romantics, hesitant when they look into the abyss of their own psyche, the nation offers an external support. The nation – an invention of the intellectuals, in order to calm their unquiet selves.

The aestheticization of the national

Even if the nation possesses an individuality that is sublime by comparison with experience of the world, an approach to this transcendent core of community is not necessarily ruled out. The old representatives of the sacred core are hardly fit for this purpose any more. They have obviously entangled themselves in particular and worldly interests. Instead of the church, art is now supposed to assume the task of approaching the sacred core of the community. F. v. Schlegel discovers in the act of artistic creation both individuality and "the divine" in itself, and Novalis affirms: "Poets and priests were originally one and the same – and only later ages have separated them. The true poet, however, is always a priest, just as the true priest has always been a poet. . . ."[43] The inimitable individuality of genius reveals itself in the act of artistic creation, just as the will of God is revealed in religious cult. "To be a people is the religion of our age," declares E.M. Arndt. The will of God and art of genius are both exalted above criticism and contradiction – they only leave people with the feeling of estrangement and admiration. Yet art does not only have the task of revealing the transcendent, but also has to educate people and lead them out of the crude, uneducated state towards the sublime.

Neither the religious nor the pedagogical function of art are Romantic inventions. Here, Romanticism can assimilate the encodings of German Classicism. Schiller's reflexions, in particular, on the aesthetic education of humankind prepared the ground. However, what is noteworthy is the connection between the religious function of art, on one side, and that of the nation, on the other, as they are produced by the Romantic intellectuals. Whereas the Enlightenment and the German classics stressed the educational function of art, in the new Romanticism the nation appears above all as a "new mythology" that must be created by the poets and artists for the people – who for their part cannot imagine transcendence and require sensory orientations. Here the nation is encoded *aesthetically*, in a double sense. First, the act of creative genius gives the artist access to the transcendent. Second, the mediation of the beyond must be carried out, for the lay person, through fiction, invention, elucidation. Novalis can thus treat the nation as a drama for the people, which must be staged by the poets.

Sometimes, however, this play comes into the vicinity of a reinforcing of prejudices and necessary deceptions. Herder already saw a sometimes favorable prejudice in "restricted nationalism": "Prejudice is good, in its day, for it brings happiness. It forces people toward their center, settles them more firmly on their ancestry, makes them blossom according to their kind, more passionate and also happier in their inclinations and purposes."[44] Peter Villaume also sees the inevitability of these prejudices:

> Uniquely, humans simply do incline to deception, and appear to have a certain preference for delusion . . . So permit us to employ the most advantageous delusions, until human reason reaches its maturity and the truth drives away every deception. If a nation had nothing to distinguish itself from every other but its name, it would not be bad, for want of anything better, to give out this name for a

national trait. And that requires no further sleight of hand than uttering this name like an honorary title.[45]

Romantics like E.M. Arndt went even further:

> . . . We must erect triple and quadruple ramparts around ourselves, so as not ultimately to become dull images resembling everything and nothing, which, having lost their shape and impress, cannot shape or form anything either.[46]

> It is an incontrovertible truth that everything that is to have life and endurance must have a definite repulsion, an antithesis, must have a hatred; that, as every people has its own innermost life element, it must equally have a firm love and a firm hate, if it is not to wither, indifferently nugatory and pitiable, and finally end under the yoke.[47]

The poets, who take on the role of priests, have brought themselves into a situation in which the deception of priesthood is almost unavoidable. Driven to the extreme, the tension between the transcendent and worldly spheres can only be borne by the man with a calling, the poet of genius. For the normal person, the layman, the sphere beyond must be translated into an order of this world, available to sensory perception and everyday things. He needs images and flags, processions and altars, and the intellectual administrators of the beyond have the task of staging and controlling precisely these profanations of the sacred. Bearing the sublime, interpreting what is strange and infinite, is reserved for the intellectuals alone. It is precisely this position in the watchtower that constitutes their power in axial ages. The necessity of staging the nation aesthetically shows that the Romantic concept of the *Volk* is ultimately not a primordial, but a universalist encoding of national identity, which must be disseminated in missionary fashion by the intellectuals in their own society.

At the turn of the nineteenth century, the German intellectuals reinforced this tension between this world and the beyond, and propagated an aesthetic *mise en scène* of the transcendental sphere for the people: national poetry. The Romantic era thus appears as a German axial age in which the nation took the place of the church, and the Romantic intellectuals took the place of the priests. With that, a structure was also created in which subsequent German intellectuals could move. Unlike their French counterparts, who could orient themselves by the position of the aristocracy and the latter's proximity to the royal court, and who therefore valued discursive elegance and the applause of the rulers whom they criticized, in the German intellectuals the dualism of priests and rulers, spirit and power, faith and worldliness, reproduces itself in a special manner. Intellectuals had to despise the vain world of the surface, and move in the essential and invisible sphere within which it was not elegance and applause that counted, but the depth and fundamentality of the priestly declaration of faith.

The revolutionary discharge: the nation at arms

At first, this Romantic idea of the nation was only a code, with which a small group of intellectuals made itself mutually intelligible and distanced itself from the public. This situation changed profoundly with the experience of the French occupation. Under the unifying pressure of foreign rule, the Romantic concept of the nation broke out of the intellectual hothouse, and became the mobilizing code for large portions of the bourgeoisie. The Romantic intellectuals gave up their distance from politics, and the "play" of the nation was staged. The great tension between this world and the beyond was discharged at the moment of rebellion, in a popular war of liberation.

The idea of the people's war as an uprising against the oppressors was certainly of French origin. The acceleration and condensation of history in the act of revolution, the people as subject of history, the *levée en masse*, the new national motivation of the soldiers, all had been enabled by the success of the Revolution in France. Now these same ideas were turned against Napoleonic rule, against France herself, acquiring a German coloration in the process. The issue was no longer that of revolting against the sovereigns within one's own society, but of an oppressor who crossed all boundaries; no longer of feudal hierarchy against equality, but of the national character under the threat of a "usurper."

The people's war or national war was to be realized initially in Austria, where Count Philipp Stadion was preparing to go to war against Napoleon. Friedrich v. Schlegel and Gentz went into Austrian service. At the same time, Görres in the Rhineland and Arndt, A. Müller and Kleist in Berlin were preparing the ground for the "God who made iron grow" (Arndt).[48] Precisely because the national uprising was at first rejected by the Prussian king, and also found little resonance among the feudal higher classes, it was attractive to the intellectuals. Hardly any of the Romantic intellectuals refused to become politically engaged after 1808. Rückert and Schlegel, Eichendorff and Arndt, Görres and Arnim all wrote songs and articles, some joined secret brotherhoods. Theodor Körner died in the ranks of the *Freikorps*. "This is no war which the crowns know about, this is a holy war" (Körner) – declared the intellectuals, and Prussian reformers like Stein or even Humboldt, who had initially contracted into the project of Enlightenment rather than Romanticism, spoke of the people having to break its chains. The fatherland was "where honor and independence" (Stein) were to be found.

Although Austria's people's war of 1808 failed and ended in defeat, and the northern German uprisings were initially of no military significance, a completely new form of military mobilization developed after Napoleon's Russian campaign, which was prepared for, in one sense, by the Prussian reformers and their idea of universal conscription; but also, and above all, was urged on by the enthusiastically nationalist intellectuals. Students and *Bürger* joined the voluntary associations, and felt that they were "a nation at arms."

Fired up and led by the intellectuals, these voluntary associations had a completely different, new motivation from that of the regular armies of the eighteenth century. One did not fight because orders, drilling and the fear of draconian punishments left no alternative, but because one personally hated the enemy, and this hatred was given a religious foundation. E.M. Arndt indeed demanded hatred as a religion of the people:

> I want hatred against the French, not only for this war, I want it for a long while, I want it for ever. Then Germany's borders will be secure even without artificial defenses, for the people will always have a unifying point as soon as the restless, thievish neighbors want to overrun them. May this hatred burn as the religion of the German people, as a sacred madness in all hearts, and always sustain us in our loyalty, honesty and courage. . .[49]

Ultimately, it was no longer a question of defending one's special character, but of the universal mission of the Germans. In his speeches to the German nation, Fichte drew up a messianic perspective for the "most aboriginal" of peoples, thereby repeating the hegemonial claim that the French Revolution had made *politically*, for German *culture*. The great, essential tension between this world and the beyond, art and politics, nation and state, collapses here in a totalitarian condensation of history. The state is to be the "discipliner into Germanness." What now counts as the guarantor of redemption is the collective will of the community, and no longer the infinite feeling of the individual. An axial-age tension that has been driven to extremes by the intellectuals is short-circuited in the national revolutionary uprising. The deed in the teeth of death, the sacrifice for the community, is seen as bridging the apparently insurmountable antitheses between the person alone and the whole, as utterly condensing of the present in the name of history, as producing the original unity.[50]

In this short-circuit through the agency of the deed, collective energies are unleashed that were unknown to the Ancien Régime, but of which the prerevolutionary Enlightenment could not have had an inkling when it viewed war as a moral institution, as an indispensable driving force of progress, as "the most potent remedy for a diseased, or, if you prefer, exhausted humanity."[51] Kant had already lauded war as something sublime in 1790, "which only makes the intellect of the people the more sublime, the more it has been exposed to dangers in which it was bravely able to assert itself; while a long peace on the contrary merely leads to the supremacy of the mercantile spirit, but with it also of base selfishness, cowardice, and softness, and to the demeaning of the people's thinking."[52] When the infinitude of the transcendent sphere is translated into violence, and the inimitability of the individual is turned to the purpose of excluding criticism, then those totalitarian demons are awakened that were to fascinate German history for a long time afterward. Its victims included precisely those intellectuals who discharged the axial-age tension in a totalizing act.

5

The people on the barricades: the democratic code

After the Napoleonic wars of liberation, the breaking out of the aesthetic concept of the people or *Volk* from the intellectual hothouse of Romanticism led to a new scenario for the construction of national identity. This scenario is generally characterized by an expansion of the carrier groups and by a concomitant trivialization[1] of the Romantic encoding itself. National consciousness was not only manifested by the educated public or the esoteric circle of the Romantics, but also by the petty bourgeoisie of the towns, and later even by the *reisende Handwerksgesellen* (journeymen craft laborers) of the *Vormärz.* Such an expanded sociostructural base could hardly apprehend itself any longer in terms of shared class origins or corporate interests. It found its common base through special forms of communication, on the one hand, and in a renewed "domestic–political" turn of national consciousness, in a united front against authority and the whims of sovereignty, on the other.

The trivialization of the national

The inclusion of the petty bourgeoisie among the carrier strata of national consciousness was initially enacted through an expansion of the institution of the *Verein*[2] – which we have already come to see as typical of the *Bildungsbürger* class in the Enlightenment period. The highbrow reading society or patriotic *Verein* of the eighteenth century was followed by the founding of large numbers of *Vereine* with various purposes and memberships: in particular, *Burschenschaften* (fraternities) among students, and *Gesangsvereine* (choral societies) and *Turnervereine* (gymnastics clubs), which looked to a petty-bourgeois public for their membership, became sites where nationalist convictions and popular consciousness could thrive.[3] However, they did not merely continue the tradition of the *Verein* among the *Bildungsbürger* class of the Enlightenment, but also took over the Romantic idea of aesthetic access to national identity – in trivialized form, of course: in song, art appreciation and physical exercise. This inclusion of the petty bourgeoisie involved a notable realignment to new forms of communication, which were able to bring large masses of people into relation with one another. The moral discourse of the patriots and aesthetic reflexion were replaced by the celebration of great festivals such as those in Wartburg or Hambach, by massed singing of songs from the national treasury, and later also erection of national memorials and the cult of the national flag.[4] These rituals of belonging are characterized precisely by their exclusion or extreme restriction of reflexion and discourse, individuality and argument. Although they had found the identity-securing ground of the national in things unnamable and unsayable, the Romantic intellectuals had approached the unutterable in linguistic fashion. The trivialized continuation of this aesthetic nation code among the petty bourgeoisie, by contrast, dispensed with linguistic refinement, celebrating the nation through collective ritual.[5] Unlike Romanticism, which sought an inimitable identity behind the merely external and reproducible, the rituals of song, of shared reverence for memorials and flags, of synchronized marches and physical exercises, produced a *uniformity* through special procedures, behind which the variety and individuality of the participants retreated. Slogans and rituals urge participation and conformity, and exclude possibilities of negation. The construction of collective identity is then no longer dependent on the fleeting success of esoteric discourses, but is staged in a manner immediately recognizable owing to its repetitiveness and intensification. Membership is flagged like a ship. This has its advantages if one wants not merely to form small groups, but also larger masses of people, so as to connect larger masses of people to one another and keep the national consciousness reproducible. In the process, a new, theatrically staged presence becomes more important. As distinct from the ratiocinations of public life, ceremonial events and festivals are only accessible through personal and physical *presence*. By its means the religious aspect is strengthened in a society where access to the written word is open to increasing numbers of people, and the public is thus no longer clearly delimited.[6]

Moreover, ritual anchoring of the national shows that the national encoding is in process of penetrating at last to the central foundation of collective identity. Here, the sacred core of collective identity must be withdrawn from the arbitrariness of individual linguistic mediation. If anything is said, it is said in a counterpoint of speaker and chorus[7] – a form in which social and individual differences vanish.

This ritual production of national identity is certainly not peculiar to the Germans. The cult of memorials and warriors' associations were just as noticeable in France during the century after Napoleon as in Germany. However, they acquire greater weight when, as in Germany, the state-political constitution is absent, and the ritual production of the national receives a quasi-political function.

The Enlightenment among the petty bourgeoisie: the teachers

In spite of this tendency toward the creation of ritual uniformity, certain sociostructural considerations were to have particular influence on the recodings of the national in the Germany of the Restoration.

The comprehensive reforms of primary schooling[8] and of *Gymnasium* (secondary school) education in the first decades of the century had led to the emergence of a relatively large group of teachers, who repeated for themselves – albeit in weakened form – the status inconsistencies of the Romantic intellectuals.[9] The poor salary, the legally and socially unclear situation of this new stratum, and the loneliness of village life were in antithesis to the high self-regard that was imparted through teachers' seminars and through the new pedagogy that derived its orientation from Pestalozzi.[10] In particular, primary school teachers not infrequently came into opposition to the traditional ranks of the pastors, to whom they were subordinate as factotums.

The teachers, however, did not overcome this disappointing life-practical situation through a transcendent deepening of individual and collective identity, i.e. through reflexion, but had recourse to the available ritual forms of communication of the bourgeoisie, while also forming a political front against the lords and rulers of the Restoration principalities. They frequented teachers' *Vereine*, visited teachers' festivals, and sang songs, thus overcoming the loneliness and insecurity of village life. The anti-traditionalist mission of education that was imparted in the teachers' seminars, the self-consciousness of the pedagogic specialist, surely also many teachers' personal history in the *Burschenschaften*, led their gaze, by way of particularist and local bigotries, beyond their own situation to the level of the general. There, positions were critically adopted with regard to the arbitrariness of the principalities, and plans were drawn up for the pedagogical correction of state and society. Posed early, the question of the revolutionary principle of public education[11] was then again critically taken up by the opposing side, who pointed to the influence of the Hegelians[12] and the "revolutionary ethos"[13] widespread among the teachers.

In this new stratum of teachers, the emancipatory Enlightenment pathos and the communication forms of the petty bourgeoisie combined not infrequently with peasant or proletarian origins, and thus indeed formed particularly favorable conditions for the reception of radical democratic ideas.[14] They underwent a special transformation of the national encoding: the nation is no longer the fatherland of the educated, and it is certainly not the unutterable mystical ground of identity, but the subject of politics, which posits itself in antithesis to the authority of the principality and of particular economic interests. The teachers became the carriers of a *democratic concept of the people*, which was to burgeon under socialism and which a populist social critique (but also the social revolutionary currents of fascism) was able to assimilate.

The distancing of the intellectuals

During the wars of liberation, the Romantic intellectuals had given up the distance from which they observed society in favor of a national, anti-French engagement. National enthusiasm increased in the act of fending off foreign rule, and took hold not only of the leading minds of Romanticism, but also of the students and of large parts of the *Bildungsbürgertum*. This idea of the people as an emancipatory subject did not remain limited to one's own nation, but also determined one's perspective on other nations.[15]

Enthusiasm for the Greek War of Liberation against the Ottoman Empire around 1820, or support for the Polish uprising against Russia in 1833, was unanimous among the educated, and stood in a barely perceived antithesis to Prussian–German administrative interests in the Grand Duchy of Poznan.[16]

This "internationalist nationalism" of the German intellectuals had as its dream the "spring-time of peoples," and also allowed Francophobia to weaken markedly after 1820.[17] France was once again seen as the cradle of the revolution, even before the July Revolution of 1830, and the ideas of Saint-Simon, later also of Baboeuf and Blanquis, found a hearing among the intellectuals in Germany relatively quickly.[18] Although it was precisely the *reisende Handwerksburschen* (journeymen) who contributed to this reception of revolutionary ideas, the German lower strata were but little moved by it until far into the *Vormärz*.[19]

In a quite different manner, similar to the Romantic reaction to Classicism, a new generation of literary intellectuals sought to dissociate themselves from late Romanticism – conceived of as simple-minded and pious – and from the Swabian school around Uhland, not to mention the blatantly reactionary inclinations of Romantic intellectuals like Adam Müller and Gentz.[20]

With explicit reference to the July Revolution of 1830 and to the transformed *Zeitgeist*, demands were raised for an "end to the Art Era," for a "young literature," for politicization and contemporary relevance, and the "Young Germany" movement was constituted.[21]

Like their literary models Heine and Börne, the inner circle of *Junges Deutschland*, i.e. Gutzkow, Laube, Mundt and Wienbarg, found themselves in a quite different situation from that of the esoteric cliques of the Romantics. They were very successful men, and reached a comparatively large audience as publishers and editors of respected periodicals.[22] Their material situation and literary reputation gave them no cause for resentment or distancing. There is no justification for seeing them as a homogeneous group, either in virtue of a common explicit program or of merely sporadic personal relations.[23] The powerful feud between Börne and Heine is by no means unique in this respect. They only found common ground because of external circumstances, through a critical commitment against the principality and philistinism, and because they were both affected by censorship, conservative criticism, and banishment. The constitution of a "group" conceived as "Young Germany" was above all the result of the famous denunciation by Menzel and the ostracism decree of the German *Bund* (the loose confederation formed after the Restoration). Only from the point of view of the state and of the public did the "Young Germans" appear as a uniform group, and it was only in relation to the state and to the public that they found a commonality which was justified neither by literary style nor by their internal communication. It took censorship and repression, the concomitants of the Restoration state, in order to individualize themselves and gain distinction as a group.[24]

Flight from the censor, ostracism or freely chosen exile, loosened the local ties of the *Vormärz* intellectuals, and facilitated a literary nomadism that refused to settle down or stabilize. "What better for homeless German literature to do than to live the life of the vagabond?"[25] This mobility did not only result from persecution by the Restoration states, but had programmatic traits. An enthusiasm for travel and for the "pleasures of the road" was cultivated,[26] and was facilitated by improvement in the infrastructure, while travel literature reported on observations and experiences. One was fascinated by the urban life of the great metropolises of Berlin, Paris, or later also Brussels, and there developed new forms of life – say, that of the *flâneur*, who without any particular goal in mind allowed himself to be driven along streams of passers-by, observed ephemera, went into wine cellars and cafes, occasionally conversing there or writing down his observations, and was permitted to do anything during the night except one thing: sleep. What was at issue was no longer the invisible world, which the intellectuals of the Romantic age had sought in their dreams, but the visible vitality of the great cities, momentary encounters, which had to be observed with extreme attentiveness. Literature was supposed to consist of "fleeting outpourings of alternating excitations."[27] The anonymity of the great cities thus presented a new form of uprooting and disengagement from solid ties for the intellectual.

It was not virtue and morals, or concord and adaptability, but ridicule and critique, "life" and "emancipation of the flesh," that became the guiding ideas of a literary Bohème that engaged itself politically, and delimited itself from the prejudices of the German petty bourgeoisie. This ironic distancing from the bourgeois public became the more important for intellectuals like Heine and Börne precisely since the public itself did not keep its distance. Unlike the early Romantics, the literati of Young Germany wrote for a broad public that was favorably disposed toward them. The literary market underwent extraordinary growth during the decades after 1830, and the professional writer who could live from his work was by no means any longer a rare exception.[28] One no longer wrote for immortality, but with a clear view to the market and one's preferences. The rewards were still comparatively low – so one wrote a lot and had little time for careful rewriting. That led to the emergence of a quite new problem for the writer: he had to solve the conflict between the requirements of the market and those of artistic autonomy through a compromise, and this compromise had to be overcome in its turn. The greater the concessions to the tastes of the market, the more apt the author was, conversely, to attempt to distance himself personally. The distance between the intellectuals and society therefore had to be created and reinforced through additional gestures – but this gesture of distancing was repeated by the public. Precisely because the readers of Heine and Börne were not the philistines whom they ridiculed, the attempt at an outward demarcation can be sensed in the public as well as in the authors. The author could create a distance to society and leave its orders through irony, satire and critique, and his readers could repeat this distancing process for themselves by means of their choice of reading matter.[29] The reading matter itself created social borders and identifications, and by no means merely depicted current sociostructural interests. The teacher could feel himself elevated from his environment, the petty bourgeois could distinguish himself from the other, "real" petty bourgeois, etc. For author and public, the same pattern held of a pronounced detachment from a society that was difficult to flee. In this attempt to gain distance from society through irony and detachment, there was a recurrence of the structural tension that Romanticism had already known.

The Young Hegelians, the second important group of *Vormärz* intellectuals,[30] also found their commonality above all in an "external" relation: the shadow of Hegel, who had given his name to the school as its founding father. For them too, it was the case that they could no longer gain their distance from the society that surrounded them through prescribed local or sociostructural marginality. On the contrary: the students of Hegel had excellent connections with the Prussian cultural ministry under Altenstein, and were able to occupy a succession of important professorial chairs, particularly during the years after 1830. They had strong allegiances to the Prussian project of state reform, and it was only gradually, and comparatively late at that, that they were prepared to enter into coalitions with Liberals against restorationist tendencies for an absolutist monarchy. The radicalization into a Hegelian Left then explicitly exploded the framework of liberalism and the "*juste-milieu*" of high society.

Not all Hegelians held professorships, however. The "second generation" of Hegelians entered an academic career crisis, and thereby also into a particular distance from the academic establishment.[31] Many Left Hegelians remained *Privatdozenten* (an unpaid academic post) or lived off journalistic activities.[32] They were just as affected by the Karlsbad Declarations as were the literati of Young Germany, and just like these, they were not only the victims, but indirectly also the benefactors of censorship. A censorship decree generated attention throughout society, and could in part be circumvented by means of appropriate publishing tricks (printing beyond the borders, simultaneous delivery of all copies, etc.).[33]

Irony, engagement and the Bohème

In their attempt to outdo the preceding generation, the literati of Young Germany first had recourse to the strategy of ironic distancing that early Romanticism had already employed. In particular, they deployed satire and irony in order to gain distance and thereby to engage themselves. Yet it was not only the preceding generation that was ridiculed, but also and above all petty-bourgeois philistinism, the authoritarian state, and censorship. The stylization of one's own intellectual identity necessitated the contrast with those who had only the appearance of learning, the suppressors of freedom of thought, with the principality, and with bourgeois society, which had united with the nation in prospect.

The form of life that converted this fundamental antithesis into deeds was the Bohème.[34] By its means, that which for the early Romantics had still been personal passion, feverish sentiment, and disorganized practice was converted into a programmatic lifestyle. As a consequence, the Bohème became the most important form of cultural distancing within Modernity.

The life-form of the Bohème no longer oriented itself by the unique and unrepeatable aesthetic achievements of genius. It was much concerned instead with a practical framework that would enable everybody to conceive of and stage themselves as "improper" and autonomous. Delimiting oneself from that which was bourgeois was thus more important than individual creativity. The Bohème was not possible as an individual arrangement, but only as a common form of individualization that contrasted with normality. In this form of life, *style* became a precondition for individuality. It thereby created a specifically modern connection between collective identity and individuality. Scorn for the majority and distance from the normal mode of living were not determined here by the attempt to salvage tradition, or to approach a charismatic personage, but rather by "avant-garde" consciousness, the temporalized aristocracy of art.[35] As a Bohemian, one could feel young and a part of tomorrow's world; the programmatic attempt to break rules opened up an infinite space of possibilities and generated a strong feeling of the new, of future and freedom. The Bohème of the *Vormärz* could in the process continue the tradition of the anti-bourgeois cliques of Romanticism.[36] As in their case, social relations within the group were largely determined by personalities; but this personal orientation manifested itself less in reciprocal sympathies than in rivalries, disfavor and envy. The group was held together above all by an external denominator: by the common rejection of bourgeois philistinism and of the principalities' arbitrary rule.

Schools, polemics, parties

For the second important group of *Vormärz* intellectuals, such an external denominator was to be found in their common relation to Hegel's *œuvre*. Initially and above all, the Hegelians had the structure of an intellectual school in which the *œuvre* of the founding father was to be treated with reverence, and could henceforth only be interpreted, applied and continued.[37] The attempt to surpass the preceding generation intellectually, which had still motivated the Romantic intellectuals, was thus fundamentally blocked. In the school of intellectuals, a new motif took the place of progress beyond the older generation: the attempt to understand the work of the founding father, to point up and fill out its central gaps, to administrate the legacy of the master and to apply it to new areas. In the shadow of the great work, the Young Hegelians in particular then developed a sectarian inclination toward argumentative mannerism and exaggerated systematization. In the process, dissension and disputes over the inheritance were carried on with a vehemence reminiscent of conflicts between relatives.[38] Membership of the group was likewise stable, and could be exposed to the strain of conflicts. Sympathy and good manners were in both cases dispensable as guarantors of the social relation. The internal communication of the intellectual school consequently oriented itself around an interest in subjecting the intellectual dignity of the others to argumentative doubt, thus excluding them as "fellow heirs."[39]

The common rejection of other social groups, and in particular also of bourgeois etiquette, remained untouched. The Young Hegelians also distanced themselves from the bourgeoisie, not merely through ridicule and satire, but also through Bohemian living conditions and a deliberate cultivation of scandal.[40] One wanted to live without the temporal rules, local ties and moral prohibitions of the bourgeoisie, and to anticipate the free life of the future by breaking the rules under the eyes of the bourgeoisie. One felt oneself to be the avant-garde, representatives of a future form of life that was given proleptic existence in the present, and future freedom served to justify all the liberties that one took in the present. In this conception of the "avant-garde" of history, the fundamental temporalization to which many sociostructural concepts were subjected at the turn of the nineteenth century is manifested: the "upper strata" were replaced by the avant-garde, upward mobility by progress, aristocracy and its frivolity by the literary Bohème and its libertinism.[41] The new privilege of the avant-garde consisted in being the first to possess the future forms of life, of future knowledge, and thereby to appear in the present as the social site of progress, the gate of entry to the future.

This Bohème of the *Vormärz* intellectuals admittedly rejected the Romantic view of subjective feeling.[42] The Young Hegelians considered feeling to be a private matter that was not directly accessible to public expression. Similar to the withdrawal of the actor's personality behind his role, personal feeling was considered to be excluded from public communication.[43]

In the wake of Hegel, this was staged for an audience as an "edifying play." Indeed, the philosophical dispute over principles often displayed theatrical traits. The most important form of argument was polemical critique. With it, philosophical confrontation was translated into an agonist personal relation – it was not only about argument, but about adopting a party stance, and the public was exhorted to take up a position.

This transition to partisanship was to an extent necessitated by the situation of the Young Hegelian school.

If one's own founding father cannot be surpassed intellectually, and exegetical communication begins to turn in circles after a certain time, then only a change of sphere offers a way out: the deed must follow the spirit, philosophy must become political, theory must become party.[44]

This step from philosophical reflexion to party-political action does not only permit the addition of a new motif to the interpretation of the great thought, but can also be grounded in the guiding Hegelian idea of "mediation." Nevertheless, the Young Hegelians were less concerned about mediation than about "*Konsequenz*" (consequence, entailment, rigor, consistency, responsibility). The "*Konsequenz*" of the theory had to be drawn in the political deed. Guided by the idea, one was to act "rigorously," etc. Partisanship was the consequence of a historical–philosophical system whose validity was achieved neither by that which prevailed, nor by the subjectivity of literary criticism.[45]

In this system, argument loses its ironic lightness. It is put on an impersonal footing and subjected to rules. Salvation was promised not by the infinitude and incomprehensibility of subjectivity and of feeling, but rather by objective knowledge. The primacy of art is at an end, the age of theory begins, and this theory is partisan.[46]

The step from school to party assimilates well into the *Vormärz* scenario, a time of party foundations, which of course rarely took on the firm contours of purposeful, rational organization, but rather corresponded to the type of the political *Verein* or *Bund*. Membership was almost exclusively tied to a common political conviction. Legally established statutes and formal hierarchies, etc. were lacking.[47] Nevertheless, the parties of the *Vormärz* distinguished themselves from the *Vereine* of Enlightenment society in one important respect. They were functionally specific entities oriented toward the participation in and possession of *political power* and sovereign authority through competition between social groups.[48] The rationality of power was no longer secured merely by the reasonableness and enlightenment of the rulers, but was predicated on the enlightened people's right to power. The task of the Enlightenment, the imparting of rationality, falls in turn to the intellectuals.[49] They are the actual guarantors of reason. They *must* become partisan in order to enable the "mediation" of state and society, to help the multiplicity of society become a reasonable unity, and so forth. The party of the intellectuals thus becomes the representative of the absolute, despite being partisan.

Of course, the certainty of standing for the absolute in history by no means prevents faction, dispute and polemic. On the contrary, certainty as a rhetorical attitude can only be sustained with comparative freedom from conflict provided that communication is subject to prior regulation by other, impersonal principles: domination or force of circumstance. In the discourse of the Young Hegelians, however, no living authority could prevent this internal conflict, and no practical pressure to act could rein in the polemic. Freed from practical necessities, but repeatedly invoking these against "utopian" ideas, the communication of the *Vormärz* intellectuals spirals into ever higher systemic spheres. The procedure which the Romantics had initiated, of generating the group only by free-floating discourse, was raised to a new level by the Young Hegelians precisely by the possibility of perpetually invoking objectivity and practical consequence, without needing to regard it as an external restriction.[50]

Unlike the objectivity of a natural-scientific finding, however, the objectivity of the dialectical argument but rarely reduces the opponent to silence. Not merely that one could continue discussing and polemicizing; one was indeed bound to do so for systemic reasons. This self-generation of the group through polemical dissent was able to succeed precisely because there were hardly any firm organizational ligatures or practical pressures to act. Within the framework of a party organization or secret league, the political dissent would have developed an explosive force leading to crisis – but on the level of an intellectual school, it secured the status quo through communication.

It is therefore only apparently paradoxical to see the social success of the Young Hegelians precisely in their failure as a party. Their situation distinguished itself thereby from that of the Saint-Simonists in France. There, the attempt to organize oneself into a sect or order was carried out with much greater rigor, and led to conflictual crises that spelled out the end of the school.[51]

With the switch to dialectical theory, behavior toward the public also changed. Unlike the case of the reading and newspaper culture of the Enlightenment, also unlike the "symphilosophical" discourse of the Romantics, the committed intellectual turned to an anonymous public, which he could *not* imagine to be on a par with himself, and which he could not expect to contradict him. Author and public were no longer linked by a systematic communicative relation, as had still been determined by the patriotic public life of the Enlightenment. The esoteric communication of early Romanticism was associated with a turn to asymmetry, to an alienation between intellectuals and the public that tended to decouple internal intellectual communication from the public. This demarcation was sharpened as soon as the intellectuals no longer owed their position merely to personal sensibility and aesthetic feeling, but could rely on a transcendentally grounded security: one commanded objectively superior knowledge. The result, unlike the case of the Romantics, was a concrete mission: the prospect of historical progress and liberation was to be revealed to uneducated, unenlightened masses.[52] With Büchner and his "Menschenfreunde" (friends of man) began a tradition of calls to a speechless and uneducated majority. The attempt was made to bridge the gulf between intellectuals and the people through argument and emphatic speech.[53] But these did not achieve the resonance that their authors had hoped for.[54] The majority of the many hunger revolts and uprisings between the Biedermeier and *Vormärz* eras were hardly inspired by early socialist ideas of radical social change, but were triggered off by naked need and remained within the traditional framework of "moral economy."[55]

The democratic nation code

The temporalization of collective identity

The situation and forms of discourse of the *Vormärz* intellectuals required new encodings of national identity. Not only the new internationalism and the new role of France, and their distance from Romanticism's trivialized forms of German folklorism, but also the aristocratic, reactionary state of the Karlsbad decrees favored a new encoding of collective identity – where the boundaries no longer ran between this world and the beyond, but right through the middle of society itself.[56] The distancing by "Young Germany" did not result from solitude and local isolation, but emerged in highly mobile living conditions; its discourses were directed toward the actual and observable world, and the encoding of the national had to do justice to this worldliness. For Heine, there were two Germanies: "the old official Germany, the moldy land of philistines" and "the real Germany, great mysterious, as 'twere anonymous Germany of the German people, of the sleeping sovereign."[57] Depending on which Germany was under consideration, the writers and the intellectuals of the *Vormärz* felt love or hatred of the fatherland. One lamented the great torn soul of one's own age,[58] the contradictions and antitheses that made the present appear as an "epoch of transition"[59] between the old and new orders. Romantics had already stressed the fragmentary character of the world of experience, but had also always asserted the invisible and other-worldly unity of the world. The radical worldliness of "Young Germany" now compelled a transformation of this encoding. The difference between this torn soul, this inward conflict, and unity was temporalized, remained in this world. The unity and order of world and society were no longer atemporal and of the world beyond, but viewed as a future state of affairs that could be realized through human action, through an acceleration of the present into the future. Orientation toward this future state of unity, of reconciliation and mediation of the antitheses, also marked the boundaries of collective identity in the present. Everyone who directed their actions and their identity toward this future unity participated in the future, formed the avant-garde of what was to come, and could therefore also call themselves "*Junges Deutschland.*"[60] Opposed to them were the representatives of the old order, of the Restoration, who sought to slow down progress into the future. Thus the past and the future were both extant, in social form, in the present.

The extraordinary intensification of the consciousness of time, and the perception of the present as a labile gateway between the past and the future, also changed the perspective on state, society and nation: the concepts of the collective were temporalized. One thought in terms of developmental stages and metaphors of movement such as emancipation; revolution and progress began their careers in social theory.[61] That which was present no longer received its significance through its relation to an eternal ontological order of the beyond, but only from the worldliness of time, from the relation to the past and to the future. The programmatic marginality of the Bohème corresponds here to the displacement of the semiopoietic center from the present into the future. Semiopoiesis, a unity that establishes meaning, cannot be realized in the present. This also holds for the collective identity of the people and of the nation. In the present, there are – according to Heine – no nations, but only parties.[62] But these mutually disputatious parties are by no means simply a result of randomly antithetical, real and particular interests. They are the social embodiment of future and past; it is only their antithesis that enables progress and history. For the Young Hegelians, partisanship is a commandment of history, for the absolute becomes historical through the party. It is understandable that, for the Young Hegelians, the absoluteness of the world spirit is assigned rather to the project of the future than to the concrete facts of the past:[63] the glance at the future makes action conscious as autonomous action; remembrance of the past points up the unalterable. The relation to the future excites and generates the tension of the uncertain, new and unprecedented, while contemplation of the past is calming and stabilizing; the party of the future is also that of the new and of the exciting.

In the act of seizing power, in the Revolution, history gets moving, reason becomes partisan, and the general is mediated through the particular. The guiding Hegelian idea of reconciliation is implemented here in a philosophy of action and of partisanship, which becomes comprehensible only as progress to the new, more acute consciousness of historicity. The intellectual plays a central role in this mediation of an absolute future and a partisan present. He is "artist, tribune, apostle,"[64] he recreates the unity of the whole through the new idea, and he overcomes the antithesis between art and life by adapting art to life, himself becoming the "unfalsified organ of the age."[65] The intellectual's knowledge will bring about salvation, theory must grab hold of the masses, philosophy must apprehend life, a new church must be founded.

Here too, the new encoding of collective identity builds on corresponding ideas of Romanticism and of the Enlightenment, but the accents are markedly displaced: one talks of organization, politics and party, instead of conjuring the powers of self-enlightenment of the individual, or the inner world of the subject. Here too, there is a parallel to the situation of the German nation in the revaluation of the intellectual. On the field of politics and of the revolutionary deed, it is held to be retrograde and remains far away from the French paradigm. In the region of the spirit, by contrast, and that now means of theory, Germany is superior.[66] Precisely this asynchrony is proof for Marx that in Germany the revolution forges ahead beyond the political sphere into the social: "Germany with its thoroughness cannot make a revolution without making it from the base. The emancipation of the German is the emancipation of the human being."[67] The German nation is therefore particularly empowered to accelerate history through a theory.

The "rehabilitation of the flesh" and the new reality

The orientation of the present toward the future was not, however, the only motif that permitted one to distance oneself from the status quo. The new cult of the senses and the "rehabilitation of the flesh," which the Saint-Simonists and Young Germany, Heine above all, cultivated, were to be just as important.[68] Sensual desire and the individual drive to freedom and self-determination were discovered as an elementary, timeless and natural source of revolt against the social order and repression. Such a revolt had in its sights not only mere liberation from the supremacy of a particular class, but things far more fundamental: the social order in itself, the servitude of the individual. Obedience to Christian morality was revoked in the name of sensuality and of an ancient pantheism.[69] The "rehabilitation of the flesh" and the immediacy of sensory experience entered into opposition with moral discipline, order and rule-following. The form of life that made this fundamental antithesis its theme was the programmatic irregularity of the Bohème, in whom art and life were to become one, and spontaneity of feeling the norm.

This "rehabilitation of the flesh" was also able to link up with Enlightenment and Romantic motifs.[70] The Enlightenment had already invoked nature as the immovable ground of reason and morality, and Romanticism saw in eroticism a dark power that fed everything, and which also redefined the position of Woman. But these themes of Romanticism were treated from a quite different and new perspective by the intellectuals of the *Vormärz*. Neither nature nor eroticism were transcendent vanishing points, but concepts of political action with which the world of the here and now could be brought into being.[71]

Allegiance to this world did not only manifest itself in politicization and partisanship, but also in a sharpened observation of reality and in enthusiasm for the new, sober and factual order of the industrial world: "Steam and railways are simply democratic forces of life. That cannot be changed."[72] Where the Romantics still sought a dark beyond in their dreams, the intellectuals of the *Vormärz* were concerned with an exact perception of the actual, with positive knowledge, with the liberating potential of technology and of science. The polemics of the Young Hegelians in particular were weighted toward objectivity and impersonal knowledge. Precisely because the discourses were fluctuating and unstable, ties were required to unquestionably valid truths, to positive, secure knowledge. This positivism and realism also recoded the collective identity of society; the new society of division of labor and of matter-of-fact necessity was counterposed against the old society of class privilege and of arbitrary rule. This was accounted the true and reasonable identity, which could be realized through the struggle of ideas and revolution. It was accounted a project of the future, while the prevailing order, by contrast, was accounted an illusion, a forgery. Here too, the intellectual once again stands in the center of the future order as the administrator of knowledge.

In this matter-of-fact order, there does not at first seem to be any place for national difference. However, it is easy to overlook the fact that during the first half of the nineteenth century, society could be conceived of above all as a nation, and concepts of any such thing as an international society were only available in vague moral outlines: the state was supposed to be a nation–state, the economy a national economy.[73] Beyond this silent presumption of what was (meanwhile) taken for granted, however, there were also fluctuations in what was understood to be a nation or a people.

The people on the barricades

Now the future order of positive knowledge and objective pragmatism could not be borne by the intellectuals alone. The unstable and fluctuating discourses required safeguards in an external terrain that could not be rendered labile by linguistic means, and the new order of matter-of-factness appeared at first to proffer such a safeguard. But like every order that claims validity, it too could in its turn be disputed – the supposed way out of the maelstrom of discourses, in other words, led back in. The uneducated and "speechless" people, the sleeping sovereign, offered itself as a social foundation that could not possibly end up discursively liquefied, that was to rise up against its suppressors, and find itself in the act of revolt. The French Revolution had created the myth of the people on the barricades, and the German intellectuals could take it over in order to anchor their restless discourses to a new carrier group. The representation of the people on the barricades subsumed the idea of salvation through revolution with partisanship for the future and the new fact of the order of labor. Just as an artificial and false morality repressed sensual desire, so the restorational order also enchained the vital energies of the people, who were the actual nation and the authentic subject of history. The nation was not determined here by inalienable peculiarities of nature or culture, but through the inalienable right to seizure of political power – a right, of course, that was not yet perceived and which was denied the people by aristocratic reaction and the new *juste-milieu*. The nation was only to emerge in the context both of repression and of revolt.[74]

This democratic code originating from the French Revolution received its special German coloration through the strong position that the intellectuals and the liberating idea assumed within it. The intellectuals obtained this powerful position because the carrier stratum of historical movement was no longer bourgeois consciousness but the pauperized masses, the uneducated people, who were not yet conscious of their power and rights, and had first to be woken up "from their dream about themselves" by "explaining to them their own actions."[75] The guiding Hegelian idea of reconciliation and mediation thus became intelligible not only for art and life or theory and practice, but also for the relation between the intellectuals and the people: a democratic nation could only arise once both groups forged an alliance. Here too, as in other encodings of collective identity, the missionary impulse was directed at one's own society. Thus the intellectuals became indispensable.[76]

This is all the more true since in Germany during the *Vormärz*, industrialization had hardly begun; yet the people only achieved consciousness of its power within a context of industrial production, as a proletariat.[77] In preindustrial Germany, on the contrary, the people was composed less of an urban proletariat than of the pauperized masses of rural areas steeped in misery. Rural pauperism was consequently also a central theme of early socialist intellectuals such as Engels, Grün or Hess in Germany. What was at stake was not merely an amelioration of poverty and misery, but a "social" democracy that guaranteed property and education not only to politically articulate citizens, but also gave a voice and power to the people excluded from the political process, who stood for labor and the material forces of the new world.[78] Admittedly, by no means did all *Vormärz* intellectuals join in this attempt to mobilize the fourth estate. Heine was far from alone in keeping a considerable distance from the "sovereign rat-king."[79] Büchner, on the contrary, not only turned to the people and against this distance of Heine's toward the people, but also against the efforts of Young Germany, who went no farther than the merely literary.

> Reform society via the Idea, from the educated class down? Impossible! Our age is purely material . . . I believe one must start out from an absolute legal principle in social matters, seek the formation of a new spiritual life in the people, and let obsolescent modern society go to the devil.[80]

But the democratic encoding of the nation did not only aim at the pauperized masses. At stake was not only a revolution of the fourth estate, but also emancipation within bourgeois society, above all, equal rights for Jews and women. Legal equality of all state citizens here becomes just as much an element of the democratic nation code as individual liberties and collective autonomy.[81] The democratic code no longer apprehends the nation as an extrahistorical and prepolitical unity, but rather as a movement of political will and political participation. The masses only become the nation by entering into history and seizing power. State and nation, things general and particular, art and life, the idea and practice of universalist openness and of particularist closure, are supposed to coincide in this movement and form a new unity. Although it aims at this unity, the democratic nation can only exist as a movement that perpetually includes and emancipates new groups, repeatedly unmasks and attempts to overcome the false status quo. As soon as this movement comes to a standstill or loses its direction, the democratic encoding enters into risky territory. It loses its eccentric attitude and runs into the sands of the status quo; the intellectuals lose their distance and their theme.

The failure of the revolution

The self-appointed mission of the intellectuals to take up the cause of the people and to help the speechless democratic nation achieve self-consciousness through theory and pedagogy was at first without success. The public that was reached was the left *Bildungsbürgertum*, and only small sections of this *Bildungsbürgertum* were prepared to bring more than intellectual curiosity to bear upon the radical democratic ideas of Saint-Simonism, for example. One supported the liberal and national movement, one read the political lyrics of Herwegh and Freiligrath, but one above all stood in a patriarchal relation to the uneducated people: charity, but otherwise social distance.[82] The people itself, the poor in the countryside and the emergent urban proletariat, reacted to the worsening of living conditions, which had always been miserable enough, with spontaneous, short-lived hunger revolts; but this was hardly inspired by the intellectuals. This is true even of the Silesian weavers' uprising of 1844, in which many democratic intellectuals saw a realization of their expectations.[83] A string of radical democratic secret societies like Hoffmann's *Deutscher Bund*, the *Bund der Gerechten* ("league of the just"), the *Bund der Geächteten* ("league of the ostracized"), or Büchner's *Gesellschaft der Menschenfreunde* ("society of the friends of man") attempted, above all in Hesse, Baden, and the Rhineland, to manufacture a connection during the thirties between the intellectuals, on the one side, and the petty bourgeoisie or tradesmen's apprentices on the other; but their agitation only met with limited success.[84] What is noteworthy here is the new form of tautly-run secret organization, which was to be the forerunner of the revolutionary party. More effective and visible than the radical democratic leagues of the *Vormärz* was the newspaper *Rheinische Zeitung,* which was founded in 1842 and controlled by radical–democratic Young Hegelians. Besides Karl Marx, M. Hess and B. Bauer, prominent members of the radical opposition wrote in this most important organ of the democratic movement. The ban on the *Rheinische Zeitung* the following year simultaneously marked the end of the hopes that democrats and liberals had attached to the investiture of the new Prussian king in 1840.[85]

What was decisive for the social resonance of the democratic national code, however, was (as already in the case of the Romantic idea of the people) a special process of historical acceleration and turbulence, in which the barriers between social groups were shattered and traditional contours of collective identity smudged: the Revolution of 1848. Although doubtless a pan-European event, it did point the way, in a particular fashion, for the liberal and democratic movement in Germany.[86]

In March 1848 the revolutionary movement seized hold not only of the radical–democratic intellectuals, but also the liberal *Bildungsbürgertum*, the petty bourgeois and tradesmen, and indeed even large parts of the peasant population, who rose up against feudal dominion, and once and for all for the emancipation of the peasantry, above all in southern Germany, Silesia and Saxony.[87] Not only the battles on the barricades in the cities, but also and precisely the rural rebellions gave the constitutional demands of the liberal bourgeoisie the necessary short-term reinforcement. The Restoration states wavered, and for a few months the vision of the intellectuals seemed to become reality. The people on the barricades allied themselves with the educated bourgeoisie, and gained consciousness and identity in the uprising. In revolutionary praxis – as it appeared – the boundaries between the various sociostructural groups disappeared: *Bildungsbürger* and peasants, craftsmen and intellectuals became one nation in the common uprising against the repressive principality.[88]

But this nation in revolt soon showed its first fissures. The spokesmen for the liberal and democratic movement were rarely to be seen on the barricades side by side with craftsmen's apprentices or the petty bourgeois, i.e. the people. The people's representatives at the Frankfurt Parliament, on the contrary, nearly all had their origins in the upper bourgeoisie: civil service lawyers, professors, attorneys. The representatives of radical–democratic and republican ideas were decidedly in the minority here. The liberals, and these were conservative liberals, outweighed them.[89]

During the course of both revolutionary years, the two sides moved ever farther apart. The liberal majority saw themselves threatened with a Jacobin rule of the gutter if the democratic demands were fulfilled. The radical–democratic fraction was embittered by the hesitation of the liberals, who did not want to relinquish the idea of constitutional monarchy. Finally, the combination of democratic and liberal movements shattered in the Revolution.[90] The peasantry in revolt was appeased by the conservative governments, and went over to their side. Town and country, the movement of the street and the debates of the national assembly, could not be coordinated. The metropolis, the central stage on which the decision might be focused, was lacking; as was the charismatic personality who might seize power, take the main chance, and assume responsibility, thereby driving the revolutionary process onward into critical phases.

The democratic encoding of social identity finally dissolved its tie with the major current of the liberal and national movement. The uprising of the Baden Republicans under Hecker's leadership attempted to realize radical–democratic ideas, and thereby put itself into opposition against the Frankfurt Parliament. Its failure was exemplary.[91]

In the second half of the century, the democratic encoding of collective identity was disjoined from the idea of the nation, and was withdrawn, on the one side, to an internal social border, while on the other being internationally expanded. National and democratic encodings of collective identity entered into an antithesis that could, it appeared, hardly be bridged under normal circumstances. Nor were the intellectuals uninvolved here. New groups took up the cause of the working class in the name of humanity.

6

The nation–state up to the founding of empire: the code of *Realpolitik*

The failure of the Revolution of 1848 entailed consequences for the democratic encoding of national identity. Threatened and persecuted by the police of the Restoration states, or simply disillusioned about the prospects of a liberal democratic unification of Germany, many radical democrats withdrew from the scene, emigrating to the United States or simply leaving the field of politics. The democratic project that had been the vehicle of so many hopes lost its attraction, and with it the direction provided by France, the flag-bearer of Revolution. So great had been the hopes, the efforts, and the subsequent defeat of the revolutionaries that their failure could no longer be interpreted as preliminary, as a first attempt of many yet to come. Beyond this, it became obvious that the collective identity of the Germans could only be vaguely defined through a concept of "the people," which ultimately was oriented more by the opposition between rulers and subjects than by national differences. The substantiation of collective identity in a philosophical system was also increasingly viewed with skepticism. The Hegelian school, which had risen, in the decade after the master's death, to the official philosophy of the Prussian reform state, and had still dominated the academic field as well as the supra-academic scene of German philosophy during the *Vormärz* period, gradually fell into discredit. A new generation of intellectuals gained their profile precisely through their abandonment of the established projects of collective identity, and focused instead upon a new – at least for Germany – construction of social unity: the nation–state.

The "German Mandarins"

The decade following the Revolution of 1848 became the formative phase for a group of historians who were later to be known as the "Prussian

School" of historical writing.[1] A few of the older ones among them, especially Dahlmann, Droysen, and Duncker, had still participated in the Frankfurt National Assembly as delegates, belonging there to the parties of the liberal or right center. They assessed the failure of the liberal constitutionalist movement as an inability to exert control over the fiscal and military means of power.[2] They had gained academic recognition already in the years preceding 1848, but their decisive works were published between 1848 and the founding of the German Reich (the "*Reichsgründung*") in 1871.

As distinct from the *Vormärz* intellectuals, from the Romantics, and also from the *Bildungsbürger* patriots of the Enlightenment, these men hardly found themselves in a socially marginal situation. Nearly all had achieved respectable positions as academic teachers early in life; their publications met with recognition, and they wrote for a large public extending beyond the borders of the academic world.[3]

Even when conflicts with state or government caused their dismissal – as was the case for both Droysen and Waitz – an appointment to a university in another German country would quickly follow. Although their liberal and national orientation at first often led to oppositional involvement and criticism of restorationism, Junkerdom, and the traditional politics of the principalities, a series of monarchs supported their work, and followed their publications with emphatic interest.[4]

Their attitude was not one of cultural distance from the statist center, but of political involvement within the framework of existing institutions. Nearly all members of the "Prussian School" acted as delegates to state parliaments or to the assembly of the German *Bund*, where they passionately advocated national and liberal opposition. They were representatives of the *Bildungsbürger* class, whose rise was narrowly coupled with that of the Prussian reform state and its administrative and university system. Thus while they did oppose the Restoration principalities and the caste-bound benightedness of the Junkers, this opposition proceeded from the self-awareness of a class that had begun to gain access to the center of state power, and become a recognized partner of government politics.

These intellectuals at the gates of power could no longer gain their identity merely through assuming the distance of culture from politics. On the contrary, the "German Mandarins"[5] had to bring the collective identity of the nation into harmony with the spheres of state and politics, for any cultural counterdesign to the world of state and power might also endanger their own position. They possessed societal prestige and political power precisely *because* they commanded culture and education, and were exemplary representatives of the *Bildungsbürgertum*.[6]

The cultural nation, the national project of the *Bildungsbürger*, was already so very much a self-aware reality by the middle of the century that it was no longer possible to use it easily as a means of subjecting the existing reality to examination.[7] The mere advocacy of German culture no longer conveyed a particular identity, either in social or temporal terms: it neither described a social margin for intellectuals to occupy, nor an extraordinary task differing from that of the previous generation.[8]

In contrast to the Hegelians, the consciousness of belonging to a common academic school was relatively weak among the *kleindeutsch* historians [*kleindeutsch* = "little German": refers to support for a Prussian-centered policy over a "Greater Germany" that included Austria – Translators note]. For all their respect for Ranke, they took pains to step out of the shadow of their master as quickly and emphatically as they could, and they did this above all by negating Ranke's separation between historiographical objectivity and involvement in current politics.[9] We will return to this below.

Although they had strong connections to Prussia through Ranke and through their Borussian orientation, the *kleindeutsch* historians lived for long periods outside the Prussian core countries: Sybel in Marburg and Munich, Dahlmann in Bonn, Waitz in Kiel and Göttingen, Droysen in Kiel and Jena, Häusser in Heidelberg, Treitschke in Leipzig and Heidelberg. They changed locations relatively often, thus experiencing the German university as a national institution superordinate to the borders of the principalities. The system of foreign-office certificates for academic appointments advanced a supralocal and strictly research-related career orientation.[10] Microstatist particularism, the "ignominy of fragmentation" (Treitschke), appeared as an unreasonable obstacle; and the shared focus on Ranke and the University of Berlin made one's own location in Kiel, Bonn, or Heidelberg seem peripheral, encouraging attitudes of inclusion and unification. Furthermore, several of the *kleindeutsch* historians grew up in "diaspora"-like situations, for example as Protestants in overwhelmingly Catholic regions.[11] This also favored a special relationship to a spatially remote center.

Geographical marginality was more than compensated for through the central social position that the German *Bildungsbürgertum* was able to claim for itself. Around the middle of the nineteenth century the *Bildungsbürgertum* was still well ahead of the industrial and commercial bourgeoisie, both in terms of sheer numbers and in relative social significance.[12] Following the great reforms, Prussia was more than ever a civil servants' state, and the university system was the most progressive and efficient in Europe. At this point we can by no means speak any longer of an uprootedness or great distance from the societal center. The income enjoyed by a full professor in Germany was unusually high.[13] The higher reaches of the *Bildungsbürgertum* thought of themselves as an aristocracy, and approached the merely economic bourgeoisie, the "nouveaux riches," with an attitude comparable to that of the French aristocracy viewing the emergent bourgeoisie on the eve of the French Revolution.[14] One maintained contact at a distance, allowed oneself to be voted into the administrative councils of stock corporations, and entered into associations by marriage, but retained a clear consciousness of one's own superiority.[15] This educational aristocracy of the nineteenth century could no longer tolerate the superior privileges of the feudal aristocracy, and were correspondingly harsh in their opposition to ideas of feudal ranking.[16]

Between the restoration and reactionary groups that held fast to the past, on the one side, and the uneducated masses desperately in need of leadership and harboring tendencies to favor radical utopias, on the other, the *Bildungsbürgertum*, and especially the "German Mandarins," viewed themselves as occupying a central position, responsible for the whole and destined for leadership. Neither the derailing of progress in the French Revolution and the democratic utopias that followed from it, nor the blind rigidity of the Restoration, could possibly live up to this responsibility for the whole – only moderate and realistic judgment, possible from a position that could mediate between tradition and emancipation, had any chance.[17] Defined this way, the middle position occupied by the *Bildungsbürger* and their recognized intellectuals facilitated a special nonpartisanship, a perspective of the indifferent third party that avoided the bigotry and radicalism of restoration and utopia, and was thus extraordinarily well suited to reaching a practical verdict. In contrast to the eccentric position of the *Vormärz* intellectuals, who had felt a similar call to passing practical political judgments, the *kleindeutsch* historians were able to deliver their verdicts from an undeniably central position, one that held the attention of a broad public.[18]

In the process, an enhanced sensitivity toward the experience of transformation and temporality is imbued with a decisive character. The downfall of the past and the acceleration of progress into the future seemed unstoppable, but there was a duty to steer the now-begun motion of history in a responsible fashion.[19] Certainly it had been the *Bildungsbürger* who had brought about this acceleration of history during the Enlightenment, but this same group now viewed the unchaining of historical transformation with disquiet and mistrust: the "self-increasing system" of social transformation[20] led, according to the prevailing belief, to "one of those greater crises that move one world epoch into another."[21] And indeed, the contours of the industrial world became visible; new classes and groups appeared on the scene, and threatened to overtake the *Bildungsbürgertum* as the motor of history. The more distinct the diagnosis that the great transformation was too rapid and could thus get out of control, the more emphatical was the corresponding call for responsible guidance.[22]

Pedagogic communication and academic controversy as models of politics

The university and academic forms of communication presented the institutional framework within which the discourses of the *kleindeutsch* historians unfolded. The public was addressed by means of a *lecture*, i.e. a monologue that excluded any reference to the individual persons among the public, while nonetheless still presupposing educational intentions on the part of the specific, actually present audience. The academic teacher did not reckon with criticism, objections, or expressions of doubt from his listeners.[23] His educational authority, strengthened by office, was the reason for the social relationship to the listeners in the first place. Despite his authority of office, it was nonetheless incumbent upon the lecturing professor to convince his listeners through arguments – by pointing out facts and presenting consistent evidence.

This special pedagogic relationship, between a professor and his listeners, is also used by the *kleindeutsch* historians in their construction of a boundary between intellectuals and their public. As distinct from the Romantics, who also occasionally entertained visions of themselves as the teachers of the nation, but could only live this out as a claim without response, the *kleindeutsch* historians did in fact command such an authority over a public willing to be educated. The tension that in the case of the Romantic intellectuals arose from the rejection they experienced was thus missing with the *kleindeutsch* historians, as was the distance from culture and politics. More still: culture and politics were narrowly coupled to each other.[24] The constitutive pedagogical difference between college tutors and listeners did not only determine the relation of the intellectuals to their public, but could also be found in the ideal of political leadership that these intellectuals strove to achieve. The claim to political leadership derived neither from tradition nor origins, nor from the maximum possible support of the voters, but was founded on the charisma of those who commanded education and reasonable insight. The freedom to exercise political power presupposed reason and education. The logics of education and politics were at first not held separate, and were carried by the same sociostructural group. This connection of cultural authority to political power directly resulted in the idea of the political responsibility of the university professor: he had to act politically, *because* he possessed cultural authority. And indeed, the *kleindeutsch* historians, like many of their colleagues, were also active politicians in local and imperial parliaments in the period between the Revolution of 1848 and the end of the seventies. Although they were liberals, their conception of politics was not primarily one of conflicting individual interests, but oriented to harmony and an idea of common welfare, ultimately derived from education and reason.[25] Later, as the political business of the Reichstag delegates was professionalized, the German intellectual withdrew to a "public supervisory office"[26] for the common welfare, and education served to substantiate and obligate public political authority.

We must once again differentiate, also in the case of the *kleindeutsch* historians, between internal communication among intellectuals and communication between intellectuals and their public. Their internal discourses were carried out primarily as *academic conflicts* between equal and absent colleagues. One struggled passionately against the opinion of another, admittedly by pointing to strictly scholarly arguments, and without attacking the representative of the opposing school of thought personally.[27]

In that process, internal communication among intellectuals took on a form that was in many ways directly contrary to the symphilosophical approach of the Romantics. While the Romantics used oral communication in an attempt to demarcate the commonalities of their clique against surrounding society, the *kleindeutsch* historians were no longer concerned with defining their commonalities. Their common theme of interest, their affiliation with a common discipline, and their regard for the same strict methodological rules were already sufficient to assure their association on a stable basis. The integration of the intellectual group was accomplished here through even stronger external boundaries than in the case of the *Vormärz* intellectuals; dissent among colleagues could thus be tolerated without posing any threat to the existence of the discipline itself.

By contrast, consensus with the (undeniably present) audiences attending academic lectures was necessary, and required constant reinforcement. One spoke to a public that had to be won over, and with reference to the dissenting opinions of one's colleagues. This sort of dissent among the carriers of cultural authority tended to endanger their authority over the public. One had to take measures against such potential losses of authority, through emphatic expression, or by professing a commonality that linked the intellectual with his public, and made his competitor look like the outsider. This is where issues of everyday politics, which affected the public, came into play, as did the construction of national identity. Sybel thus could play the national card in his conflict with Ficker: in contrast to his opponent, *he* had the interests of the nation in mind.[28] The nation thus offered an additional reason to solidify the consensus between intellectuals and their public, and deny the legitimacy of their competitors.

This basic structure of debate among peers with respect to a public can be found in historical scholarship and in parliamentary politics alike. At stake in both cases was not the conversion of one's opponent to one's own point of view, but winning over the third party: the public, the listeners, the voters. In both cases, personal antagonism had to be hidden behind factual arguments. That the *kleindeutsch* historians were able to so closely merge research into the past with problems of the present, academic with current political discourses, and seminars with parliaments, becomes less astounding when one keeps the structural similarities between the two forms of discourse in mind.[29]

But the particular discursive form of the "German Mandarins" was by no means limited to lectures and academic controversy. Both forms only gain their significance given the background of a *great work*, with which historiography took up the legacy of the grand systems of German philosophy.[30] Its specialty was not necessarily rooted in an original and pointed thesis, with which one could provoke stands and counterstands in daily political conflict, but in the exhaustive description of an epoch, or of an overarching historical process. Paying regard to the rules of verifying evidence was a self-evident part of that process. Decisive, however, was the talent for impressive literary depiction of a complex process. The principle according to which the mass of material was ordered and weighted arose from the development and formative history (*Bildungsgeschichte*) of one or several historical individuals. The comprehensive portrayal of historical individuation was less a matter of daily politics than of education ("*Bildung*" = "education" *and* "formation") – understood as a fundamental process of encounter and conflict with the cultural and political movements of a given time. Here history primarily became *Bildungsgeschichte* – the history of an education, and historical writing as pedagogy.[31]

In the labor of many years, sometimes repeatedly interrupted, involved in creating a great work, the historian found himself in a situation of dialogue with himself, in which the potential readership largely lost its outlines, far more than would be the case in lectures or academic debates. On returning to his work after a longer interruption, the historian thus also encountered a piece of his own history. No external obligation or organization, only the continuity of his own interest in the theme, was the glue that held the stuff together, and assured the continuation of the work.

In this long-term and lonely occupation of the historian, it is natural that the principle of an individual's continuity is also discovered in the historical material. As the intellectual wrote his life's work, he saw in the historical processes that he described the workings of the same principle – of the development and perfection of an individual – as that which drove him to pursue his work in the first place.[32] There was one important difference, however: history was primarily understood as the history of collective individuals – of nations, peoples, and states.[33] The state in particular was considered a "personality in a historical–moral sense."[34]

The orientation of the great work to the individual was founded in the *idea* of education, which was sharply distinguished from the acquisition of mere technical knowledge. Sophisticated education was not simply a matter of practical usefulness – of instrumental rationality, economic interests, or "healthy human understanding." It was its own goal, and it aimed at the whole. It created a "spiritual" or "intellectual" unity (*Geist*) and fulfilled itself in the encounter of an individual with history, with the powers of custom, the cultural currents of a time, all of which had themselves arisen from the "power(s) of mind (*Geist*) emanating from fundamental individuals."[35] Only through the opening of the individual to the formative forces, which were conceived as collective individuals, meaning through a synthesis of personal identity with collective identity, could spirit and history, individual and society, be comprehended. In this fundamental process of mediation, the nation played a decisive role. It posed the unsurpassable collective identity, around which individuals could form themselves; an identity in which they found the highest culmination and farthest horizon of their will to education and formation (*Bildungswillen*).[36]

The *Realpolitik* encoding of the national

Historical scholarship as national pedagogy

Historical scholarship rose to the status of a key discipline around the middle of the century, driving philosophy from that position.[37] The grand system of Hegel could no longer be surpassed by the subsequent generation. Academic philosophy fell back into repetition and exegesis, and engaged reflexion outside the universities turned to the praxis of political or technological action.[38]

By contrast, historical scholarship had begun securing, with its strict research methodology, that which increasingly seemed questionable and fragile in the midst of Modernity's rapid transformations: the past as history, i.e., as a current of events moved forward by action and agency.

The modern perspective of the world had not only opened up the future as a field of action and uncertainty,[39] which one attempted to handle by expressing agency in the present; it had also released the past from its traditional guarantees. No longer did either the hand of God or the uninterrupted certainty of narrative suffice to secure the view of the past. Just like the future, the past opened up as a space for possible action – in that it could well have been *thus*, but might also have been *that way*. Not only was the past no longer a source of lessons for the future – since the future did not merely repeat the past, but was supposed to bring forth the new, the unprecedented – but this past uncoupled from future itself became uncertain, and demanding of comprehension.[40] Only through methodical effort, objective processes of gathering evidence, and a critical approach to sources could the facts of the past be revealed and determined.

Reconstructing the past with regard to the factual and true, however, did not yet mean that the past was being perceived as history. The past first becomes history when it is narrated as past action, and it is in this *narrative form of linking* true events of agency that we see the difference between mere determination of facts, and true historical perspective.[41]

A narrative form of reconstruction nonetheless poses the problem of an uncertain and contingent past on a new level: a mass of assured facts does not yet force an obvious narrative, but can be connected to each other through a large number of alternative, also possible, equally plausible narratives. The past, as a narrated historical past, remains contingent even when one takes all effort to report "how it really was" (Ranke).

One solution to this problem of contingence is to have recourse to the present, to the obvious, to certainties that are present to the narrator and his listeners. Historical writing therefore does not presuppose that we must forget the present so as to be immersed in the past, but is in fact only possible through the present.[42] This applies not only to the observation and perception of past facts, but also precisely with respect to the line of the narrative, the problems superordinate to plot, and the meaning of what occurred.

The *kleindeutsch* historians, above all Droysen, were well aware that historical narrative related to the present, and was bound to a conscious subject.[43] That the narrative of the past could be distorted or colored by the present interests of the narrator was naturally not a new recognition. What was new, however, was that these bonds of perspectivity were no longer viewed either as obstacles that were impossible to overcome, or as mistakes that could be avoided through methodological care, but as fundamentally unavoidable, and indeed fertile, heuristic principles in the production of the narrated past.[44]

History, according to Sybel, had to be written "cum ira et studio." For Droysen there was only the "relative truth of my standpoint, as my fatherland, my political or my religious conviction, or my serious studies have taken to convey to me." Objectivity as "released from all ties of nationality" was dismissed as being "castrated."[45] Only the present, the evident reality, offered a foundation from which the uncertain territory of the past could be explored. Sybel therefore could, in his famous argument with Ficker over the Italian campaigns of the Kaiser in the German Middle Ages, criticize this past because it served as a poor forerunner to the present. The point was not to reconstruct past history as a forerunner of the present in order to orient the present to the past – as the traditional "historia magistra vitae" conception attempts – but in order to link the past to the present. This present-centering of the "Prussian School" was by no means naively held, but the consequence of historiographical considerations.

Decisive significance in that process is given not only to the relation between present and past, but also to that between the cognitive subject and the historical object, or between the unity of reason and the variety of reality. Only when the cognitive subject orders the materials according to its measure, or when reason permeates reality, does historical truth show itself. Such a theory of historical cognition certainly has Hegelian roots; and the turn to the present and practical judgment, indeed to partisanship, had indeed already been carried out by the Young Hegelians.[46] New here, by contrast, is the strict methodological inclusion of historical cognition. But even the hermeneutical method of historiography again shows an active interest on the historian's part. Since history consists of actions, it can only be explored in the present by means of active interests.

Why have historical scholarship at all, however, if it can only be pursued by proceeding from present interests? For the *kleindeutsch* historians, the answer cannot possibly be found in an antiquarian interest in the past itself. The past is not interesting merely because it is simply past, but because it can be presented to the outside, to a public, with a *pedagogical* intention.[47] The German Mandarins won their exceptional status among the *Bildungsbürger* precisely through this pedagogical difference between the initiated teachers, aware of their responsibility, and the people, in need of upbringing and guidance. The *nation is presented as a pupil* to be helped by historians, through their narration of history, on its way to self-awareness and agency. This national–pedagogical intention defines the historical narratives from Sybel and Häusser as much as those from Treitschke and Dahlmann.

The nation–state as autonomous power concern

Dahlmann, Droysen, and Sybel had experienced firsthand, while acting as delegates of the liberal *Bildungsbürgertum* in the Frankfurt National Assembly, how the power of conviction inherent in ideas can still fail because of a lack of real political strength. Military and fiscal power could not be overcome through simple enthusiasm for freedom and constitutionalism.[48] The subsequent encoding of the national identity took this experience into account, effecting a reversal in the relation between culture and politics. While Enlightenment, Romantic, and *Vormärz* intellectuals still attempted to get political history moving in the name of an autonomous cultural authority, the political sphere now appeared more and more as a separate realm with its own laws, and no further need of substantiation – as an ultimate purpose that could be neither exceeded, nor shaken, through morality or art. That was, however, at first not the intention of the German Mandarins, who founded their authority and political engagement precisely on the insufficient differentiation between culture and politics.

At first, the "unfolding of free formation of will in a bourgeois constitutional state"[49] or the "freedom of the educated masses"[50] was set up as the priority of history. Reason and reality were to combine into a "moral power" in the state.[51] This subordination of the state to moral goals, and its orientation towards the goal of bourgeois emancipation, nonetheless became ever weaker, among the *kleindeutsch* historians, during the two decades preceding the founding of the German *Reich.* The attempt to research political history with an emancipatory motivation, while at the same time strictly respecting the rules of source verification, made the independence of political action, according to its own laws, ever more obvious. "The law of the stronger [exercised] a similar rule over state life as the law of gravity on the world of bodies."[52] The effort to determine a maximum, unsurpassable and irreducible reference horizon for political action culminated in the absolute sovereignty of the state.

This sovereign state was based ever more completely on simple reality, i.e. on its own power: the sphere of state action becomes autonomous. In Modernity,

> the state, arising from an embodiment of social and legal conditions already given and inherent in themselves, and transformed into an institution to generate and exercise power, swallows the autonomy of all lower circles, needs and demands the omnipotence to use everyone and everything in every moment according to this highest goal, to define and define again, to mobilize.[53]

The state decouples itself from cultural foundations, and appears as a system that only relates to itself and its own dynamics of growth. The measure of the state's exercise of power is ultimately only that of its long-term political success, i.e. the growth of that power itself.[54] Political action loses superordinate values or goals, and is oriented only by its own measure: it becomes pure will, which increases itself as the will to be able to will ever more, in short: as the will to power.[55] The will to power supplants partisanship, the decisive practical verdict, as the "motion metaphor" for history.[56]

If the state is no longer a means for the realization of individual freedom but itself the ultimate purpose, if it is seen as the expression of pure power, then a new perspective arises for the historian: the past is the past of possible state power organizations, and the current historian's mission is to reveal the potentials for the possible development of state power that had existed in the past. The point of departure for such a perspective is self-evidently the present, and present views on the formation of state power. And these views speak for the understanding of the national as it was held by the *kleindeutsch*, for in the situation as given, that understanding offered the best chances for a strong (because homogeneous) state.

The national movement proved, at the middle of the century, to be the strongest political force moving towards the conglomeration of the German microstates, and thus towards larger concentrations of power.[57] Following the Congress of Vienna, dynastic interests were bound through European-wide arrangements, and hardly suitable for pursuing the expansion and concentration of state power in central Europe. Only the idea of the nation offered a strong motif for state unification, without which no relative advantage could be gained within the overall European system of power.

If, in the middle of the century, an increase of power only seemed possible within the framework of national unification, then this did not mean that the nation was comprehended as a prepolitical and transhistorical matter. The nation won its identity solely through the fact that it behaved as a real power; the German nation was a nation only as a political movement, as a possible nation–state, or else it was merely the dreaming of a handful of lyric visionaries.[58]

The nation–state as conceived by the *kleindeutsch* historians was nonetheless quite distinct from the western European idea of the political nation. Quite in contrast to, for example, Renan's famous sentence, "La nation – c'est le plébiscit de tous les jours," the *kleindeutsch* concept of nation lacked reference to the process of forming a democratic will.[59] Anything whatsoever, given that it had success as a will to power, could lay claim to being the true embodiment of the state and its dynamic foundation, the nation. That applied just as much to charismatic individuals as to popular movements. According to the "Prussian School," binding the state to the mere opinion of the majority risked the irresponsible rule of a mob, and this was already thought to have been confirmed in the final phase of the Revolution of 1848. The nation–state was an *autonomous power concern* – bound neither to cultural nor moral bases, nor to mere formal majorities.[60]

The nation fulfilled a special function for this autonomous power concern. The priority was now no longer to help the subjugated nation – which was considered to have always existed – to its rights, i.e. to its form as a state. That would be to understand the state as the means by which a nation becomes. The *kleindeutsch* adopted the reverse position: the nation was to be employed as the means of the state's becoming.[61] The national encoding was what gave the self-organizing power system of the state an awareness of itself. Fundamentally, the nation was only one of several possible encodings by which this process – of forming state power – could observe and describe itself; but the national encoding was especially suitable to the situation in the middle of the nineteenth century. Thus was the liberal conception of the dissolution of the state in society ultimately realized: the state created its own society, the nation.[62]

An encoding in this manner has the decisive advantage that it suggests an actor as the source of willed action for political processes – power-agency as pure self-organization, without a deliberate actor, was hard for the *kleindeutsch* historians to imagine, and not just for them. In this way, the idea of the nation created the necessary voluntary basis for a process of power organization; for power agency could only be conceived as willed action, and will presupposes someone who wills, i.e. a person.[63] The pure will to power in this way finds its expression in a nation–state purified of all reference to concrete individuals and concrete majorities. The diversity and mutability of majorities weakens the development of state power; the state must therefore be freed from these limitations upon its potentials. In contrast to the political nation of western Europe, this concept of the nation–state completes the decoupling of collective will from domestic conflict and real diversity. The national encoding allows the various and contradictory to appear unified and cohesive, *without* requiring that the freedom of the citizens is suppressed in the process.[64] As distinct from despotic rule, in which the will of the despot forces together the variety of citizens from the outside, the nation–state commands a foundation of integration and unity without force, shifted onto the individual citizen and in agreement with his freedom. It thus not only fulfills the liberal profession of the citizen's individual rights to liberty, but also the conservative conception of internal harmony between social groups. The indisputable sense of belonging to the same nation brings a people together in non-violent fashion, and so increases the power of the state in absolute comparison to other states.[65]

This brings us to the referent actually considered decisive for the development of power: foreign policy.[66] If there is no true unity conceivable above and beyond the state, nothing higher that could gain and increase power for itself, then the relations between states become the ultimate field for the exercise of power, and all else, especially the domestic relations of a society, must be subordinated to foreign policy. Adopted from Ranke, this primacy of foreign policy is absolute, and narrowly associated with the glorification of war as the act of power that cannot be surpassed.[67] Here too, the development of military power outwards and the bridging of conflicts internally stand in complementary relation. Only national unification can facilitate the greatest possible mobilization and maximum effort that create advantage in war, and only military conflict with an enemy can facilitate the ultimate experiencing of one's own national identity. The nation–state thus marks the outermost border between inside and outside, war and peace, opponents and allies, that could be conceived with respect to the autonomous unfolding of power. This border simultaneously facilitates the civilization of forms of communication within society.[68] Violence and power are removed from domestic social relations, and shifted beyond the borders, to relations between states: society as a sphere of the regulated free self-determination of individuals, international anarchy as the realm of pure violence and will to power.

The nation as a homogeneous society: the "Little German" solution

The national unification of Germany could not possibly, in the view of the *kleindeutsch* historians, succeed as an effort to actualize a cultural identity through politics and in the constitution of a nation–state; it had to be instead based on the real power potentials in the actual historical situation. A look at the relations of power at the middle of the century quickly shows that it was primarily the two great powers of central Europe, Prussia and Austria, who could be considered as potential cores of a national unification driven by *Realpolitik*.[69] The state territory of Prussia included by far the largest part of northern Germany. Prussia could thus not be excluded from a national unification. The Austro-Hungarian Dual Monarchy was clearly superior to Prussia both in territory and in population, but that population was German only in the Austrian core areas. A "Greater

German" solution that included Austria would have therefore created an ambiguous situation in several ways. Spreading far beyond the German-speaking countries, the Dual Monarchy's imperial interests would have come into conflict with those of the German nation–state. The greater German nation–state would thus have had to live with an open and blurred southeastern border.[70] The nation–state's advantage in power politics, of creating a clear and unbridgeable boundary between inside and outside, would have thus been surrendered. Beyond this, the rivalry of the two inner-German great powers would have created conflicts and thus weakened foreign policy. And, finally, to a *Bildungsbürgertum* who felt responsible for history, post-reform Prussia offered far more of the image of a modern state on the rise, with its impersonal administration and highly developed system of education, than did Austria and Metternich and Schwarzenberg. Thus did arguments of power politics speak for a nation–state only if it would be centered on Prussia, and exclude Austria. Anything else would have endangered the homogeneity of the nation–state and the clarity of its borders. This conception of the internal harmony and homogeneity of a society gained in significance for the liberal–conservative historians to the same degree as functional differentiation and individualization increased, and the variety of societal processes threatened to elude comprehension. National encoding alone offered the prospect of creating the desired internal harmony, and this harmony required homogeneity as its precondition.[71]

The demand for homogeneity was not only meant politically, but also and especially with respect to a demarcation that had taken on a fundamental significance in central Europe since the Thirty Years War: the confessional split between Protestants and Catholics. The western European nation–states all arose from civil wars over faith and confession, and these had, in each case, ultimately led to the clear dominance of a single confession within the state territory.

In contrast to that, a greater German solution that included Austria would not only involve a political bipolarity, but also a balanced relation between Protestants and Catholics within the German nation–state. This would have provided substantiation for internal conflicts, and weakened any chances for bridging social oppositions through a common moral horizon. An exclusive orientation to Prussia thus not only provided the direct advantage of power politics, but was also justified in the dominance of Protestant–Lutheran ideas of virtue. A "Greater German" solution including Austria would instead have endangered Prussian–Protestant introversion and sense of duty, asceticism, and bourgeois freedom through the Catholic counterproject, which was seen as reactionary, hostile to reason, deceitful and superstitious.[72]

But the primary accusation leveled against Catholicism was its connection to the Vatican. Catholics had to place the authority of the Vatican above that of nation–states: "There is no space for secular sovereignty alongside the jurisdiction of the Church."[73] Such manner of "ultramontane" obligation was unbearable in the power-political perspective of the *kleindeutsch* historians. The nation–state was to be viewed as the unsurpassable collective identity, and every attempt to move beyond it posed dangers, not only to the autonomy of the political, but also to the bourgeois freedoms that carried politics. Sybel's criticism of *Ultramontanismus* in particular at first stood clearly within the Enlightenment tradition of Rhineland liberalism and its confrontation with reactionary and clerical tendencies.[74]

The primary concern, however, was to prevent the "dissolution and destruction of the state in favor of the church."[75] It was not the church that was to be ordered above the state, but the state above the church. Just like other areas of culture, religion had to be subjected to state control.[76] The state, and only the state, stood for the reasonable encompassing collective, and epitomized the "form for social existence";[77] all other collectives were considered particular, as mere parts of society.

The *kleindeutsch* historians' demand for homogeneity was directed not only against the Catholics, but also against every form of collective identity that exceeded the horizons of the nation–state, and thus endangered the unity of the state. It was just as much against feudal–aristocratic identity as against the cosmopolitanism of the Enlightenment, against the radical democrats of the *Vormärz* as against the Jews – whom above all Treitschke treated as foreign intruders.[78] As a power-political perspective, national unification assumed not only the empowerment of a statist central authority, but also the persecution of all forms of identity that could weaken internal homogeneity or the exclusiveness of the nation–state's claim.

These conceptions of national identity were not yet substantiated in biological or organic claims, however. It was not provenance that decided here over foreignness or affiliation, but a cultural identity, something that could admittedly be changed. Even Treitschke still differentiated between German citizens of Jewish faith and the "culturally foreign" Jews. This insistence on cultural homogeneity demonstrated the continuing significance of the cultural–national encoding, against which the *kleindeutsch* historians were holding up their real-political project. The turn to pure power politics could not completely disregard the effectiveness of cultural identity. If cultural identities did not accept the demarcations as drawn by state power, the nation–state would answer with their exclusion. Under a liberal constitution, this exclusion could admittedly not be simply carried out as a legal discrimination, but required instead a cultural substantiation, through intellectuals.

Bismarck and the founding of the *Reich*

The politics of German unification pursued by Bismarck led to the 1871 proclamation of the German Empire, in the Hall of Mirrors of the Palace of Versailles. Heinrich von Sybel commented upon the event in a brief passage that has become famous:

> Through what has one earned the mercy of God, to be allowed to live through such great and mighty things? And how will one live after? That which was the content of all desires and efforts for twenty years, is now fulfilled in such an infinitely magnificent way! From what should one as advanced in age as I still draw new content for living on?[79]

Indeed, the founding of the *Reich* represented a nearly perfect fulfillment of the national conceptions formulated by the Borussian historians.[80] Bismarck's policy of national unification was a power- and state-centered *Realpolitik* driven to its ultimate extreme, using the national idea not as a prepolitical motif for the motion of history, but as a vehicle for strengthening an autonomous state drive for power.[81] The point of departure was the particular statist interest of Prussia and the Prussian crown, but this Prussian–Hohenzollern framework was not constraining: "Prussia's German mission" also required the respect of the southern German states, and worked against a limitless politics of annexation following the victory over France. The "Little German" solution favored a national homogeneity of the state, and could not afford the risks of including a large French minority, as Sybel had determined in 1870.[82] The national and *kleindeutsch* orientation of Bismarckian politics arises not from a cultural definition of German identity, but through *Realpolitik* cunning in an autonomous state power concern. National unification offered a chance for power expansion, and also defused a noisy political movement. The Bismarckian principle of national "revolution from above," in the interests of the state, corresponded to the ideas of the Borussian historians, as clearly as did the adopted solution of a "Little Germany," and the undisputed primacy of foreign policy – which accomplished German unity by way of three victorious wars (against Denmark, the Austro-Hungarian Empire, and France).

The hymnal enthusiasm over Bismarck's policy of national unification admittedly contrasts strongly with the harsh criticism leveled by the liberal historians only a few years before, during the Prussian constitutional crisis, against Bismarck's governing without a parliamentary foundation. Both positions subsequently ended up approaching each other. The liberal and national *Bildungsbürgertum*, weakened through the elections of 1866, gave up its liberal reservations and voted for the 1871 indemnity clause against France; while Bismarck gave up his former stand of reactionary Prussian Junker, and conceded that he had not governed in accordance with constitutionalism. The actual reconciliation between the national–liberal *Bildungsbürgertum* and the Prussian crown and/or Prussian state, as represented by Bismarck, was effected not in the debate over the indemnity clause, but in the joyous celebrations of the victory over France and the founding of the German Empire.[83]

The general enthusiasm over the success of national unification nonetheless concealed the circumstance that the military event of founding took place not as a "revolution from below," but as a "revolution from above" – one which assured the continuity of the center of power, and preceded, took priority over, any revolutionary renewal of that center. As a consequence the *Bildungsbürgertum* could no longer behave indisputably as the likely basis and social carrier of national identity.[84] With the realization of the German nation–state coming not through cultural mission or liberal ideas, but through Bismarck's maxim of "blood and iron," the *Bildungsbürgertum* and the intellectuals lost the chance of constructing cultural identity through the national issue, in opposition to the existing order. The great axial-age tension, that had held the German *Bildungsbürgertum* in constant national movement for over a century, collapsed. As distinct from all previous attempts to defuse that tension, through the realization of a cultural project of national identity by an act of political revolution, Bismarck's "gamble without principles" was successful, but this political success also signaled a crisis for any cultural foundation of national identity. The nation was now no longer a cultural project, but a saber-rattling statist reality, one that found expression in societally encompassing rituals, in monument cults and war veterans' associations, in honoring the Kaiser and colonial expansion; but all that could no longer stir the engaged discourses of intellectuals.[85]

Nevertheless, only a handful of intellectuals recognized the mounting crisis of the German cultural nation in the midst of national jubilation over the founding of empire. Nietzsche, for example, wrote with great foresight about the public mistake following the victory over the French,

> that the German culture was also victorious in that battle, and therefore must also be decorated with the laurels due to such extraordinary undertakings and successes. This madness is extremely corruptive: . . . for it could transform our victory into a complete defeat: in the defeat, indeed extirpation, of the German spirit in the name of the "German Empire."[86]

After the founding of the *Reich*, the intellectuals dissolved the link between identity-creating culture and nation. They reconstructed the critical tension between culture, on the one side, and the existing order and secular world, on the other, through cultural pessimism, but the nation had clearly changed sides to the secular. From that moment, the nation became the issue of politics in the field of conflict between leaders and masses.

7

The national identity of the Germans: attempt at a conclusion

The century between 1770 and 1870 set up the foundation for the identity of the Germans. For all the differences between the scenarios and encodings that we have sketched herein, this identity certainly shows remarkable consistencies. The always difficult and simplifying attempt to summarize these common points in a single, ideal type of German identity leads to the following six propositions:

1. The identity of the Germans, although it was conceived as a comprehensive national identity, is carried by a particular social group: the *Bildungsbürgertum*, and here above all certain *groups of intellectuals*, each in their turn designing new encodings for national identity. *Bildungsbürgertum* and intellectuals find themselves in a situation decoupled from all other social groups, but are also able to think of themselves as especially central. One maintains distance to the particular and limited interests of the other groups or partial societal realms, and therefore commands an undistorted view of the general, the *Allgemeine*, the encompassing societal collective. Intellectual distancing and social uprootedness thus become the prerequisite for recognition of the encompassing collectivity or national identity.

2. The construction of the national identity by the *Bildungsbürgertum* and the intellectuals runs into tension with the specific, the existing, and the present. The national identity of the Germans during the century we have examined here is not only a cultural identity, but also an identity that *transcends* the present moment, individual formulation of will, or empirical experience. It posits itself in contrast to "normal" social life, whose horizons are considered to be limited and temporary. The tension between the cultural identity of the nation, which assures continuity, unity, and the encompassing collective, on the one side, and the variety of the empirical, individual, and temporal, on the other, has its effects feeding back upon the

sociostructural level. There the tension precipitates as a split between those who stand for the eternal and invisible *Allgemeine*, and those who are entangled in the visible, temporary, specific (*das Besondere*). This internal societal split into two "camps" recalls the confessional split that determined central European politics from the beginning of the early modern age and had not, in Germany, ever led to the clear dominance of a single religion.

3. The constructed identity of the Germans, as carried by the *Bildungsbürgertum* and intellectuals, is normally *apolitical* (the *kleindeutsch* historians pose a special exception). Like money and economy, politics stands for the realm of specific interests, from which distance must be maintained. The boundary between the *Allgemeine* and the *Besondere*, between general cultural identity and specific political business, is therefore only crossed in exceptional cases, of great tension and most extreme involvement: then one enters into unknown and unholy territory. The cultural–national identity of the Germans therefore expresses itself above all in heterodox forms of political involvement, in revolutions and demonstrations, or remains limited to activities beneath the threshold of official political institutions, to *Vereine* and publicity. From this perspective, the Germans cannot understand themselves as a "belated nation." The distance to the political becoming of the nation is not comprehended as a historic retardation, but as a guarantee of identity.

4. The cultural identity of the German nation not only results in a split between two camps, but also in the attempt to enlighten outsiders, and convey to them a consciousness of the true identity. This urge to missionary action within one's own society can be found not only in the relations between *Bildungsbürgertum*, the carriers of the cultural national identity, and the surrounding society, but also within the *Bildungsbürgertum* in the relations between intellectuals and their public. In both cases, the *cultural mission* runs into resistance, and in both cases the relations of the educators to their potential pupils are ambivalent. The former do want to convince the latter and find agreement, but at the same time do not want to surrender the constitutive distance between intellectuals and their public, between *Bildungsbürgertum* and other social groups. Should the attempts to proselytize and educate the outsiders succeed, then the borders between inside and outside, the tensions between the encompassing collectivity and the specific concern, collapse.

5. This ambivalence between missionary expansion and constitutive distancing can be overcome over axial time. As soon as a cultural encoding of national identity is received by the public and taken up by other social groups, the form by which it is communicatively moved also changes.

Institutional routines and everyday *trivializations* supplant intellectual discourse. New generations of intellectuals assume their distance from precisely these trivializations, which indicate a loss of the *Allgemeine* in the *Besondere*. As a rule, the intellectuals attempt to construct new, more demanding conceptions in distinction to the "failed" cultural projects of national identity, reconstructing the original tension and distance. This exchange between trivialization and new construction determines the transformations of the German identity through the various scenarios considered here.

6. As soon as unification of the nation–state is realized, i.e. in our case with the *Reichsgründung* of 1871, the elementary tension between cultural identity and the particularism of state and politics largely collapses. The basis for unity and identity shifts away from the cultural discourses of the intellectuals to the institutional "ground floor" of the state and its political goals. The intellectuals react to this loss of compensatory function by taking up new issues. The national code is supplanted as the ultimate encoding of collective identity and moving force of history by such other concepts as class, race, and society.

Epilogue: German identity between 1945 and 1990

The catastrophic crash of German history in the Second World War and the Holocaust created an entirely new situation, to which the encoding of the national and its carrier groups had to adjust. It was not just that the Third *Reich* had discredited the German nation–state far beyond its borders. The pressure felt to establish a demarcation against the generation of the fathers, who bore responsibility for the disaster, also made it difficult for the subsequent generation to identify with the state nation. The political division of Germany was felt to be the just punishment for political nationalism.[1] Eight decades of a unified German nation–state thus came to an end. As in the eighteenth and nineteenth centuries, German identity could no longer find support in the unity of the state, and was once again dependent upon a cultural substantiation.

a) The intellectuals who found themselves in this situation reacted by reconstructing the constitutive tension of the cultural nation – a cultural nation that was viewed not only as always having stood in opposition to the existing order, but which had also gone into exile during the Nazi barbarism, and now returned from emigration.

Thomas Mann spoke of an "invisible nation," whose duty had never been to power, but always to culture. The retreat to introversion and to the "simple things" was celebrated.[2] After a few years of "literature among the ruins," of a sparse overcoming of the "demolition," a period of reflexion about the German past began. The intellectuals of the new Bundesrepublik (Federal Republic) – from the writers in the "Group of '47" to the critical theorists of the Frankfurt School – gained their collective identity by focusing upon the nation's still-unaddressed past. Acting in the name of a European democratic humanism and employing literary means, they engaged themselves against the nation–state and against dyed-in-the-wool representatives of national ritual: only in acknowledgment of the Holocaust, in the attempt to live with that unspeakable terror, with the unprecedented crime of history, could a new foundation for national identity be approached. This new reference point was indeed unique and inalienable. Language failed in the attempt to describe it, and could at first only approach it through a meager description of the monstrous in the everyday. Starting from this fundamental demarcation with respect to the Holocaust past, the construction of societal unity was carried out as a pedagogic attempt at reeducation towards democracy. One was called upon to learn from the mistakes of the past; anyone who preferred to make compromises there tended to fall silent. The intellectuals were certain of themselves: only through reference to the Holocaust could national identity be found. The involvement of the at first "skeptical," then "critical" generation of youth followed in their wake. This involvement provided a guarantee of identity for the new generation, above all because the silent majority of their elders rightly stood under suspicion of having tolerated, denied, or suppressed the terrible truth. Thus the new identity of the Germans once again resulted not from an undistanced adoption of the existing order, but from a criticism of reality.

New, however, was that the object of criticism was not only the present, but also and precisely the past – the realm which until then had provided the guarantee of identity. The chance for national identity was not seen in the continuation of tradition, but solely in overcoming and coping with the past: in the attempt to save the present from the past. Thus the identity of the Germans, to a far greater degree than that of their western European neighbors, was an open identity, oriented to the future, not based upon a continuity between past and future, but upon the radical discontinuity of a new beginning.

Next to this openness to the future, a further characteristic of the new German identity must be noted: the German postwar identity arose more from an orientation by the demonic and catastrophic than by conceptions of the sacred, or of fulfillment of a collective happiness. The new encodings consisted less of a catalogue of national virtues than of collective avoidance imperatives. This construction of national identity *ex negativo*, accomplished through an exclusion of threat instead of a positive symbolization, had the advantage of embodying a special form of Modernity. It left to individuals a free space in which to design their own identity, although any association of the individual with a particular characteristic that secured this affiliation tended to limit precisely that individual diversity.[3] A shared involved consternation ["*Betroffenheit*," an attitude that has come to be seen, especially by its detractors, as a kind of German bourgeois institution – Translator's note] of this kind facilitates a binding of individual variety with collective identity, more easily than would demands that members of the collectivity share the same ancestry, same professions of faith, or same lifestyle.

However, the construction of collective identity through consternation did not merely tend to allow greater individual variety, but also tended to create greater openings for outsiders. The new identity of the Germans defined itself more clearly than before through cultural and moral encodings, and lived off the tension between the cultural project assigned to the future, and the unreasonableness and bigotry of the existing order. As distinct from primordial determinations of national identity, the boundaries of a universally encoded identity are subject to pressures of expansion: one can and must convince others to open their eyes, see the invisible threat, and join the universal crusade. Like all universalist encodings of collective identity, the new forms of German identity therefore also provided impulse for missionary movements that lived from this constitutive difference – between those who have already recognized the demonic, and those who still need to be enlightened. Should this opposition ever be defused – because everyone has, in the meantime, become enlightened and been convinced – then the missionary tension of a universal encoding collapses. Turns to the ritual, to trivializations and positive symbolizations of affiliation, then become probable. This flowing of a universal movement towards the trivial and banal normally prompts the intellectuals and advanced portions of the *Bildungsbürgertum* to assume distance, and search for new encodings of collective identity. A new transformation of national identity then becomes likely.

The temporalization of the new German identity also had consequences for the self-demarcation of its carriers. The boundary between the generations was, at first, still far more important than the traditional anchoring of the cultural national code in the *Bildungsbürgertum.* But as had been the case in the past, the *Bildungsbürgertum* and the intellectuals remained the carriers of the new cultural encoding of identity. Sociostructurally, the *Bildungsbürgertum* of the postwar era was hardly distinguishable from the group's traditional pattern. Its forms of communication were those of the classically educated public. One wrote or held lectures, one read or debated in small groups. *Vereine* and parties, ritual solemnities and demonstrations, were all at first felt as deindividualizations, and therefore played a lesser role. The initiated instead met in more sophisticated associations, in *Goethe-Vereine* and *Volkshochschulen* (the extensive system of public open universities), in theaters and concert halls. They did their best to uphold distance from the *Raffkes* ("money-grubbers") and new rich, from the construction barons or "captains of industry" who were forming themselves as the new economic bourgeoisie after the currency reform of 1948. Not all members of the *Bildungsbürgertum* were equally prepared to announce their grief and share of responsibility for the Holocaust; many distinguished between the Germany of Goethe and Kant, and that of the uncultured barbarians who had followed Hitler, the "Bohemian corporal." But it was nonetheless primarily members of the *Bildungsbürgertum* who presented themselves to the public as the Group of '47, and (next to the remnants of the traditional workers' movement) were prepared to make recent German history into a public issue. This opening of the *Bildungsbürgertum* to the Holocaust past was reinforced through the circumstance that the "coping with the past" [*Vergangenheitsbewältigung*, nearly tantamount to an official postwar institution – Translator's note] was carried out through enlightenment and education, and took place to no mean degree in the schools. Next to the intellectuals, it was above all a new generation of teachers who took up the role as the carriers of "Holocaust consciousness" in the Bundesrepublik.

By contrast, the carrier groups of a nation–state encoding in a narrower sense – the refugee associations from eastern Prussia and the Sudetenland, the war veterans' associations and "reunification committees" – found no right-wing counterpart in the realm of intellectual reflexion. Here the reproduction of national identity correspondingly slid down to the level of ritual, of the Sunday sermon, of professions of faith and formalistic invocations: candles for Christmas, memorial celebrations, observing the Day of German Unity [held every 17 June from 1954 to 1990 to commemorate the failed June Uprising of 1953 in East Berlin – Translator's note] Even the demand for the reunification of Germany, as written into the constitution of the Bundesrepublik, required anti-Communist and anti-totalitarian arguments if it was to approach the faculty of reflexion. In the anti-Communist path followed by the "official" national consciousness, one can still see the search for something that could stand in for the totalitarianism of the Third *Reich*: this time, the chance to take up the struggle against evil should not be allowed to pass.

Over the years, this anti-Communist "freedom-rhetoric" of the national tended to use itself up. The state-political sphere was occupied by a stable "provisorium," while the international political situation submerged any prospects for the unity of the nation–state over the long term. The national encoding was therefore diverted into a sphere that it had rarely commanded in the tradition of the *Bildungsbürgertum*: the economy. In the nineteenth century, decades of economic integration, of a nation fragmented into many states, had preceded the founding of the German *Reich*. In the post-

Second World War period, however, the issue was not that of bridging the new German borders through economic relations, but of establishing an economically substantiated, "positive" national consciousness in the west. If it was obviously difficult to feel a national pride about history and politics, and if the cultural definition of the national attempted to cope with the past instead of surpassing the present order, then what remained – next to success in sports – as a means to achieve reconciliation with the nation's present, and construct a collective identity for the majority who did not belong to the *Bildungsbürgertum*, was only the "indisputable" economic success of the new Bundesrepublik. The second code of national identity in postwar Germany was thus that of economic prosperity, the *Wirtschaftswunder* ("economic miracle") and a corresponding rejection of all things "ideological." The mistakes of the past were located in the ideological seduction of the masses. A repetition was to be avoided through limitation to the factual, to the existing and impartial, and through a rigorous disbelief in the "overextended" ideas of any intellectuals who aimed at comprehending the whole.

The carrier of this new "*Wirtschaftswunder* code" was the petty bourgeoisie of the new republic, who also included the traditional, but now "embourgeoisied" group of highly skilled workers: in Schelsky's words, the "leveled middle-class society." This leveled middle-class society generated its collective identity through nonideological and modest rituals, of evenings spent in front of the television, of leisure time and consumption, occasions and places where everyone did the same thing, but each only for themselves and with their families. Precisely this modest, limited satisfaction with that which was already achieved provided the object of intellectual distancing and criticism. Adorno mocked the "warm security in provincialism," and writers like Jaspers (philosopher and author of *Wohin treibt die Bundesrepublik?*, "Where is the Federal Republic headed?") stressed the old opposition between *Geist* (intellect, spirit) and power, or between morality and wealth. The *Wirtschaftswunder* nation was diagnosed as "unable to grieve" (*mitscherlich*), and accused of rapidly forgetting the identity-guarantee of morality in its "consumerist thrill." Disturbed in its contentment, the middle-class society reacted with annoyance and expressions of exclusion, as from Ludwig Erhard ["architect of the *Wirtschaftswunder*," CDU finance minister under the "Father of the Republic" Konrad Adenauer, and later briefly Chancellor himself – Translator's note].

Parallels to the situation of the German *Vormärz* can certainly be drawn: on the side of the "*Wirtschaftswunder* nation" majority, we see the hardly reflexive and undistanced exaggeration of what had already been achieved, the *Adenauerscher Biedermeier* [mock term, roughly like "Eisenhower middle-class straight" – Translator's note] and the pathos of "Einigkeit und Recht und Freiheit" ["Unity and justice and freedom," first strophe of the section of the "Deutschlandlied" which became the Bundesrepublik's national anthem, excluding the formerly popular stanzas which begin with "Deutschland über alles" – Translator's note] On the side of the intellectual minority, we see the only putatively antinational sketch of a morally pure (or purified) nation, a distance from bourgeois consumerist ritual, an emphatic engagement for the self-determination of other nations (in nineteenth-century Poland, in twentieth-century Vietnam), a return to "the people" as the suppressed subject of history, etc.

b) Both codes of national identity conflicted directly and vehemently in the student revolt of the "1968 Generation." A second postwar generation entered stage left. It insisted on a radical, moral rejection of the legacies of the war generation, and eschewed the halfheartedness with which the leveled middle-class society "coped with the past" and settled into its leisure-time rituals. Even the political institutions of postwar democratic Germany were subjected to moral suspicion.[4] The task was to surpass the established democratic institutions in revolutionary fashion; critical alternatives were considered necessary. One was happy at being a "small radical minority," and issued broadly based philosophical criticisms of the social system. And once again, the high priests of criticism were students of Hegel.

With the student revolt, the socially critical reflexions of these intellectuals became practical matters – much like the ideas of the *Vormärz* intellectuals could be implemented in the praxis of the political conflicts of 1848.[5] The tension between the moral mission of the Holocaust nation and the *Wirtschaftswunder* nation was staged using sophisticated reflexive claims and new forms of political communication. One was provocative with open demonstrations of free sexuality and rituals of public resistance. Here as well, the cultural national identity was able to cross the borders between culture and politics only through heterodox, nonparliamentary forms of action (the "*außerparlamentarische Opposition*"), and not through any "normal" political activity.

The distance of the student movement from the established forms of politics, from parliamentarianism and parties, was made all the more dramatic through their reflexive connection to philosophical foundations that some representatives of the *Wirtschaftswunder* nation viewed as a dangerous and foreign ideology, if not as an "enemy to the constitution" (*Verfassungsfeind*) outright: Marxism. Marxism was condemned much in the way that in its time the "Enlightenment" had been rejected by parts of the

Bildungsbürgertum for being too French. The German student movement gained its effectiveness and particularity above all as a movement that advocated "revolution," meaning a radical departure from the past and violent acceleration of the present into the future. One trusted in the explosive power of the utopian idea, and attempted, in a new approach, to finally lead the project of a revolutionary break with tradition to success, following the failures of the Revolutions of 1848 and 1918. The "people on the barricades" was the conception of collective identity that the student revolt once again hoped to adopt.

But the failure of this attempt as a revolutionary movement was exemplary. It remained an esoteric movement of intellectuals, who appealed, in their enlightening tones, to a "bigoted" society, but in this asymmetrical relationship could simply not be understood. Much like the *Vormärz* intellectuals, the theoreticians of the student cultural revolution also encountered a public that was willing to learn, among the *Bildungsbürger*; but this public was of no concern to the students. They wanted the "oppressed" to rise up against their "rulers," and precisely this people – the desirously courted working class – reacted with rejection, and indeed anger, at the agitational attempts of the intellectuals.

The failure of the student cultural revolution of 1968 had quite a sobering effect on questions of organization and power. The nonparliamentary standpoint was surrendered. Parts of the student movement culminated in formal organizations of political activity, and thus not only completed an adaptation to the realm of strategic action, but also underwent a traditionalist shift to the old forms of the workers' movement, to Leninist or social-democratic party structures. This return to classical forms of political organization, as well as the reform-oriented call to undertake a "march through the institutions," defused and institutionalized the cultural revolutionary movement. In the end, the issues of concern were no longer the tensions between a moral project and established politics, but instead became questions of organization, and of dealing with the power of functionaries who had grown apart from the student movement.

But if one examines the student movement not as an attempt at revolution, but as a reform-oriented political movement, then it was thoroughly successful. From the periphery, it penetrated to the center of power, and set into motion institutional reforms that ultimately altered the sociostructural balance. There was a price to pay for participation in power, however, and it consisted in the loss of the tension between culture and politics.

c) A new generation gradually assumed distance from these institutionalized forms of party-political engagement. One moved away from the cities to the country, one sought the simplicity and natural life of premodern technology, and the self-determination and directness of rural forms of life and work. In this distancing there resurfaced the Romantic conception, of a harmony between culture and nature in distinction from a corrupt society, of an aesthetic foundation of life and an idealization of simplicity and introversion.

This retreat to the private and personal was carried by new aspects of reflexion that in a sense crossed well beyond the level of conflict over power within a single society. Efforts to secure peace or save nature were directed against threats that not only faced the single nation with which one was affiliated, but the whole of humanity. In contrast to the meanwhile institutionalized parts of the student movement, this generation of the "alternative movement," the peace movement and the ecological movement, gained a new perspective, from which the accustomed political conflicts between left and right might appear as particularist conflicts of interest. In range and urgency, the concern of the new social movements exceeded all classical differences. The issue was everything, the end of nature and history. Everyone was affected, and no partisanship, no special interest, could be brought up against this form of encompassing collectivity.[6] Beyond that, this sort of involved consternation was not located in the willfulness of the individual. One was affected as a member of a species, and although one could close one's eyes to the threat, one could hardly ban it from the world.

The new social movements distinguished themselves from the student movement not only in that aspect, overarching all else and allowing the gaining of a collective identity; but also through their new relationship to the past and future. While the student movement was still oriented by the classical model of progress under Modernity, the new social movements represented an increasingly obvious fundamental reversal of temporal perspective: expectations of revolution, so filled with the certainty of progress, disappeared to make room for the "German *angst*." The future was no longer an open area of progress, but a realm of imminent crises and catastrophes. The point was no longer to accelerate history through action in the present, but to prevent the coming of future catastrophes through timely action.

This axial reversal from utopia to apocalypse arises not only from a perception of real crises, but also from the logic of the national identity of the Germans: the Holocaust identity drew a border against the past, and founded identity on an attempt to prevent a repetition of the catastrophe.[7] As its referent this avoidance attitude had precisely the same time horizon by which the modern perspective oriented itself: the future. Collective identity arises here from the same consternation felt by everyone at the ultimate, unsurpassable catastrophe of the future, and through the shared attempt to avoid the worst. Unlike concrete hopes of progress, such an ultimate catastrophe – regardless of whether past or future – cannot be coped with through strategic action: it limits the horizons of possible experience and expectation, it is superordinate to every particular empirical consideration and individual decision, and thus it establishes collective identity – an identity, certainly, that, while arising from national encodings, has dissolved itself from national referents.

If future – just as much as past – history is occupied by catastrophes, then the search for reconciliation can find its way out of history only in the realm that modern consciousness sets up against history, as that of paradise and timelessness: nature. The neo-Romantic identity of the new social movements finds its retreat in the idea of pure, harmonic, and timeless nature, which requires defense against the threatening attack of history, of human activity and temporality.[8] This pure nature assumes the role of a transcendental retreat, much like the certainty of the coming catastrophe.

The new social movements could not, however, depend only upon the radically presented and discursively accelerated idea of apocalypse for very long. In contrast to the student movement, their central theses did find an echo, in a more moderate form, outside the intellectual circle. Much thought was given to the prospect of global catastrophes. To the degree that its following grew, however, the alternative movement's reflexive discourse was outweighed by ritual forms of integration.

This dissemination of the sociostructural basis was carried out less through the direct proselytization of a public than through the extraordinary expansion of the educational system in the years following 1975. The students of the alternative generation moved into educational institutions as teachers. Together with social workers, public-sector doctors, etc., and also unemployed academics, they became the core of a new, leftist *Bildungsbürgertum.* Often civil servants or at salaried jobs, without economic career perspectives, but also withdrawn from the vicissitudes of the market, they oriented their activities to a common welfare. Through this tension between morality and reality, between nature and society, and from the distance to the political center of society, a collective identity could be gained.

The new *Bildungsbürgertum* nonetheless also found itself in a central sociostructural situation. It was firmly established as one of the pillars of the new welfare-state-regulated society. The rhetoric of critical distancing thus set forth the tradition of cultural–moral codes of national identity, and concealed the circumstance that with the expansion of the new *Bildungsbürgertum*, petty bourgeois forms of communication had also found entry: *Vereine* and citizens' initiatives (*Bürgerinitiativen*), human chains and protest pickets.

Here as well the crossing of the boundaries between culture and politics is accomplished in heterodox forms. The code of the Holocaust nation, and its transformation into a catastrophe consciousness, undergo, even in heterodox fields, a petty bourgeois trivialization, showing quite similar features to the transmission of the transcendent–aesthetic Romantic nation code to the petty bourgeoisie of the Restoration. Collective identity becomes less discursive than ritually constructed, and the intellectuals increasingly become peripheral figures on the scene.

Even when the communication of this new "juste-milieu" hardly shows explicit references to the nation, at best by making antinational points, it nonetheless represents the accomplishment of a construction of national identity. At issue here is the German special path (*deutscher Sonderweg*) – the uniqueness and absoluteness of German history, which cannot be confused by any concern from abroad, and allows no comparison. At issue here is the "German calling to peace." Admittedly: here as well, the basic tension between culture and politics is defused. The diffusion of pacifist and ecological themes all the way into the "family values" hit-parade world (as in the song "A little bit of peace . . .") and advertisements for detergents (Slogan: "Out of a Love of Nature") took the "alternative" out of alternative consciousness, and paved the way to the center of political power.

d) This was the situation as the central European revolutions and German unification of 1989 and 1990 arrived.[9] These changed the tension between culture and power, between Holocaust identity and *Wirtschaftswunder* identity, in a fundamental fashion, and effected a new transformation of national identity. Characteristic of this new transformation is the decoupling of the conception of collective identity from its received social foundation. This especially applies to the intellectuals; in unified Germany, they lost their assignment of constructing unity and identity.

In the GDR as well, from whose territory the movement for unification emerged, the tension between Holocaust nation and *Wirtschaftswunder* nation had determined the field of national identification – from a very different perspective, however. Anti-Fascism was the official state ideology of the GDR – and one was very proud of having, through a radical new beginning, demarcated the boundaries against the Holocaust past so obviously that questions of guilt and vengeance could be shifted to the other German state, beyond the "anti-Fascist protective wall." But with the state claiming a monopoly on anti-Fascist representation, the Holocaust identity faded as a moral project. State-carrying rhetoric and official forms of speech trivialized the Holocaust identity, and took away its chance of setting socialist reality under tension. Instead, it was the unachievable *Wirtschaftswunder* beyond the western borders that played the role, for the citizens of the GDR, of a utopian counterdesign to the banality and routine of "anti-Fascist" reality. This "transcendent" consumer world became a graspable and palpable reality for GDR citizens after the German Revolution of 1989.

The carriers of this revolution were at first not the consumption-enthused masses, but a small, unbending moral elite: the East German civil-rights groups (the *Bürgerrechtler*). In exemplary fashion, they stood for the German *Bildungsbürgertum*, for church people, college teachers, and other intellectuals who held up a moral project against the state-socialist reality, and attempted to save the Holocaust identity from the all-encompassing power of the state.

After the winter of 1989–90, this civil rights movement, which brought down the Socialist regime with moral strictness and rituals of resistance taken over from the West[10] – and thus actually facilitated a revival of the Holocaust nation – was nonetheless forced entirely to the background, and had to clear the field for the "*Wirtschaftswunder* nation." The slogan "*We* are the People!," which stressed moral opposition to the state apparatus, became that of "We are *one* People!," which meant participation, after the fact, in the *Wirtschaftswunder* nation. The chance to revive the Holocaust identity, an attempt in which the western German left *Bildungsbürgertum* would not have hesitated to support and include the eastern German civil rights movement, was thus never taken up.

The irreversible collapse of "real-existing socialism" as an economic system and political regime left the until-then so publicly oriented *Bildungsbürgertum* of the old Bundesrepublik behind, indecisive and nearly speechless. The idea of democratic resistance urged them to an emphatic support for the civil-rights movements in the socialist countries. But the socialist system had also served as a "real existing support" for their moral criticism of the reigning order in the West. Certainly, the socialist reality had provided much reason for critique, and did not exactly invite identification, but one had been prepared, from a distance, to overlook a great deal, and derive, from a common opposition to the anti-Communist *Wirtschaftswunder* Germans, a certain kind of alliance with the GDR – a country which, for all its practical imperfections, at least advocated the "right principles." The cultural distancing of the West German intellectuals had thus found a support beyond the borders – a nearly unreal place that one tended not to visit, but from which *Wirtschaftswunder* Germany could at least be put under pressure.

This support was now gone, and the whirlpool of the German unification process blurred the lines of demarcation that had lent form and foundation to the opposition between Holocaust identity and *Wirtschaftswunder* identity. The encoding of national identity changed carrier groups. Parts of the new *Bildungsbürgertum*, until now carriers of the moral identity of the Holocaust nation, were morally discredited through their all-too obvious leaning on the "real Socialist" reality. More still: many among the *Bildungsbürgertum* could only articulate their reservations about unification – i.e., against the collapse of tension between moral vision and political reality – by pointing to particular economic interests, to the costs of unification, the number of unemployed and, in short, the threat posed by unification to the *Wirtschaftswunder* nation. Thus the identity of the *Wirtschaftswunder* nation was unwillingly adopted, and reinforced, by those who had until then endeavored to distance themselves from it. For the eastern German population, however, that identity was already the only one that set the standard.

The representatives of the *Wirtschaftswunder* nation, until then rather speechless in intellectual terms, followed the fashion of the times, and emphasized the universal moral duty to "Einigkeit und Recht und Freiheit." The *Wirtschaftswunder* identity had proven to be overwhelmingly attractive, and the conservative carrier groups of this identity could feel themselves blown forward by the winds of history as they turned to moral appeals for solidarity within the united nation. The unexpectedly rapid success of unification recalled the founding of the German *Reich*, which had turned liberal critics into enthusiastic admirers of Bismarck, and made all past reservations appear to be petty and morally bankrupt. Now, following unification, the Prussian tradition was positively symbolized by the ceremonial moving of the remains of the Hohenzollern kings to their tombs in Potsdam, attended by the current personages of state. In short: a surprising turn of history unexpectedly dealt the conservative carriers of the economic nation a primacy in the morally symbolic construction of national identity, a realm that had until then been under the claim of the left *Bildungsbürgertum*.

The formerly cut-and-dried camps of the German public thus began to dissolve. The turbulences of the year 1990 created an incomprehensible situation in which everything, a new beginning, a reconciliation between Holocaust identity and *Wirtschaftswunder* identity, seemed possible.[11]

For a brief time, the hour of the intellectuals had arrived. In a great and sophisticated debate [i.e., primarily during the uncertain period in the first half of 1990, before the course of unification was set – Translator's note], the chances of the new beginning and the risks of the nation–state, the end of the German *Sonderweg* and the new perspective of German national identity, all became issues. Perhaps for the last time, the intellectuals behaved as the constructors of national identity, but the unstoppable drive to a unified currency and political unity overtook their deliberations. In the end, unity was no longer a cultural project, but a political and administrative fact. This change from the cultural construction of identity to a statist reality of unity had consequences for the position of the intellectuals, to which we shall return.

Unification had hardly been effected when the sophisticated public discussion about German identity and its state constitution was replaced by a debate that seemed once again to be oriented by the traditional division between Holocaust nation and *Wirtschaftswunder* nation. The debate revolved around the Persian Gulf crisis and war of 1990–91. This gave the new left *Bildungsbürgertum*, made so uncertain by German unification, a renewed opportunity to ritually establish its own collective identity: pickets, peace marches, a powerful mobilization of a peace movement that had seemed to lose its issue with the end of the Cold War. The refusal and unwavering certainty of the Germans against foreign influences, the insistence of a special German position obligated to peace because of history, again pointed to a national identity based in the German *Sonderweg*, the "German calling" to peace.[12] Not political cunning, let alone economic interests (petroleum), but "life," the preservation of all life, the purity of peace, were once again defined as the foundation of collective identity.

In the attempt to revive the strict moral project of the Holocaust nation, however, the German peace movement ran into contradiction with the memory of the Holocaust itself, revived by the threat of Iraqi gas attacks on Israel. They could answer this contradictory situation only by emphasizing the uniqueness and inimitability of the Holocaust. The identity of the Holocaust nation was thus further reinforced and deepened, but at the same time depoliticized. The trauma of the Holocaust becomes the inalienable property of the Germans, and political considerations cannot touch this German identity. This view also stands in the tradition of the German cultural nation. Political action is only legitimate here as an extraordinary crossing of borders, as an uprising or great conflict, but not as a normal activity of political interest.

In contrast to the rigorism of the peace movement, a series of intellectuals also cited the Holocaust identity and Germany's special responsibility as they came out *for* supporting the war against the Iraqi dictator. Since most of them had previously been known as "left" intellectuals, the entire indignation of the peace movement was directed against this heretical standpoint. The harshness of the debate makes it clear that the Holocaust identity could obviously no longer secure clear political commonalities. The intellectuals began to dissolve their links to the established *Bildungsbürgertum.* The separation of two large sociostructural groups, who had each taken up particular encodings of national identity, gave way to an incomprehensible series of changing images and overlapping conflicts, from which no new moral construction of national identity seemed likely to emerge in the short term.

A further opportunity to revive the moral encoding of the national identity seemed to come with the public debate over the involvement of the Stasi (the all-powerful GDR State Security) with former citizens of the GDR. In this process, the Stasi system of "informal co-workers" is taken as representative of the complete control exercised by the GDR's totalitarian state, and the moral entanglement of the individual citizen within this system. In the attempt to draw a definitive border against the morally despicable past, and to comprehend the national identity as a project of the future, the public debate over the "Stasi past" moved within the framework of a code that had already defined the Holocaust identity. At stake once again is a "coping with the past" through a moral purification. Here as well, the headmasters of de-Stasification [a term consciously recalling the earlier "de-Nazification" – Translator's note] come from the outside. The existing laws once again offer only ambiguous criteria against acts of denunciation and collaboration. The gray zone, between naked opportunism and a responsibly undertaken readiness to compromise with the realities of the state, must once again be evaluated on a case-by-case basis. And the public debate about shared guilt and responsibility in dealing with the "Stasi past" once again focuses primarily on politicians who concealed their Stasi involvements over longer periods. The high level of public agitation over this debate indicates that the issue here is not just one of actionable crimes, but entirely elemental: the radical demarcation between past and future, the moral purification of the national identity won through the new beginning. In this construction of moral identity by means of "dealing with the Stasi past," the constructors are no longer the new *Bildungsbürgertum*, however, who had until then acted as carriers of the Holocaust identity, but instead conservative intellectuals and the opposition figures who had been affected by Stasi rule. These groups insist on an unrelenting self-purification, while representatives of the western German left tend to instead focus upon entanglements and intangibles, and emphasize the powerlessness of the individual against a totalitarian state.

Most of the eastern German population did not support a radical persecution of the Stasi system. Too many had been included in the organization, and even some of the most highly reputable public representatives of the new democratic politics were revealed to have been "informal collaborators" [*informelle Mitarbeiter* or "IMs"] of the Stasi. After the initial euphoria faded away, the gray and unpleasant reality of competitive labor markets took over, and disappointed those who expected that Chancellor Kohl's promise of "flourishing regions" would be accomplished within a matter of months. The mainstream of the eastern German *Bildungsbürgertum* in particular – teachers and officials in public service, academics and also more than a few intellectuals who had been the carriers of the GDR regime – were now all facing the grim situation of unemployment, and could not reasonably expect a better future. Like all others who lost their status and their jobs in the transformation of the outdated economy and the *Abwickelung* (dissolution) of the gigantic governmental organization, they sought relief in a nostalgic view of the coziness and solidarity of everyday life in the GDR. What was always missing in the times of the old regime was now developing strongly: a new collective identity of eastern Germans, based on shared local origin and the implicit rules of personal networks. The wall and the barbed wire had been torn down, and a new divide of mentality and affiliation rose up in its place. The boundaries between East and West were mostly constructed by silence: the outsiders would never be able to understand, the project of unification was much too popular to be publicly questioned, and the political system of the GDR was much too discredited to be publicly advocated. Even the post-communist successor to the ruling Socialist Unity Party, the PDS, presented itself in clear distinction to the past regime. But in contrast to its modernized image, most of its members were the supporters of the overthrown socialist system, and continued the old organizational networks on a local level. Because the PDS clearly advocated the cause of the disadvantaged east German population, and attacked the ruthlessness of capitalism, it ascended to a major political force on a regional and local level. The PDS attracted not only unemployed teachers and former party officials who were now driving taxis, but also intellectuals and writers like Stefan Heym – who had not enjoyed the privileges of official protection under the old regime. But it never appealed to west German intellectuals. The new collective identity of east Germans blended primordial and traditional codes; it has considerable difficulties in overcoming its local and regional confines.

In contrast to this strong regional cleavage between east and west, the outburst of right-wing extremism and *Ausländerfeindlichkeit* (xenophobia) in the early nineties provided a moral cause to be addressed in a campaign across society. A new rightist movement of youth in eastern and western Germany spread out, revived the Nazi symbols, attacked immigrants, and burnt their homes. Although not very large in numbers, the new extreme-right groups were highly mobilized, armed and ready for violent action. Their ideological basis was fuzzy, and their prime motive was more a generational revolt than an elaborated racism: hitting the taboos of the liberal left *Bildungsbürgertum* by publicly visible militant actions was more important to them than a political strategy for a neo-Nazi society. The response of the German *Bildungsbürgertum* to this blunt assault on the Holocaust identity was impressive. Immediately after the pogrom attacks on immigrant homes, several hundred thousand Germans joined the rallies mourning the victims and protesting against *Ausländerfeindlichkeit* – one of the largest rallies ever in Western societies. Intellectuals and the *Bildungsbürgertum* again were the opinion leaders in the defense of the German Holocaust identity, but their public support went far beyond the confines of the traditional *Bildungsbürgertum.* The horror of the past that was now again showing its ugly face was confronted with a determined majority, which silenced those few voices among the intellectuals who tried to sympathize with a primordial coding of the nation. Although the support for right-wing radicalism in Germany was certainly not larger than in other European nations, the Holocaust identity made a profound difference, and required a strong public response. The overwhelming support for the campaign, however, and its success in intimidating the neo-Nazi activists, subsequently weakened the attraction of the issue for intellectuals. A moral consensus which is supported by almost everyone does not convey distinction, and does not provide a promising cause for debates. The campaigns against Nazism continued in a ritualized manner on the level of local groups, and the immigration issue passed from the arena of agitated public debates to the round table of politicians. New causes, like the war in Bosnia, mobilized the German public and divided the intellectuals. Here appeals to the Holocaust identity seemed to yield entirely different political options: one group of intellectuals claimed that Germany had a special moral responsibility to help persecuted minorities, and therefore advocated military support to the Bosnian Muslims. By contrast others pointed to the Nazi past in order to bar any kind of military intervention. Irrespective of political camps, the Holocaust past is accepted in contemporary German public discourse as the reference of national identity, because appealing to it provides an unchallengeable value commitment. The Holocaust identity serves as the reference for entirely different political positions, and is no longer the exclusive project of a particular social carrier – the *Bildungsbürgertum.*

The *Wirtschaftswunder* identity also went through a transformation following German unification. The binding of national identity to economic self-confidence is no longer carried out through the simple "we are again somebody" feeling of the early postwar age, but in a fiscal redistribution in favor of the new German states. Here national identity is not marked through spectacular rituals, but comes in the form of an intangible additional argument to substantiate a redistribution of wealth, an argument that goes beyond the bounds of economic rationalism or mere regulatory guidelines. This "intangible" is defined as the point where the exchange of arguments ends, where the "partisan quarreling" breaks off, where solidarity is so self-evident it need no longer even be professed. The field of this national identity is today determined by ministerial bureaucracies, in which the routes of institutional restructuring are drawn up and the costs of unity calculated, recalculated, and financed in more or less artificial manner. Here we again see a decoupling of the encodings from their traditional carrier groups. It is by no means only the traditional carriers of the *Wirtschaftswunder* identity who participate in this process of the fiscal construction of the nation; broad parts of the *Bildungsbürgertum* also play a role. Here as well, German unification has given rise to a transformation in the encoding of national identity running contrary to the lines dividing the traditional camps. The formerly clear attributions of particular encodings of national identity to center and periphery, to specific carrier groups and social policy camps, are dissolved.

This dissolution of links between the traditional social carriers and their projects of national identity can be seen also with respect to the recent German debate over European monetary union. At stake was the Deutsche Mark, the strongest and most unchallenged symbol of Germany's economic strength, and hence of the *Wirtschaftswunder* identity. Germany's managerial class and its government strongly advocated monetary union, and Chancellor Kohl, a committed European, even referred to Germany's dark past when he praised the monetary union as a way of taming and binding the new, strong Germany. More ambivalent was the response of the unions and the *Bildungsbürgertum*, who expected increasing competition, wage cuts, and risks for the large public sector. Although reluctant to engage publicly in straight economic nationalism, they abstained from supporting the official pro-Maastricht campaign. The European Union of the Brussels Eurocrats was under suspicion of being a construction of instrumental reason, leveling regional and local differences of culture. Again "Geist und Macht," culture and money, could be pitted against each other. However, in their distance to the monetary union, parts of the *Bildungsbürgertum* joined the nationalist defenders of the Deutsche Mark among the petty bourgeoisie – the many who were afraid of a devaluation of their savings, and the few who made use of economic fears in order to fuel their political ambitions. The prospect of monetary union affected the national identity of Germany more so than of other European nations; its ambivalent support and divided reception impaired German confidence in the nation's economic strength in a manner similar to the tiresome and expensive reconstruction of the East. Germany was no longer a proud model for other European nations; others had modernized their institutions and taken the economic lead. This erosion of the *Wirtschaftswunder* identity engendered uneasiness among those who once backed this code of German postwar identity, and may possibly weaken their ties to the national pattern of collective identity in general.

The national identity of the Germans is thus no longer the exclusive domain of the intellectuals and the *Bildungsbürgertum.* Those who for over two centuries determined the construction of German identity, and constantly brought forth new conceptions of the encompassing societal collectivity, now lose this special function as the constructors of the nation's cultural identity. The reasons that the intellectuals and the *Bildungsbürgertum* can no longer solely determine national identity can above all be located in the fact of state unification itself. Since the Enlightenment, the tradition of the cultural nation, administrated by the *Bildungsbürgertum*, lived from the contradiction between the particularity of state relations and the universalism of morality and culture. Only culture could safeguard the unity of the whole, the self-awareness and identity of the nation. Once unity and integration are created on the level of the state, however, the compensatory mission of culture becomes superfluous. The great tension between the existing order and what is possible, between the this-worldly and the other-worldly, between culture and power, from which the classical intellectuals drew their significance, collapses with respect to the identity and unity of the society. If the whole is already real, and if this reality becomes self-evident and overwhelmingly powerful, then the task that arises for intellectuals is much more that of helping diversity and difference to their rights, than of generating the missing unity of the nation–state by cultural means. The construction of national identity can then surrender its cultural substantiation, and relate itself exclusively to the sheer positivism of societal processes.

Quite beyond that, the sphere of culture, in societies on their way to post-Modernism, has become less and less a matter of an education that is oriented to the whole, and that finds its counterpart in a particular form of personality. That sphere instead increasingly becomes a matter of cultural production, of a specialized business directed at an anonymous market, of a rapid turnover and consumption of cultural goods. The *Bildungsbürgertum* and classical intellectuals gained their particularity precisely from their distance to the world of markets and production. They saw themselves as an aristocracy of enlightenment, and not as a specialized functional elite. They produced themselves through education and upbringing, and not according to common market interests. This fall of the *Bildungsbürgertum* and the classical intellectuals is certainly a long-term and general process, but German unification makes it all the more obvious, and accelerates it in an exceptional fashion.

Notes

Introduction: the nation in social science and history

1 This discovery can naturally be linked to the preparatory works of the eighteenth century, but only becomes generally valid in the nineteenth century, following the *Sattelzeit* as described by Koselleck [i.e., according to Koselleck, the period in which understandings of basic sociopolitical concepts moved irreversibly "over the ridge" into their modern forms – Translator's note]. Cf. W. Conze, "Nation und Gesellschaft – Zwei Grundbegriffe der revolutionären Epoche" [nation and society – two basic concepts of the revolutionary age], in: *Historische Zeitschrift*, 198, 1964, pp. 1–16.

2 On the connection between nation-building and modernization, cf. S.N. Eisenstadt and S. Rokkan (eds.), *Building States and Nations*, Vol. I and II, Beverly Hills 1973; K. W. Deutsch, *Nationalism and Social Communication*, Cambridge, MA. 1953; K. W. Deutsch, *Nationalism and its Alternatives*, New York 1969; R. Dahrendorf, *Gesellschaft und Demokratie in Deutschland* [available in English as *Society and Democracy in Germany*, Garden City, NY 1967], Munich 1965; R. L. Merrit, "Nation-Building in America: The Colonial Years," in: K.W. Deutsch *et al.*, *Nation-Building*, New York 1963, pp. 56–72; D. Lerner, *The Passing of Traditional Society. Modernizing the Middle East*, New York 1958; S. Rokkan *et al.*, "Nationbuilding – A Review of Recent Comparative Research and a Selected Bibliography of Analytical Studies," in: *Current Sociology*, 19, 1971, pp. 1–86. On the more recent discussion, see, among others, E. A. Tiryakian, "Nationalism, Modernity, and Sociology," in: *Sociologia Internationalis*, I, 1988, pp. 1–17.

3 For a critical retrospective, if only of a certain part of these studies, cf. U. Menzel, "Das Ende der 'Dritten Welt' und das Scheitern der großen Theorien. Zur Soziologie einer Disziplin in auch selbstkritischer Absicht" [the end of the "Third World" and the failure of grand theories; towards a self-critical sociology of a discipline], in: *Politische Vierteljahresschrift*, 32, 1991, pp. 4–33.

4 Cf. also P. Chatterjee, *Nationalist Thought and the Colonial World – A Derivative Discourse?*, London 1986.

5 C. Geertz, "After the Revolution: The Fate of Nationalism in the New States," in: Geertz, *The Interpretation of Cultures*, New York 1973, pp. 234–254.
6 For a defense of acknowledging at least one of these factors in modernization theory, cf. W. Zapf, "Der Untergang der DDR und die soziologische Theorie der Modernisierung" [the fall of the GDR and the sociological theory of modernization], in: B. Giesen and C. Leggewie (eds.), *Experiment Vereinigung* [the unification experiment], Berlin 1991, pp. 38–51.
7 On this cf., for example, H. Kohn, *The Mind of Germany*, London 1965; E. Kedourie, *Nationalism*, London 1966; C. Graf v. Krockow, *Nationalismus als deutsches Problem* [nationalism as a German problem], Munich 1970.
8 This is where Jürgen Habermas follows in a language-pragmatic, modernized form, i.e. provisionally, without debts to history or transcendent philosophy. In this connection cf. especially "Können komplexe Gesellschaften eine vernünftige Identität ausbilden?" [can complex societies form a reasonable identity?] in: Habermas, *Zur Rekonstruktion des Historischen Materialismus* [towards a reconstruction of historical materialism], Frankfurt am Main, 1976, pp. 92–126.
9 Although Helmuth Plessner succeeds in placing this jumble in a thematically unified context, his analysis nonetheless remains differentiated in its individual considerations, even if his title of the "Verspätete Nation" ("the delayed nation") has become a catchword. He hesitates before sweeping condemnations like the ones found in popular treatments of the subject, such as in A. Finkielkraut, *La Défaite de la pensée*, Paris 1987. Drawing such continuities is of course by no means a "foreign" invention, therefore cf. instead A. Gehlen, "Deutschtum und Christentum bei Fichte" [Germanness and Christendom in Fichte], in: Gehlen, *Gesamtausgabe*, Vol. II, Frankfurt am Main 1980, pp. 215–293.
10 A. D. Smith, *Theories of Nationalism*, London 1971, p. 262.
11 On this central distinction cf. especially R. Bendix, *Freiheit und historisches Schicksal* [freedom and historical destiny], Frankfurt am Main 1982, pp. 120ff.
12 M. Hroch, "Das Erwachen kleiner Nationen als Problem der komparativen Forschung" [the awakening of small nations as a problem in comparative research], in: H. A. Winkler (ed.), *Nationalismus*, 2nd expanded edition, Königstein am Taunus 1985, pp. 155–172; H. Kohn, *Die Slawen und der Westen* [the Slavs and the West], Vienna 1956.
13 Perhaps this drawing of types can be found in all national movements. At any rate, today it can no longer be assumed to only apply to eastern Europe, and not to the west. On the attempts by English patriots, for example, at disassociating from their "Frenchifying" rulers, cf. G. Newman, *The Rise of English Nationalism. A Cultural History 1740–1830*, New York 1987.
14 Cf. F. Meinecke, *Weltbürgertum und Nationalstaat. Studien zur Genesis des deutschen Nationalstaats* [cosmopolitanism and nation–state; studies on the genesis of the German nation–state], Munich and Berlin 1908.
15 For example, cf. H. Seton-Watson, *Nations and States: An Enquiry into the*

Origins of Nations and the Politics of Nationalism, Boulder, CO 1977. Good analyses of the problems of transposing terms such as "the people" or *Volk* and "nation" to non-European cultures can be found especially in W. E. Mühlmann, *Homo Creator. Abhandlungen zur Soziologie, Anthropologie und Ethnologie* [treatises on sociology, anthropology and ethnology], Wiesbaden 1962, pp. 409ff.

16 Especially cf. T. Nairn, *The Break-up of Britain*, London 1977.

17 M. Hechter, *Internal Colonialism. The Celtic Fringe in British National Development, 1536–1966*, Berkeley and Los Angeles 1975; by the same author, "Group Formation and the Cultural Division of Labor," in: *American Journal of Sociology*, 84, 1978, pp. 293–318; and "Internal Colonialism Revisited," in: E. A. Tiryakian and R. Rogowski (eds.), *New Nationalisms in the Developed West*, London 1985, pp. 17–26. Hechter began his analyses with a rather structuralist approach, but has by now reformed this into a strict rational-choice design. Also along these lines, and fascinating for their unified systematism, are the analyses of M. Banton, *Racial and Ethnic Competition*, Cambridge 1983. In addition, cf. J. Nagel and S. Olzak, "Ethnic Mobilization in New and Old States: An Extension of the Competition Model," in: *Social Problems*, 30, 1982, pp. 127–143; and, for an overview, F. Nielsen, "Toward a Theory of Ethnic Solidarity in Modern Societies," in: *American Sociological Review*, 50, 1985, pp. 133–149. Within German-language research, Hartmut Esser especially has distinguished himself with a similar approach; cf., for example, "Ethnische Differenzierung und moderne Gesellschaft" [ethnic differentiation and modern society], in: *Zeitschrift für Soziologie*, 17, 1988, pp. 235–248.

18 Here we might point to a series of similar considerations by other authors; cf. especially: E. Gellner, "Nationalism," in: Gellner, *Thought and Change*, London 1964, pp. 147–178; by the same author, *Nations and Nationalism*, Oxford 1983; cf. also B. Anderson, *Imagined Communities*, 2nd revised edition, London 1991; O. Dann, "Nationalismus und sozialer Wandel in Deutschland 1806–1850" [nationalism and social change in Germany 1806–1850], in: Dann (ed.), *Nationalismus und sozialer Wandel*, Hamburg 1978, pp. 77–128; cf. also the works by K. W. Deutsch referred to in note 2 above.

19 An issue that today, given great migrational movements and demands for multiculturalism, is once again current, especially in the USA; cf. E.D. Hirsch, *Cultural Literacy. What Every American Needs to Know*, New York 1988.

20 Cf. F. Coulmas, *Sprache und Staat. Studien zur Sprachplanung* [language and state; studies on language planning], Berlin and New York 1985; and *Die Wirtschaft mit der Sprache* [the language business], Frankfurt am Main 1992.

21 Cf. G.L. Mosse, *Die Nationalisierung der Massen. Politische Symbolik und Massenbewegung in Deutschland von den napoleonischen Kriegen bis zum 3. Reich* [nationalization of the masses; political symbolism and mass movement in Germany from the Napoleonic Wars to the Third Reich], Frankfurt am Main and Berlin 1976.

22 W.E. Mühlmann, "Chiliasmus, Nativismus, Nationalismus," in: *Soziologie und*

moderne Gesellschaft. Verhandlungen des 14. Deutschen Soziologentages [sociology and modern society; proceedings of the 14th conference of German sociologists], Stuttgart 1966, pp. 228–242; and (ed.), *Chiliasmus und Nativismus*, Berlin 1961.

23 An extensive theoretical development of this model and its placement within a comprehensive sociological – better: evolutionary – theoretical structure, as well as bibliographical recommendations, which I shall therefore largely forgo here, can be found in: B. Giesen, *Die Entdinglichung des Sozialen. Eine evolutionstheoretische Perspektive auf die Postmoderne* [the dereification of the social; a developmental-theory perspective on post-Modernism], Frankfurt am Main 1991; also "Code, Process and Situation in Cultural Selection," in: Giesen, *Cultural Dynamic*, 4, 2, 1991, pp. 172–185. Another evolutionary, theoretical model, comparable in detail but entirely different in basic orientation, was applied by Klaus Eder to similar historic material in a comprehensive study. In contrast to the present work, Eder's primary concern, for all the historic distinctions among his single analyses, is drawn from classical developmental theory. In this view, societal progress and cultural advancement are to be explained through a theory of collective moral learning. And in the process, Eder also attempts to reformulate the thesis of the "special German path." From the perspective of the present work, it is possible to agree with his diagnosis – that the way to post-conventional morality, already inherent in the associations preceding 1848, was blocked by an increasing orientation towards utility and power in the second half of the nineteenth century – without needing to adopt his evolutionary perspective of the necessity of moral advancement. The present work also takes collective learning experiences into account, but understands these not in terms of an "external" criterion of progress, but as the disappointment of one generation of intellectuals at the previous attempts to construct collective identity. The underlying paradigm is not – as with Eder – a transhistorical model of higher moral development, but a generationally sequenced, working model of social differentiation and identity construction. In addition, the present work does not treat the whole of society as a discursive community, but takes the particular sociostructural embeddings and delimitations of discourses into account. It might be considered a defect that only the intellectuals, and no other societal groups, are considered; but this is explained through the exceptional "seedbed" function played by intellectuals in the formulation of collective identity. Cf. K. Eder, *Geschichte als Lernprozeß? Zur Pathogenese politischer Modernität in Deutschland* [history as a learning process; on the pathogenesis of political modernity in Germany], Frankfurt am Main 1985.

24 The literature on the "special German path" is by now nearly impossible to summarize. The following works were highly stimulating for the present work, even if in part only as the object of critical distancing: H. Plessner, *Die verspätete Nation*, Stuttgart 1959; Dahrendorf, *Gesellschaft und Demokratie;* N. Elias, *The Germans. Studies of Power, Struggles, and the Development of Habitus in the Nineteenth and Twentieth Centuries*, New York 1996; F. K. Ringer, *Die*

Gelehrten. Der Niedergang der deutschen Mandarine 1850–1933 [the learned; the fall of the German mandarins], Munich 1987; R. Münch, *Die Kultur der Moderne* [culture of Modernism], Vol. II: *Ihre Entwicklung in Frankreich und Deutschland* [its development in France and Germany], Frankfurt am Main 1986; and K. Eder as in note 23. The discussion is summarized from a historical perspective in: H.A. Winkler, "Der deutsche Sonderweg. Eine Nachlese," in: *Merkur*, 35, 1981, pp. 793–804.

1 The construction of collective identity: proposal for a new analysis

1 But for a more recent overview, cf. A. P. Cohen, *The Symbolic Construction of Community*, London 1985. Quite in contrast to older formulations, community is viewed therein not as a natural substructure, but understood as symbolic construct. The more recent discussion on the status of culture has meanwhile also allowed for a redefinition of the relation between culture, community, and society. Here I shall especially point to the works of M. Archer, such as *Culture and Agency. The Place of Culture in Social Theory*, Cambridge 1990.

2 It remains Georg Simmel's achievement that he was the first to recognize this clearly for sociology; cf. especially *Der Krieg und die geistige Entscheidung* [war and decisions of intellect], Munich 1917. The problem is formulated with the same clarity in Max Weber, especially in his writings on the sociology of religion. In his political texts, however, because of their function as position papers, it paradoxically remains hidden beneath a sometimes imploring tone; cf. for example "Der Nationalstaat und die Volkswirtschaftspolitik" [nation–state and national economic policy], in: Weber, *Gesammelte politische Schriften* [collected political works], Tübingen 1988, pp. 1–25, pp. 13f.

3 E. Zerubavel, *The Fine Line. Making Distinctions in Everyday Life*, New York 1991.

4 In literature the map is a tried-and-true metaphor for portraying epistemological problems. Whilst acknowledging Jorge Luis Borges, cf. especially Umberto Eco's parodic treatment of "a map of the empire in 1:1 scale" in: *Diario minimo,* Milan 1963. An absolute map is impossible, and this is why theorists are also well advised to occasionally draw "dotted lines and confessions of ignorance" instead of issuing blanket warnings about "cannibals," as Grahame Greene remarked about an old American map of Liberia in *Journey Without Maps*, Harmondsworth 1978, pp. 46f.

5 Reinhart Koselleck proposes a rather differently weighted triad of differences, specifically: earlier/later, inside/outside, and over/under; cf. "Sprachwandel und Ereignisgeschichte" [transformation of language and history of events], in: *Merkur*, 43, 1989, pp. 657–673. As is well known, Niklas Luhmann prefers the triad "temporal–factual–social," and a rather differently accentuated categorization can be found in Carl Schmitt, "Nehmen/Teilen/Weiden" [taking, sharing, grazing], in: *Verfassungsrechtliche Aufsätze aus den Jahren 1924–1954* [essays on constitutional law, 1924–1954], Berlin 1985, pp. 489–504.

6 On recent discussion about construction of categories and their relation to biological or situational givens, cf. especially G. Lakoff, *Women, Fire and Dangerous Things. What Categories Reveal about the Mind*, Chicago and London 1987.

7 Here we take up, with slight variations, considerations from Lévi-Strauss, but without adopting the precise detail of his theoretical apparatus. Cf. especially "Les Organisations dualistes existent-elles?" [do dualist organizations exist?] in: C. Lévi-Strauss, *Anthropologie structurale*, Vol. I, Paris 1958, pp. 147–180.

8 Ethnomethodologists therefore speak of a necessary "indexicality" of all social occurrences – corresponding here to the actually processed code in each case. For a classic treatment, cf. H. Garfinkel, *Studies in Ethnomethodology*, Englewood Cliffs, NJ 1967, pp. 4ff.

9 The levels of code, process, and situation can be traced back to the triadic relation of signs in Peircean semiotics. The "code" here corresponds to the Peircean "sign." The "objects" described there are elements of "situation" here, and are selected from it through the act of description. Finally, the serial association of acts of using signs constitutes the signing process, the "semiosis," in which signs are related to other signs as their "interpretants." For a concentrated formulation of triadic sign relations, see C. S. Peirce's "Syllabus of Certain Topics of Logic" [has not been published fully in English, but is available in German as *Phänomen und Logik der Zeichen* (phenomenon and logic of signs), edited and translated by H. Pape, Frankfurt am Main 1983, here p. 64]; cf. also K. Oehler, "Idee und Grundriß der Peirceschen Semiotik" [idea and outline of Peircean semiotics], in: M. Krampen, R. Posner, and T. v. Uexküll (eds.), *Die Welt als Zeichen. Klassiker der modernen Semiotik* [the world as sign; classics of modern semiotics], Berlin 1981, pp. 15–49, here p. 23ff.

10 To prevent any misunderstanding that might arise from the partly phenomenological-seeming vocabulary employed here, it should be noted that I am naturally not adopting Husserl directly, but connecting to a later Husserl at most, one as received within sociology in the main through Schütz (some phenomenologists would say "distorted"). The issue here can no longer be *epoché*, free variation, or display of essence. On the contrary, contingent experience conveyed through signs, always historically formed, makes up the hardly avoidable starting point of our considerations.

11 On the difficulty of formulating an isolated conception of process and code (or repetition and difference) and thus ultimately of gaining access to situation, i.e. the referent, cf. the many impulses, admonishments, and dilemmas detailed by Gilles Deleuze, *Différence et répétition*, Paris 1968.

12 Here we follow the widely disseminated theoretical figure of self-organization. For a new variant cf. especially: H. R. Maturana, *Erkennen: Die Organisation und Verkörperung von Wirklichkeit. Arbeiten zum Radikalen Konstruktivismus* [cognition: organization and embodiment of reality; works on radical constructivism], Braunschweig and Wiesbaden 1982. For further, more general treatments cf. G. Roth and H. Schwedler (eds.), *Self-Organizing Systems. An Interdisciplinary Approach*, Frankfurt am Main 1981; W. Krohn and G. Küppers

(eds.), *Emergenz: Die Entstehung von Ordnung, Organisation und Bedeutung* [emergence: origins of order, organization, and meaning], Frankfurt am Main 1992; S.J. Schmidt (ed.), *Der Diskurs des Radikalen Konstruktivismus*, Frankfurt am Main 1990. As the classical sociological work on this issue, see P.L. Berger and T. Luckmann, *The Social Construction of Reality: a Treatise in the Sociology of Knowledge*, Garden City, NY 1966.

13 The constitutive role negation plays in all forms of socialization has been distinguished especially well by Niklas Luhmann through his combination of phenomenological and systems-theory concepts; cf. "Über die Funktion der Negation in sinnkonstituierenden Systemen" [on the function of negation in meaning-constituting systems] in: *Soziologische Aufklärung*, Vol. 3, Opladen 1981, pp. 35–49. Also, "Diskussion als System," in: J. Habermas and N. Luhmann, *Theorie der Gesellschaft oder Sozialtechnologie?* [theory of society or social technology?], Frankfurt am Main 1971, pp. 316–341, pp. 323f.

14 On the concept of decoupling, see Giesen, *Die Entdinglichung des Sozialen*.

15 An overview of the state of research on orality and literacy can be found in W. J. Ong, *Orality and Literacy – The Technologizing of the Word*, London 1982. Numerous signposts, which I have partly followed here, can be found in the work of Lévi-Strauss, especially chapter 28 of *Tristes Tropiques*, London 1955.

16 On the consequences of the rise of written language, see J. Goody, *The Domestication of the Savage Mind*, Cambridge 1977.

17 To echo Odo Marquard, the issue here is typically that of incompetence-compensation competence: cf. "Inkompetenzkompensationskompetenz. Über Kompetenz und Inkompetenz der Philosophie," in: Marquard, *Abschied vom Prinzipiellen* [farewell to the principal point], Stuttgart 1981, pp. 23–38. In this fashion reality, specifically as socially constructed reality with situation-resistant tendencies, moves over into the fictive; therefore cf. the same author's "Kunst als Antifiktion – Versuch über den Weg der Wirklichkeit ins Fiktive" [art as anti-fiction; an attempt to reach the fictive over the path of reality], in: Marquard, *Aesthetica und Anaesthetica*, Paderborn, pp. 82–99.

18 With just a few exceptions, social philosophical reflexion on the "other" has placed priority on the you–me relationship, or the problem of understanding, while the question of the genesis of a collective identity, a "we," has rarely been understood in terms of encounter with an "other." Instead, attempts were usually made to explain collective identity endogenously. Among the more recent and stimulating attempts to overcome this narrowing of the question, cf. especially J. Kristeva, *Fremde sind wir uns selbst* [we are the others to ourselves], Frankfurt am Main 1990, and J.A. Boon, *Other Tribes, Other Scribes. Symbolic Anthropology in the Comparative Study of Cultures, Histories, Religions and Texts*, Cambridge 1982. Approaching the problem much more from a Foucauldian perspective are the many movements towards "imaginative geography" in E. Said, *Orientalism*, New York 1978, especially pp. 49ff.

19 Not without reason does the concept of seduction occupy a key role in the works of Jean Baudrillard whenever he considers the constitution and genesis

of meaning. Otherness attracts and seems seductive only as long as it is other, and constantly withdraws from contact; cf. especially *Les Stratégies fatales*, Paris 1983.

20 On this cf. also C. Geertz, "The Integrative Revolution: Primordial Sentiment and Civil Politics in the New States," in: Geertz, *The Interpretation of Cultures*, New York 1973, pp. 255–310.

21 The literature on borders and limits is relatively sparse, despite their constitutive function in the building of all systems. And that does not just apply to sociology. For example there is no entry for the word *Grenzen* in the dictionary of basic historical terms (*Geschichtliche Grundbegriffe*). Still of interest therefore is J. Grimm, "Deutsche Grenzalterthümer" [borders in early German histories], in: Grimm, *Abhandlungen zur Mythologie und Sittenkunde* [considerations on mythology and ethics], *Kleinere Schriften*, Vol. II, Berlin 1965, pp. 30–74. But for a sociological and/or anthropological view, cf. also F. Barth (ed.), *Ethnic Groups and Boundaries: The Social Organization of Cultural Difference*, Boston 1969.

22 Cf. the still well worth reading A. van Gennep, *The Rites of Passage*, London 1960; as well as V. T. Turner, *Das Ritual. Struktur und Anti-Struktur*, Cologne 1989. Of more recent works cf. also H.-G. Soeffner, *Die Ordnung der Rituale. Die Auslegung des Alltags 2* [the order of rituals; interpretation of everyday life 2], Frankfurt am Main 1992.

23 In this connection Ernest Gellner speaks of a kind of social "entropy"; cf. *Nations and Nationalism*, pp. 64ff.

24 Such naturalizations are naturally not found only in premodern societies. Processes of naturalization remain omnipresent today, not only as national myths, but also as everyday ones. Cf. the now-classic analyses in R. Barthes, *Mythologies*, Paris 1957.

25 E. Shils, "Personal, Primordial, Sacred and Civil Ties," in: Shils, *Center and Periphery. Essays on Macrosociology*, Chicago 1975, pp. 111–126.

26 On the problem of the "other" in this connection, cf. the two classic works, one by Georg Simmel, "Exkurs über den Fremden," in: Simmel, *Soziologie. Untersuchungen über die Formen der Vergesellschaftung* [sociology; forms of socialization], 4th edition, Berlin 1958, pp. 509–512; and Alfred Schütz, "Der Fremde," in: Schütz, *Gesammelte Aufsätze*, Vol. II, The Hague 1972, pp. 53–69. An overview of more recent literature can be found in L. D. Harman, *The Modern Stranger – On Language and Membership*, Berlin, New York and Amsterdam 1988.

27 But the story can take unexpected turns, even when one attempts to account for all observed peculiarities of "others," as the example of Captain Cook demonstrates. Marshall Sahlins's account of what Cook and his crew experienced on their two journeys to the Hawaiian Islands at times reads like a thriller; cf. *Historical Metaphors and Mythical Realities*, Ann Arbor, MI 1981 [the German version is even called "The Death of Captain Cook" – translator's note].

28 The following considerations are indebted to K. Löwith, *Weltgeschichte und*

Heilsgeschehen [world history and God's saving grace], Stuttgart 1953. In the wake of the Enlightenment, specific nations became the forerunners of a history of the world as a tale of redemption.

29 Friedrich Tenbruck even goes so far as to postulate sociology itself, above all the dominant American theory of modernization, as a specific, secular variant of cultural proselytization. Above all cf. *Die unbewältigten Sozialwissenschaften oder die Abschaffung des Menschen* [the unfinished social sciences, or the abolition of the human], Graz 1984; as well as "Der Traum der säkularen Ökumene. Sinn und Grenze der Entwicklungsvision" [dream of the secular priesthood; meaning and limits of the vision of development], in: Tenbruck, *Die kulturellen Grundlagen der Gesellschaft* [cultural foundations of society], Opladen 1989, pp. 291–307.

30 Here we adopt considerations stemming from the sociology of science. Compare Thomas Kuhn, *Die Entstehung des Neuen* [origins of the novel], Frankfurt am Main 1978.

31 Randall Collins has announced a broad and ambitious effort to reconstruct the history of ideas as the history of dynamic, social networks of intellectuals. The publications so far are impressive and promising. There are many points of agreement with the efforts made here, albeit within a far narrower historical perspective. Cf. "A Micro-Macro Theory of Intellectual Creativity: The Case of German Idealist Philosophy," in: *Sociological Theory*, 1987, pp. 47–69.

32 This formulation follows upon the conception of an "axial age" as developed by Eisenstadt in succession to Karl Jaspers; cf. especially S. N. Eisenstadt, "The Axial Age: The Emergence of Transcendental Visions and the Rise of Clerics," in: *European Journal of Sociology*, 23, 2, 1982, pp. 299–314, as well as the collection by the same author (ed.), *Kulturen der Achsenzeit*, 2 Vols., Frankfurt am Main 1987.

33 R. Michels, "Historisch-kritische Untersuchungen zum politischen Verhalten der Intellektuellen" [historical/critical examinations of the political behavior of intellectuals], in: Michels, *Masse, Führer, Intellektuelle* [masses, leaders, intellectuals], Frankfurt am Main and New York 1987, pp. 189–213, here p. 189.

34 K. Mannheim, *Ideologie und Utopie*, Frankfurt am Main 1952, p. 11 [available in English as *Ideology and Utopia: An Introduction to the Sociology of Knowledge*, San Diego 1985]; E. Shils, "Intellectuals, Public Opinion and Economic Development," in: *World Politics*, 10, 1958, pp. 232–255; E. Shils, "Intellectuals, Tradition, and the Tradition of Intellectuals: Some Preliminary Considerations," in: Shils, *Center and Periphery. Essays on Macrosociology*, Chicago 1975, pp. 21–35; S. M. Lipset, *Political Man*, New York 1960, p. 311.

35 In Weber this opposition is found not only in the texts on the sociology of the world religions, but also in a strict separation between politics and science, indeed even between the ethics of conviction (*Gesinnungsethik*) and the ethics of responsibility (*Verantwortungsethik*). German sociology always assigned great weight to the tension between spirit and power, between "*Geist*" and "*Macht.*" Cf. T. Geiger, *Aufgaben und Stellung der Intelligenz in der Gesellschaft* [tasks and

place of the intelligence in society], Stuttgart 1949, p. 79; M. R. Lepsius, "Kritik als Beruf. Zur Soziologie der Intellektuellen" [criticism as a profession; on the sociology of intellectuals] in: Lepsius, *Interessen, Ideen und Institutionen*, Opladen 1990, pp. 273ff.

36 Not without reason does Helmut Schelsky explicitly speak of the "priestly rule" of the intellectuals in *Die Arbeit tun die anderen. Klassenkampf und Priesterherrschaft der Intellektuellen* [others do the work; class conflict and priestly rule of the intellectuals], Opladen 1975. For a critical view however, cf. R. Löwenthal, "Neues Mittelalter oder anomische Kulturkrise" [new Middle Ages or anomic cultural crisis] in: Löwenthal, *Gesellschaftswandel und Kulturkrise* [change in society and cultural crisis], Frankfurt am Main 1979, pp. 37–57.

37 Cf., also generally, G. Konrád and I. Szelényi, *The Intellectuals on the Road to Class Power*, New York 1979. The authors mainly focus on the position and function of the *intelligentsia* in Eastern Europe. They formulate their approach as an analogy to the Marxian theory of the Asian mode of production, and see themselves in this tradition. A criticism of their work and an alternative more in the mainstream of sociology, combining humanist and conservative as well as Marxist elements, can be found in Alvin Gouldner, *The Future of Intellectuals and the Rise of the New Class: A Frame of Reference, Theses, Conjectures, Arguments, and an Historical Perspective on the Role of Intellectuals and Intelligentsia in the International Class Contest of the Modern Era,* New York 1979.

38 The Gramscian term "organic intellectuals" in particular has been the subject of much discussion, and can serve here as a contrasting foil. The early Romantics and pre-1848 intellectuals, analyzed in the main part of this book, were never "organic intellectuals" in Gramsci's sense. They lacked the social ties, the "more or less narrow relation to a basic social group" and hence anything "organic" – a fact that Gramsci also turned into an accusation against his intellectual contemporaries, whom he likened to "something unbound from the people, floating in the air, a caste and not a part of the people with organic functions": cf. A. Gramsci, *Zu Politik, Geschichte und Kultur*, Frankfurt am Main 1980, pp. 222–230, p. 228. On the isolation of Italian intellectuals and their lack of popular appeal, see *Ibid.*, pp. 235–243, p. 239. Neither the German Romantics nor the pre-1848 writers succeeded in becoming organically integrated speakers of a particular social stratum. They primarily spoke for themselves, and found a resonance of only short duration. But the concept of "organic intellectuals" does seem to apply to the patriots before them, and the mandarins who followed. The intellectual discourse of the patriots remained narrowly tied to the expanding administrative system; that of the mandarins to an educational system that was unique by international comparison, especially the *Gymnasien* [grammar schools] and universities.

39 Cf. Geiger, *Aufgaben und Stellung*; Konrád and Szelényi, *Intellectuals*, pp. 32f. The question of ties between intellectuals and other sociostructural groups, strata, or classes is a central theme in the sociology of intellectuals. Between

Marx and Gramsci, who see intellectuals narrowly coupled to the interests of other groups, and Mannheim, who understands intellectuals as social free-floaters, there is a wide field for intermediate positions.

40 On the relation between intellectuals and politicians, cf. the impressive work by Z. Bauman, *Legislators and Interpreters. On Modernity, Postmodernity and Intellectuals*, Ithaca, NY 1987.

41 Ralf Dahrendorf thus distinguished between "classical" (state-carrying) and romantic (apolitical) intellectuals, contrasting both to the over-distanced, tragic intellectuals of the Exile during the Nazi period and the liberal/critical intellectuals; cf. *Gesellschaft und Demokratie*, pp. 311–324.

42 Intellectuals are thus a "decrying class" in a double sense: they criticize the order of society while also complaining about the lack of public understanding for their complaints and criticism; cf. W. Lepenies, *Aufstieg und Fall der Intellektuellen in Europa* [rise and fall of European intellectuals], Frankfurt am Main and New York, 1992.

43 From this point forward there arises a possibility of understanding the crisis phenomena in this area sociologically; cf. R. Collins, "On the Sociology of Intellectual Stagnation: The Late Twentieth Century in Perspective," in: *Theory, Culture and Society*, vol. IX, 1992, pp. 73–96.

44 There is a wide-ranging literature on the discourse rituals of intellectuals, for example on the technique of "debunking," of claiming a difference in being from appearance; cf. K. Burke, "The Virtues and Limitations of Debunking," in: Burke, *The Philosophy of Literary Form*, Berkeley and Los Angeles 1973, pp. 168–190. On the technique of advocating the oppressed, the inexpressible, or the natural, cf. W. Empson, *Some Versions of Pastoral*, London 1986. This tradition, which in particular is linked to Burke's dramaturgy, has more recently been set forth by authors like H. White as in his *Tropics of Discourse. Essays in Cultural Criticism*, Baltimore and London 1978; and by C. Geertz, *Works and Lives: The Anthropologist as Author*, Cambridge 1988. The microlevel of argumentative technique, in a work in turn also strongly influenced by Burke, is explored by E. Goffman, "The Lecture," in: Goffman, *Forms of Talk*, Pennsylvania 1981, pp. 160–195 (including, on the theme of free-floating intellectualism covered here, a few revealing observations about the use of parenthetical remarks and footnotes; how these allow an observation of what is said or written from a different angle: pp. 175ff). In addition, linguistic criticism – while being thoroughly frowned upon for its "positivism" – still contains numerous stimuli: cf. especially G. Degenkolbe, "Über logische Strukturen und gesellschaftliche Funktionen von Leerformeln" [on the logical structures and social functions of empty phrases], in: *Kölner Zeitschrift für Soziologie und Sozialpsychologie*, 17, 1965, pp. 327–338; M. Schmid, *Leerformeln und Ideologiekritik* [empty phrases and the criticism of ideology], Tübingen 1972. On the self-celebratory techniques of modern "television intellectuals" – more or less as forced by the media – cf. R. Debray, *Teachers, Writers, Celebrities. The Intellectuals of Modern France*, London 1981.

45 Cf. E. L. Eisenstein, *The Printing Press as an Agent of Change – Communications*

and Cultural Transformations in Early-Modern Europe, Cambridge 1982; M. Giesecke, *Der Buchdruck in der frühen Neuzeit. Eine historische Fallstudie über die Durchsetzung neuer Informations- und Kommunikationstechnologien* [printing in early modernity; a historical case study on the triumph of new information and communications technologies], Frankfurt am Main 1991.

46 Cf. G. H. Mead, *Mind, Self, and Society. From the Standpoint of a Social Behaviorist*, Chicago 1967.

47 Walter J. Ong therefore speaks in this connection of the decay of dialogue; cf. *Ramus, Method, and the Decay of Dialog*, Cambridge, MA 1958.

48 It is therefore certainly no coincidence that reflexions on solitude and melancholy first appear with the text culture associated with the printing press; cf. W. Lepenies, *Melancholie und Gesellschaft*, Frankfurt am Main 1969.

49 For this thought I am indebted to Harold Garfinkel for the several extended discussions we had at UCLA.

50 Philosophy therefore began only with the invention of writing, especially of alphabetic writing; cf. E. A. Havelock, *Preface to Plato*, Cambridge, MA 1982 (originally 1963).

51 Not without reason did Helmut Shelsky choose to call his treatise on the German university *Einsamkeit und Freiheit* [solitude and freedom], Hamburg 1963.

52 "Each of these demons regarded itself rather often in a paper mirror; therein it saw the highest and lowest of all creatures," according to Paul Valéry, *Herr Teste [Soirée avec Monsieur Teste]*, Frankfurt am Main 1984, p. 56. The interlocutor, the alter ego, and ultimately one's own self are all encountered in book and paper.

53 Cf. K. Mannheim, *Ideology and Utopia*; and *Essays on the Sociology of Culture*, London 1956, p. 170. Schumpeter views intellectuals' lack of a duty to take action rather more critically. According to him, intellectuals can be distinguished from other literate persons in that they have no responsibility for practical things, lack knowledge from first-hand experience, and have their greatest chances for success in their value as disruptive factors; cf. J. A. Schumpeter, *Kapitalismus, Sozialismus, Demokratie*, Berne 1946, p. 237 [available in English as *Capitalism, Socialism, and Democracy*, 5th edition, London 1976].

54 Arnold Gehlen therefore polemically started saying "humanitarianism" instead of humanism; cf. *Moral und Hypermoral. Eine pluralistische Ethik*, Wiesbaden 1986.

55 In his broad-based and ambitious comparison of the various paths to modernity, Richard Münch therefore distinguished solitude as the characteristic quality of German intellectuals. Against that, it is argued here that the distinguishing of certain discourse rituals – including the reflexive dialogue with an invisible interlocutor – represents a defining quality of intellectual communication. But that the present typification especially has the German case in mind should by no means be ignored; cf. Münch, *Die Kultur der Moderne*, Vol. II, pp. 742ff., pp. 756ff.

56 Cf. Eisenstadt, *Kulturen der Achsenzeit*.

2 Prelude: the encounter with otherness

1 Verrazano, quoted in: U. Bitterli, *Alte Welt – neue Welt. Formen des europäisch-überseeischen Kontakts vom 15. bis zum 18. Jahrhundert* [old world–new world; forms of European overseas contact in the fifteenth to eighteenth centuries], Munich 1986, p. 18.

2 *Ibid.*, pp. 18ff. Already in the sixteenth century, travel instructions therefore advised seafarers to be as friendly as possible to the residents of the New World.

3 Even if they were seen as contractual partners, they had entirely different ideas of the rights foreseen in the contract. According to the Indians, one could not sell land, only generously grant residence and extensive use of it. The construction of fixed settlements was therefore seen as a breach of contract, and an act of war. This led to the notorious Virginia massacres of 1622; *ibid.*, p. 29.

4 Cf. the definitive work by A. Lovejoy, *The Great Chain of Being*, Cambridge, MA 1982.

5 And ultimately turn into actual "humans" through baptism. Here we can distinguish clear differences in the course of events on each of the two American continents. In the Spanish colonies, the "natives" had a chance, through baptism, to at least take a place at the "bottom" of the hierarchy, whereas they remained entirely excluded in the Anglo-Saxon colonies. Cf. O. Paz, *El laberinto de la soledad* (ed. Enrico Mario Santi), Madrid 1993.

6 Cf. the more wide-ranging portrayal and analysis of the debate, only outlined here, in T. Todorov, *Die Eroberung Amerikas. Das Problem des Anderen* [conquest of America; the problem of the other], Frankfurt am Main, 1985.

7 Cf. Lévi-Strauss, *Tristes Tropiques*.

8 Cf. K.-H. Kohl, *Entzauberter Blick. Das Bild vom Guten Wilden und die Erfahrung der Zivilisation* [the demystified gaze; images of the noble savage and the experience of civilization], Frankfurt am Main 1986, p. 21ff.

9 Because the biological mixing of the Portuguese with the natives began nearly at the same time as colonization, discrimination against the indigenous peoples in Brazil never reached the dichotomous severity known to us from the other countries of America. Cf. G. Freyre, *Herrenhaus und Sklavenhütte. Ein Bild der brasilianischen Gesellschaft* [master's house and slave's hut; a picture of Brazilian society], Stuttgart 1982, pp. 81ff.

10 Cf. J. C. Alexander, "Core Solidarity, Ethnic Outgroup, and Social Differentiation: A Multidimensional Model of Inclusion in Modern Societies," in: J. Dofny and A. Akiwowo (eds.), *National and Ethnic Movements*, Beverly Hills and London 1980, pp. 5–28.

11 The German language lacks a fitting word for these resident "aliens." "Denizens" is the term that English-language sociology seems to be adopting at the moment. Cf. T. Hammar, *Democracy and the Nation State – Aliens, Denizens and Citizens in a World of International Migration* (Research in Ethnic Relations Series), Aldershot 1990.

12 On this figure, cf. also: C. Wiedemann, " 'Supplement seines Daseins?' Zu den

kultur- und identitätsgeschichtlichen Voraussetzungen deutscher Schriftstellerreisen nach Rom–Paris–London seit Winckelmann" ['Supplement to his existence?' On presuppositions of culture and identity in German writers' journeys to Rome, Paris, and London since Winckelmann] in: Weidemann (ed.), *Rom–Paris–London. Erfahrung und Selbsterfahrung deutscher Schriftsteller und Künstler in den fremden Metropolen – Ein Symposium* [symposium on German writers' and artists' experiences and self-discoveries in foreign metropolises], Stuttgart 1988, pp. 1–20. Similar in its argumentative structure is G. Oesterle, "F. Schlegel in Paris oder die romantische Gegenrevolution" [Schlegel in Paris or the romantic counterrevolution], in: G.-L. Fink (ed.), "Die deutsche Romantik und die Französische Revolution," in *Actes du Colloque International, Collection Recherches Germaniques*, 3, Strasbourg 1989, pp. 163–179. For yet further variations, cf. the collection of essays edited by K. J. Bade (ed.), *Deutsche im Ausland – Fremde in Deutschland. Migration in Geschichte und Gegenwart* [Germans abroad – strangers in Germany; migration in history and the present], Munich 1992.

3 The nation as invisible public: the patriotic code

1 Cf. V. Packard, *A Nation of Strangers*, New York 1972. Of related interest: Harman, *The Modern Stranger*.
2 To put it in Hirschman's terms: the exit options increase by comparison with the voice options. Cf. A. O. Hirschman, *Exit, Voice and Loyalty – Responses to Declines in Firms, Organizations and States*, Cambridge, MA 1970.
3 Cf. the summary by Winkler, "Der deutsche Sonderweg."
4 Cf. T. Nipperdey, "Probleme der Modernisierung in Deutschland" [problems of modernization in Germany], in: Nipperdey, *Nachdenken über die deutsche Geschichte* [reflexions on German history], Munich 1990, pp. 52–70; R. Vierhaus, "Umrisse einer Sozialgeschichte der Gebildeten in Deutschland" [sketches of a social history of the educated class in Germany], in: Vierhaus, *Deutschland im 18. Jahrhundert*, Göttingen 1987, pp. 167–182; M. R. Lepsius, "Der Europäische Nationalstaat: Erbe und Zukunft" [the European nation–state: legacy and future], in: Lepsius, *Interessen, Ideen und Institutionen*, Opladen 1990, pp. 256–269; U. Engelhardt, *Bildungsbürgertum, Begriffs- und Dogmengeschichte eines Etiketts* [*Bildungsbürgertum*, a history of the concepts and dogmas attaching to a label], Stuttgart 1986.
5 In his impressive and comprehensive cultural comparison influenced by Parsons, Richard Münch has also proposed the thesis that the German road to modernity was decisively determined by the officialdom among the *Bildungsbürgertum* and their distance from the world of particular interests. Cf. Münch, *Die Kultur der Moderne*, *passim.* By contrast with Münch's work, our starting point here is not a homogeneous tradition created by a few founding fathers (Luther, Kant, Hegel), which endured without breaks or crises. Instead, several encodings of the national community are introduced, each carried by the

discursive practice of specific groups of intellectuals. This is intended partly to improve the historical resolution, partly also to invert the question. It is not a matter of subsuming social groups or historical developments under a cultural tradition that has always been posited, and which is in principle unchanged, but of reconstructing various cultural representations of social unity from particular historical situations. Beyond that, the present attempt tries to comprehend cultural traditions not as the homogeneous creations of individuals, but as partly inconsistent reconstructions, the result of a social process subject to considerable crises.

6 Cf. J. Ben-David, *The Scientist's Role in Society – A Comparative Study*, 2nd edition, London 1984.

7 L. Gall, *Bürgertum in Deutschland*, Berlin 1989; J. Kocka, "Bürgertum und Bürgerlichkeit als Probleme der deutschen Geschichte vom späten 18. zum frühen 20. Jahrhundert" [*Bürgertum* and its ethos as problems of German history from the late eighteenth to the early twentieth century], in: Kocka (ed.), *Bürger und Bürgerlichkeit im 19. Jahrhundert* [the *Bürger* and bourgeois ethos in the nineteenth century], Göttingen 1987, pp. 21–63, here p. 26.

8 Cf. M. Walker, *German Home-Towns*, Ithaca, NY 1971.

9 H. Schilling, *Die Geschichte der nördlichen Niederlande* [history of the northern Netherlands], in: *Geschichte und Gesellschaft*, 8, 1982, pp. 475–517.

10 Kocka, "Bürgertum und Bürgerlichkeit," p. 25.

11 M. Stolleis, *Geschichte des öffentlichen Rechts in Deutschland* [history of public law in Germany], Munich 1988, p. 402.

12 Cf. R. Koselleck, *Preußen zwischen Reform und Revolution. Allgemeines Landrecht, Verwaltung und soziale Bewegung 1791–1848* [Prussia between reform and revolution; general property law, administration, social movement 1791–1848], 2nd edition, Stuttgart 1981, pp. 78ff.

13 Quoted from R. Vierhaus, *Staaten und Stände. Vom Westfälischen bis zum Hubertusberger Frieden 1648 bis 1763* [states and estates; from the Westphalian to the Hubertusberg armistice 1648 to 1763], Frankfurt am Main and Berlin 1990, p. 125.

14 Cf. D. Rüschemeyer, "Bourgeoisie, Staat und Bildungsbürgertum. Idealtypische Modelle für die vergleichende Erforschung von Bürgertum und Bürgerlichkeit" [bourgeoisie, state, *Bildungsbürgertum*; models for comparative research into *Bürgertum* and its ethos], in: J. Kocka (ed.), *Bürger und Bürgerlichkeit im 19. Jahrhundert* [*Bürger* and their ethos in the nineteenth century], Göttingen 1987, pp. 101–120.

15 K. Eder by contrast stresses the oppositional and secret, i.e. public and nonstatist, character of the Enlightenment associations after 1870; cf. *Geschichte als Lernprozeß?*, pp. 155ff.

16 Cf. J. G. Büsch, "Von dem Unnatürlichen in dem Umgange der Gelehrten und Ungelehrten" [on the unnatural aspects of any intercourse between scholars and the uneducated], in: Büsch, *Vermischte Abhandlungen,* Part 2, Hamburg 1777, pp. 509–524, p. 511.

17 Walker, *German Home-Towns*, pp. 119ff., speaks in this connection of these new groups of "movers and doers" who acted as foreign bodies in the traditional urban bourgeoisie.
18 Vierhaus, *Staaten und Stände*, p. 137.
19 Madame de Staël, *Über Deutschland* [*De l'Allemagne*, On Germany], ed. M. Bosse, Frankfurt am Main 1985, p. 97.
20 C. Garve, "Ueber die Maxime Rochefoucaulds: das bürgerliche Air verliert sich zuweilen bey der Armee, niemals am Hofe" [on the maxims of Rochefoucauld: the bourgeois manner is sometimes lost in the army, never at court], in: Garve, *Versuche über verschiedene Gegenstände aus der Moral, der Literatur und dem gesellschaftlichen Leben* [essays on various subjects taken from morality, literature and social life], Part 1, Breslau 1792, pp. 295–452, here pp. 303–306.
21 Büsch, "Von dem Unnatürlichen," p. 511; cf. also B. E. Brandes, *Über den Einfluß und die Wirkungen des Zeitgeistes auf die höheren Stände Deutschlands* [on influence and effects of *Zeitgeist* on the higher classes of Germany], Part 2, Hanover 1810, p. 250; A. Frhr. v. Knigge, *Über den Umgang mit Menschen* [on manners] (1788), ed. G. Ueding, 3rd edition, Frankfurt am Main 1982, p. 25.
22 Cf. R. Stichweh, *Der frühmoderne Staat und die europäische Universität* [early modern state and European university], Frankfurt am Main 1991.
23 Cf. Ben-David, *Scientist's Role*; E. Zilsel, *Die sozialen Ursprünge der neuzeitlichen Wissenschaft* [social origins of modern science], Frankfurt am Main 1976.
24 A "supreme examination committee" of officials was soon to decide on the intake and training of the new generation of officialdom. This decoupling from the direct influence of the king encouraged self-recruitment by the bureaucracy.
25 Cf. H.-U. Wehler, *Deutsche Gesellschaftsgeschichte* [German social history], Vol. I: *Vom Feudalismus des Alten Reiches bis zur Defensiven Modernisierung der Reformära 1700–1815* [from "Holy Roman" feudalism to defensive modernization in the reform era 1700–1815], Munich 1987, p. 292.
26 H. Möller, *Vernunft und Kritik – Deutsche Aufklärung im 17. und 18. Jahrhundert* [reason and critique – German Enlightenment in the seventeenth and eighteenth centuries], Frankfurt am Main 1986, p. 242; cf. also H. Brunschwig, *Gesellschaft und Romantik in Preußen im 18. Jahrhundert. Die Krise des preußischen Staates am Ende des 18. Jahrhunderts und die Entstehung der romantischen Mentalität* [society and Romanticism in Prussia in the eighteenth century, the crisis of the Prussian state at the end of the eighteenth century and the emergence of Romantic mentality], Frankfurt am Main, Berlin and Vienna 1975 (1976), pp. 228ff.
27 Cf. M. R. Lepsius, "Zur Soziologie des Bürgertums und der Bürgerlichkeit" [on the sociology of the *Bürger* class and its ethos], in: J. Kocka (ed.), *Bürger und Bürgerlichkeit im 19. Jahrhundert*, Göttingen 1987, pp. 79–100.
28 Cf. T. Nipperdey, "Der Verein als soziale Struktur in Deutschland im späten 18. und frühen 19. Jahrhundert" [the Verein as social structure in Germany in the late eighteenth and early nineteenth centuries], in: Nipperdey, *Gesellschaft,*

Kultur, Theorie, Göttingen 1976, pp. 174–205; F. Tenbruck, "Modernisierung – Vergesellschaftung – Gruppenbildung – Vereinswesen" [modernization, socialization, group formation, associations], in: Tenbruck, *Die kulturellen Grundlagen der Gesellschaft* [cultural foundations of society], Opladen 1989, pp. 215–226; O. Dann, "Einleitung" [Introduction], in: Dann (ed.), *Lesegesellschaften und bürgerliche Emanzipation – Ein europäischer Vergleich* [reading societies and bourgeois emancipation – a European comparison], Munich 1981, pp. 9–28.

29 Christian Garves, "Betrachtungen zu den französischen Clubs" [reflexions on the French clubs] can certainly be applied, albeit in a weakened form, to the German *Verein;* cf. Garves, "Clubs," in: Z. Batscha *et al.* (eds.), *Von der ständischen zur bürgerlichen Gesellschaft* [from feudal to bourgeois society], Frankfurt am Main 1981, pp. 279–288.

30 H. J. Haferkorn, "Zur Entstehung der bürgerlich-literarischen Intelligenz und des Schriftstellers in Deutschland zwischen 1750 und 1800" [on emergence of bourgeois–literary intelligentsia and of the writer in Germany between 1750 and 1800], in: B. Lutz (ed.), *Deutsches Bürgertum und literarische Intelligenz 1750–1800* [*Bürger* class and literary intelligentsia, 1750–1800], *Literaturwissenschaft und Sozialwissenschaften* 3, Stuttgart 1974, pp. 113–275, here pp. 190ff.

31 Starting out from a Habermasian perspective, K. Eder also stresses the combination of equality and discursive communication practice; cf. *Geschichte als Lernprozeß? Zur Pathogenese politischer Modernität in Deutschland* [history as learning process? On the pathogenesis of political modernity in Germany], Frankfurt am Main 1985, p. 159.

32 M. Welke, "Gemeinsame Lektüre und frühe Formen von Gruppenbildungen im 17. und 18. Jahrhundert: Zeitungslesen in Deutschland" [shared reading matter and early modes of group formation in the seventeenth and eighteenth centuries: newspaper reading in Germany], in: Dann (ed.), *Lesegesellschaften und bürgerliche Emanzipation*, pp. 29–53.

33 R. Engelsing, *Der Bürger als Leser* [the bourgeois as reader], Stuttgart, 1974; Engelsing, "Die Perioden der Lesergeschichte in der Neuzeit" [periods of reading history in modern times], in: Engelsing, *Zur Sozialgeschichte deutscher Mittel- und Unterschichten* [on the social history of German middle and lower classes], 2nd expanded edition, Göttingen 1978, pp. 112–154.

34 Cf. Möller, *Vernunft und Kritik*, p. 269; Welke, "Gemeinsame Lektüre," p. 30.

35 Möller, *Vernunft und Kritik*, pp. 273f.

36 Cf. generally J. Habermas, *The Structural Transformation of the Public Sphere: An Inquiry into a Category of Bourgeois Society*, Cambridge, MA 1989; also R. Williams, *The Long Revolution*, Harmondsworth 1961; R. van Dülmen, *Die Gesellschaft der Aufklärer* [society of the Enlightenment thinkers], Frankfurt am Main 1986.

37 J. G. Herder, "Ideen zur Philosophie der Geschichte der Menschheit" [ideas for a philosophy of the history of humankind], in: *Johann Gottfried Herders sämtliche Werke*, ed. B. Suphan, Vol. XIII, Berlin 1887, p. 5; P. Honigsheim, "Soziologie der Kunst, Musik und Literatur" [sociology of art, music and liter-

ature], in: G. Eisermann (ed.), *Die Lehre von der Gesellschaft* [the doctrine of society], Stuttgart 1958, pp. 338–373, p. 346.

38 W. Woesler, "Die Idee der deutschen Nationalliteratur in der zweiten Hälfte des 18. Jahrhunderts" [the idea of German national literature in the second half of the eighteenth century], in: K. Garber (ed.), *Nation und Literatur im Europa der Frühen Neuzeit, Akten des I. Internationalen Osnabrücker Kongresses zur Kulturgeschichte der frühen Neuzeit* [nation and literature in early modern Europe; proceedings of the 1st international Osnabrück "Congress on Cultural History"], Tübingen 1989, pp. 716–733.

39 This decoupling is simultaneously at the center of a crucial sociohistorical process, namely the destruction of inherited monopolies of communication; cf. N. Wegmann, *Diskurse der Empfindsamkeit. Zur Geschichte eines Gefühls in der Literatur des 18. Jahrhunderts* [discourses on sensibility; on the history of feeling in the literature of the eighteenth century], Stuttgart 1988, p. 17. For the first historical processes in which the ruling elite's monopoly on communications is undermined, cf. C. Hill, "Protestantismus, Pamphlete, Patriotismus and öffentliche Meinung im England des 16. und 17. Jahrhunderts" [Protestantism, pamphlets, patriotism and public opinion in sixteenth- and seventeenth-century England]; also: H. Grabes, "England oder die Königin? Öffentlicher Meinungsstreit und nationale Identität unter Mary Tudor" [England or the queen? Public disputes and national identity under Mary Tudor]; both articles in: B. Giesen (ed.), *Nationale und kulturelle Identität. Studien zur Entwicklung des kollektiven Bewußtseins in der Neuzeit* [national and cultural identity; studies on the development of collective consciousness in modern times], Frankfurt am Main 1991, pp. 100–120 and 121–168. Specifically on Kant's idea of a public, cf. Kant, "Beantwortung der Frage: Was ist Aufklärung?" [Answering the question: what is Enlightenment?], in: Kant, *Werke,* ed. by E. Cassirer, Vol. IV, Berlin 1922, pp. 171f. Cf. also H. E. Bödeker, "Aufklärung als Kommunikationsprozeß" [Enlightenment as a communication process], in: R. Vierhaus (ed.), *Aufklärung als Prozeß*, Hamburg 1988, pp. 89–111, here p. 89.

40 Cf. R. Vierhaus, "Patriotismus," in: Vierhaus, *Deutschland im 18. Jahrhundert*, Göttingen 1987, pp. 96–109; C. Prignitz, *Vaterlandsliebe und Freiheit. Deutscher Patriotismus von 1750–1850* [love of the fatherland and freedom; German patriotism 1750–1850], Wiesbaden 1981; J. Schmitt-Sasse, "Der Patriot und sein Vaterland. Aufklärer und Reformer im sächsischen Rétablissement" [the patriot and his fatherland; enlighteners and reformers in the Saxonian *rétablissement*], in: H. E. Bödeker and U. Herrmann (eds.), *Aufklärung als Politisierung – Politisierung als Aufklärung* [Enlightenment as politicization; politicization as Enlightenment], Hamburg 1987, pp. 237–252.

41 P. Fuchs, "Historisch-systematische Analyse des Nationencodes in der deutschen Öffentlichkeit zwischen 1770 und 1850" [historical–systematic analysis of the nation code in German public life between 1770 and 1850], working paper in the research project "Nation als Publikum" [nation as public], MS University of Gießen 1989.

42 Community is posited against anonymous communications networks, and this is precisely the point at which F. Tönnies (*Gemeinschaft und Gesellschaft. Grundbegriffe der reinen Soziologie* [community and society; basic concepts of pure sociology] (1887), Berlin 1912) later developed a dichotomy that was to have far-reaching consequences. It is symptomatic of the period under consideration that this idiosyncrasy leads to an augmentation of letter-writing culture – of course not only in the epistolary form. The genesis of types of sociality specific to the eighteenth century will occupy us below. Let us just note here that the yearning for closeness, for a specific interactional density, extends right into the refinements of the bourgeois culture of domestic architecture. Of particular significance here is the furnishing of a study or *Expeditionsraum* [dispatch room], where the master of the house can read and cultivate his correspondence without losing the possibility of contact with the living room. Cf. J. Gessinger, *Sprache und Bürgertum. Sozialgeschichte sprachlicher Verkehrsformen im Deutschland des 18. Jahrhunderts* [language and bourgeoisie; social history of forms of speech in Germany during the eighteenth century], Stuttgart 1980, pp. 17ff.

43 Cf. especially G. Kaiser, *Pietismus und Patriotismus im literarischen Deutschland: Ein Beitrag zum Problem der Säkularisierung* [Pietism and patriotism in literary Germany: a contribution to the problem of secularization], Wiesbaden 1961.

44 Structurally this corresponds to the *Bildungsbürgertum*'s widening of the horizons of experience. This horizon becomes supraregional. The boundaries of interaction and of constricted feudal forms of communication are crossed, the vastness of the social space becomes palpable. Bourgeois theater takes this into account by exploding the topological and temporal unity of the drama.

45 One could say that the modern form of patriotism is characterized by a substitution of "virtue" for "recourse to ancestry and tradition." Patriotism begins its modern career as a doctrine of virtue that laments the falling away of virtue. For an example of this, see Anonymous, "Moralische Schilderung des ehemals altfränkischen itzt ***artigen Frauenzimmers. Von einem altväterschen, aber redlich denkenden Patrioten entworfen, An. 1740" [moral depiction of the formerly old Franconian, now ***(nasty) wench; written by a patriarchal, but decent-thinking patriot], in: *Schweizerisches Museum,* 3, 1, 1784, pp. 740–752.

46 W. A. Teller, "Ueber Patriotismus," in: *Berlinische Monatsschrift*, vol. 22, 1793, pp. 431–447, p. 442.

47 *Ibid.*, p. 436.

48 For sample texts, cf. G. F. Palm, "Politisch-Moralische Reflexionen" [political and moral reflexions], in: *Neues Hannoverisches Magazin*, Year 4, 1794, pp. 353–368, here p. 367f.; Anonymous, "Von den Vortheilen für Industrie, Moralität, Patriotismus und Bevölkerung, wenn die Bauerngüter getheilt werden" [on the advantages for industry, morality, patriotism and the population if the farms are divided], in: *Neues Hannoverisches Magazin*, Year 5, 1795, pp. 1243–1248 and 1249–1270. For an explicit linking of enlightened patriotism with morality, cf. Anonymous, "Rede, gehalten in der vaterländischen

Gesellschaft zu B. . .," [speech delivered to the Patriotic society at B. . .], in: *Neues Hannoverisches Magazin,* 7, Year 6, 1796, pp. 97–116, p. 100.

49 Patriotism is even capable of having recourse to the texts of the ancestors, if the issue is one of subjecting a "lord" to patriotic morality.
Treuherziger Patriotischer Rath aus dem sechszehnten Jahrhundert.

> Ein Herr der soll nicht allezeit,
> was ihm sein Sinn und Willen geit, (gelüstet)
> sich auszurichten unterstehen,
> vilmehr in allweg dahin sehen,
> Auf daß er thu, was ehrlich sey
> und halt ob dem, was recht dabey.
> O Keiserliche Majestät,
> Dir will ich geben diesen Rath:
> Daß Du wollst helfen jedermann,
> Und nicht zu Herzen lassen gahn
> Dein eigen Nutz; und so du was
> Geboten hast, daßselbig laß
> Dir selbst auch mit befohlen seyn,
> Dann wirst Du Deine Unterthan
> Gar leichtlich im Gehorsam han,
> Wenn sie Dich sehen halten das
> Was Du Ihnen befohlen hast. . .
>
> *Patriotisches Archiv für Deutschland,* vol. 5, 1786, p. 481.

Loyalhearted patriotic counseyl from the sixteenth century.

> A master sholde nat everich deye,
> allowen himselne to performe
> that for whiche he lustie yse
> rathere in alweye seyne
> that he doone whiche honeste bee
> and stoppe with thatte whyche yse richte,
> o empeyreal maggestie
> to thee wol I geve this counsyle:
> That if yew wol be as thine fadre
> do nat onlye counsel yore servants
> but rathere holpen everich manne
> and nat let pyrce ye thro the herte
> yore owne uses: and shalt thou
> refreyne fro that ye have forbide
> Be commanded yorseelfe to yore command
> then you wol have yore serveynte
> easilye in yore obedience
> if theye seyen ye kepe
> that ye have biden theme.

By Amos Weisz.

50 C. S. L. v. Beyer, "Ueber Kosmopolitismus und Patriotismus" [cosmopolitanism and patriotism], in: *Deutsche Monatsschrift,* 1, 1795, pp. 223–230, pp. 226ff.
51 H. Zimmer, *Auf dem Altar des Vaterlandes. Religion und Patriotismus in der deutschen Kriegslyrik des 19. Jahrhunderts* [on the altar of the fatherland; religion and patriotism in German war lyrics of the nineteenth century], Frankfurt am Main 1971, p. 17.
52 Cf. Prignitz, *Vaterlandsliebe und Freiheit*, pp. 66f.

4 The nation as Holy Grail of the intellectuals: the transcendental code of Romanticism

1 H. Kiesel and P. Münch, *Gesellschaft und Literatur im 18. Jahrhundert. Voraussetzungen und Entstehung des literarischen Markts in Deutschland* [society and literature in the eighteenth century; preconditions for and emergence of the literary market in Germany], Munich 1977, pp. 78f.
2 Cf. J. Schulte-Sasse, "Das Konzept bürgerlich-literarische Öffentlichkeit und die historischen Gründe seines Zerfalls" [concept of the bourgeois–literary public and historical reasons for its decay], in: C. Bürger *et al.* (eds.), *Aufklärung und literarische Öffentlichkeit*, [Enlightenment and the literary public], Frankfurt am Main 1980, pp. 83–115.
3 For the following, cf. especially Haferkorn, "Zur Entstehung der bürgerlich-literarischen Intelligenz."
4 Cf. H. Gerth, *Bürgerliche Intelligenz um 1800* [bourgeois intelligentsia around 1800], Göttingen 1976, p. 87.
5 Cf., for example, R. Vierhaus, "Heinrich von Kleist und die Krise des preußischen Staates um 1800" [Heinrich von Kleist and the crisis of the Prussian state around 1800], in: Vierhaus, *Deutschland im 18. Jahrhundert*, Göttingen 1987, pp. 216–234, p. 226.
6 C. Brentano, *Ausgewählte Werke*, ed. M. Morris, Vol. III, Leipzig 1904, p. 92.
7 All quotes from Haferkorn, "Zur Entstehung der bürgerlich-literarischen Intelligenz," pp. 229ff.
8 Both quotes from E.C. Mason, *Deutsche und englische Romantik* [German and English Romanticism], Göttingen 1966, pp. 39f.
9 J. P. Eckermann, *Gespräche mit Goethe* [conversations with Goethe], Berlin 1956, p. 226.
10 Cf. L. Fertig, "Die Hofmeister. Befunde, Thesen, Fragen" [tutors; findings, theses, questions], in: U. Hermann (ed.), *Die Bildung des Bürgers. Die Formierung der bürgerlichen Gesellschaft und die Gebildeten im 18. Jahrhundert* [education of the citizen; formation of bourgeois society and the educated in the eighteenth century], Weinheim and Basel 1982, pp. 322–328; Gerth, *Bürgerliche Intelligenz*, pp. 51–60.
11 F. Hölderlin, letter to his brother of 12.2.1789, in: Hölderlin, *Sämtliche Werke*, ed. F. Beißner, Vol. VI.1, Stuttgart 1954, No. 152, p. 264.
12 Münch traces German *Innerlichkeit* (inwardness) back to Lutheran piety: *Die Kultur der Moderne*, Vol. II, pp. 686ff. Romanticism, however, drove Luther's

idea of the individual as the "vessel of the divine" into a new transformation: in the turn of the gaze inwards, one finds neither the word of God nor the peace of God, but nameless and unquiet abysses. The Protestant idea of finding steadfastness in oneself in the name of God is entirely relinquished here.

13 Cf. I. Hoffmann-Axthelm, *Geisterfamilie – Studien zur Geselligkeit der Frühromantik* [family of ghosts; on the sociability of the early Romantic era], Frankfurt am Main 1973.

14 H. Tyrell, "Romantische Liebe – Überlegegungen zu ihrer 'quantitativen Bestimmtheit'" [romantic love; on its "quantitative determination"], in D. Baecker *et al.* (eds.), *Theorie als Passion. Niklas Luhmann zum 60. Geburtstag*, Frankfurt am Main 1987, pp. 570–599, p. 577.

15 Cf. Brunschwig, *Gesellschaft und Romantik*, pp. 325ff.

16 Novalis, *Schriften. Die Werke Friedrich von Hardenbergs*, eds. P. Kluckhohn and R. Samuel (critical edition), Vol. III, 3rd expanded and revised edition, Darmstadt 1977, section IX, HKA No. 50, p. 248.

17 Brunschwig, *Gesellschaft und Romantik*, p. 341.

18 Quoted in *ibid.*, p. 342.

19 Cf. P. Hocks and P. Schmidt, *Literarische und politische Zeitschriften 1789–1805* [literary and political journals 1789–1805], Stuttgart 1975.

20 Cf. Hoffmann-Axthelm, *Geisterfamilie*.

21 Cf. B. Nedelmann, "Georg Simmel – Emotion und Wechselwirkung in intimen Gruppen" [Georg Simmel – emotion and interaction in intimate groups], in: F. Neidhardt (ed.), *Gruppensoziologie. Perspektiven und Materialien*, special issue No. 25 of the *Kölner Zeitschrift für Soziologie und Sozialpsychologie*, Opladen 1983, pp. 174–209; A. Hahn, "Konsensfiktionen in Kleingruppen. Dargestellt am Beispiel von jungen Ehen" [consensus fictions in small groups; sample sketch of young married couples], in: *ibid.*, pp. 210–232.

22 The philosophical technique of ironization is at times exemplified in unvarnished ridicule. According to a letter of Caroline von Schlegel, the circle around the Schlegels "nearly fell off their seats laughing" after a reading of Schiller's "Glocke" ("The Bell"). Schiller, conversely, had already assumed his position through aesthetic arguments against Bürger's ideas of the *Volksdichter* or "bard of the people," and Klopstock had turned his poetic vocation, which he conceived of in religious terms, against Goethe's hunger for experience. On the Schlegels, cf. E. Behler, *Friedrich Schlegel in Selbstzeugnissen und Bilddokumenten* [Friedrich Schlegel in his own words and in contemporary pictures], Reinbek 1988, pp. 44ff.

23 Thus Schelling and Görres: cf. P. Kluckhohn, "Voraussetzungen und Verlauf der romantischen Bewegung" [preconditions and trajectory of the romantic movement], in: T. Steinbüchel (ed.), *Romantik. Ein Zyklus Tübinger Vorlesungen* [Romanticism; a cycle of Tübingen lectures], Tübingen and Stuttgart 1958, pp. 13–26, p. 21.

24 From the posthumous works of F. v. Schlegel, quoted by F. N. Mennemeier, "Fragment und Ironie beim jungen Friedrich Schlegel. Versuch der Konstruktion einer nicht geschriebenen Theorie" [on irony and the fragmentary

in the young Friedrich Schlegel; attempt to construct an unwritten theory] (1968), in K. Peter (ed.), *Romantikforschung seit 1945* [research into Romanticism since 1945], Königstein (Taunus) 1990, pp. 229–250.

25 F. v. Schlegel, quoted in *ibid.*, p. 229.

26 Novalis, "Fragmente und Studien 1797–1798," No. 37, in: Novalis, *Werke*, ed. G. Schulz, Munich 1969, pp. 384f.

27 F. v. Schlegel, quoted by Mennemeier, "Fragment und Ironie," p. 229.

28 F. W. J. Schelling, "Über das Verhältnis der bildenden Künste zur Natur" [on the relation of the visual arts to nature] (1807), in: Schelling, *Ausgewählte Schriften*, Vol. II: *Schriften 1801–1803*, Frankfurt am Main 1985, pp. 579–619.

29 Quoted by W. Sughe, *Saint-Simonismus und Junges Deutschland. Das Saint-Simonistische System in der deutschen Literatur der ersten Hälfte des 19. Jahrhunderts* [Saint-Simonism and young Germany; his system in the German literature of the first half of the eighteenth century], Berlin 1935, p. 52.

30 J. G. Fichte, "Reden an die deutsche Nation" [speeches to the German nation], in: *Johann Gottlieb Fichtes sämtliche Werke*, ed. I.H. Fichte, Berlin 1845/46, Vol. VII, pp. 257–502; here, the eighth speech, p. 384.

31 "Our old nationality was, as it seems to me, authentically Roman-natural, because we arose on precisely the same path as the Romans – and so the name of Roman Empire would probably be a decent coincidence, pregnant with meaning." Novalis, "Vermischte Bemerkungen (Blütenstaub)" [mingled aperçus (pollen dust)], 1797–1798, in: Novalis, *Schriften. Die Werke Friedrich von Hardenbergs*, eds. P. Kluckhohn and R. Samuel (critical edition), Vol. II, 3rd expanded and revised edition, Darmstadt 1977, section VI, HKA No. 267.

32 Cf. C. Wiedemann, "Römische Staatsnation und griechische Kulturnation" [Roman state nation and Greek cultural nation], in: *Akten des VII. Internat. Germanisten-Kongresses Göttingen 1985*, Tübingen 1986, pp. 173-178.

33 F. v. Schlegel, "Über das Studium der griechischen Poesie" [on the study of Greek poetry], in: Schlegel, *Schriften zur Literatur*, ed. W. Rasch, Munich 1972, pp. 84–192, here p. 190.

34 Novalis, "Vermischte Bemerkungen (Blütenstaub)," HKA No. 280.

35 O. Marquard, "Über einige Beziehungen zwischen Ästhetik und Therapeutik in der Philosophie des 19. Jahrhunderts" [on certain relations between aesthetics and therapeutics in nineteenth-century philosophy], in: Marquard, *Schwierigkeiten mit der Geschichtsphilosophie* [difficulties with the philosophy of history], Frankfurt am Main 1973, pp. 85–106, here pp. 103ff.

36 A. Müller, "Die Elemente der Staatskunst" [elements of statecraft], in: K. Peter (ed.), *Die politische Romantik in Deutschland – Eine Textsammlung* [anthology of Romantic political texts], Stuttgart 1985, pp. 280–300.

37 J. Görres, "Teutschland und die Revolution" [Teutonia and the revolution] (1819), in: Görres, *Politische Schriften*, ed. M. Görres, Vol. IV, Munich 1856, pp. 65–244, p. 167.

38 F. L. Jahn, "Einleitung in die allgemeine Volkstumskunde" [roughly: introduction to general anthropology], in: Jahn, *Deutsches Volkstum*, Leipzig 1936, pp. 27–45.

39 J. G. Herder, "Briefe zur Beförderung der Humanität" [letters for the advancement of humanity], in: Herder, *Johann Gottfried Herders sämtliche Werke*, ed. B. Suphan, Vol. XVII, 7th letter, Berlin 1881, pp. 28–33.
40 Fichte, "Reden an die deutsche Nation"; here, the fourth speech, p. 325.
41 M. Frank, *Einführung in die frühromantische Ästhetik* [introduction to early romantic aesthetics], Frankfurt am Main 1989, p. 81.
42 H. v. Kleist, "Katechismus der Deutschen, abgefaßt nach dem Spanischen zum Gebrauch für Kinder und Alte" [catechism of the Germans, translated from the Spanish, for children and old people alike], in: Kleist, *Sämtliche Werke und Briefe*, ed. H. Sembdner, Vol. II, 2nd edition, Munich 1961, pp. 350–360, p. 351.
43 Novalis, "Vermischte Bemerkungen (Blütenstaub)," HKA No. 347.
44 J. G. Herder, "Auch eine Philosophie zur Bildung der Menschheit. Beytrag zu vielen Beyträgen des Jahrhunderts" [another philosophy for the education of mankind; contribution to many contributions of this century] (1774), in: *Johann Gottfried Herders sämtliche Werke*, ed. B. Suphan, Vol. V, Berlin 1891, pp. 475–594, p. 510.
45 P. Villaume, "Patriotismus und Konstitutionalismus," in: Z. Batscha *et al.* (eds.), *Von der ständischen zur bürgerlichen Gesellschaft* [from feudal to bourgeois society], Frankfurt am Main 1981, pp. 267–276, p. 272.
46 E. M. Arndt, "Über den Volkshaß und über den Gebrauch einer fremden Sprache" [on the people's hatred and on the use of a foreign language] (1803), reprinted in: H. Vogt (ed.), *Nationalismus gestern und heute* [nationalism yesterday and today], Opladen 1967, pp. 102–105; here, p. 105.
47 *Ibid.*, p. 102.
48 On the following, cf. Prignitz, *Vaterlandsliebe und Freiheit*, pp. 101ff.
49 Arndt, "Über den Volkshaß," p. 104.
50 Bettina von Arnim reports that the actual military gain thanks to the intellectuals' taking up arms was if anything laughable, and that the highly excited intellectuals under arms seemed at times rather ridiculous.
51 Article on "Krieg" (war), in: *Deutsche Encyclopädie oder Allgemeines Real-Wörterbuch aller Künste und Wissenschaften* [German encyclopedia or general dictionary of all arts and sciences], ed. H. M. G. Köster and J. F. Roos, Vol. XXIII, Frankfurt am Main 1804, pp. 170–188, p. 170; cf. also J. Kunisch, "Von der gezähmten zur entfesselten Bellona. Die Umwertung des Krieges im Zeitalter der Revolutions- und Freiheitskriege" [from Bellona tamed to Bellona unleashed; reevaluation of war in the age of revolutionary and liberation wars], in *Kleist-Jahrbuch 1988/89*, ed. H. J. Kreutzer, Berlin 1988, pp. 44–63.
52 I. Kant, "Kritik der Urteilskraft" [critique of judgment], in: Kant, *Werke*, Vol. V, Berlin 1968, pp. 165–485, p. 263.

5 The people on the barricades: the democratic code

1 Regarding the concept of trivialization, cf. especially F. Tenbruck, "Der Fortschritt der Wissenschaft als Trivialisierungsprozeß" [scientific progress as a

process of trivialization], in: Tenbruck, *Die kulturellen Grundlagen der Gesellschaft* [cultural foundations of society], Opladen 1989, pp. 143–174.

2 On this subject, cf. Nipperdey, "Der Verein als soziale Struktur"; Tenbruck, "Modernisierung"; Dann, "Einleitung."

3 Cf. D. Düding, *Organisierter gesellschaftlicher Nationalismus 1808–1847. Bedeutung und Funktion der Turner- und Sängervereine für die deutsche Nationalbewegung* [organized societal nationalism 1808–1847; significance and function of the gymnasts' and choral *Vereine* for the German national movement], Munich 1984.

4 Cf. T. Nipperdey, "Nationalidee und Nationaldenkmal in Deutschland im 19. Jahrhundert" [national idea and national memorial in Germany during the nineteenth century], in: Nipperdey, *Gesellschaft, Kultur, Theorie*, pp. 133–173; R. Koselleck, "Die Kriegerdenkmäler als Identitätsstiftung für Überlebende" [warriors' memorials as creation of identity for survivors], in O. Marquard and K.-H. Stierle (eds.), *Identität*, Munich 1979, pp. 255–276; D. Düding, P. Friedmann and P. Münch (eds.), *Öffentliche Festkultur. Politische Feste in Deutschland von der Aufklärung bis zum ersten Weltkrieg* [public festival culture; political festivals in Germany from the Enlightenment to the First World War], Reinbek 1988.

5 Cf. Mosse, *Die Nationalisierung der Massen.*

6 Official presence at festivals and on petitions no less than recourse to traditional forms of social protest (caterwauling, freedom trees) could be employed for demonstrations and popularization of oppositional efforts. Cf. C. Foerster, "Sozialstruktur und Organizationsformen des deutschen Preß- und Vaterlandsvereins von 1832/33" [social structure and organizational forms of the German fatherland *Verein* of 1832/33], in W. Schieder (ed.), *Liberalismus in der Gesellschaft des deutschen Vormärz* [liberalism in German *Vormärz* society], Göttingen 1983, pp. 147–166.

7 Thus Frederick William IV also employed the form of a sacred address to his *Volk*, and owes his popularity to the misunderstandings thereby unleashed.

8 Cf. T. Nipperdey, "Volksschule und Revolution im Vormärz. Eine Fallstudie zur Modernisierung II" [primary school and revolution in the *Vormärz*; a case study of modernization], in: Nipperdey, *Gesellschaft, Kultur, Theorie*, pp. 206–227; F. Baumgart, "Lehrer und Lehrervereine während der Revolution von 1848/49" [teachers and teachers' *Vereine* during the revolution of 1848/49], in: *Mentalitäten und Lebensverhältnisse. Beispiele aus der Sozialgeschichte. R. Vierhaus zum 60. Geburtstag* [mentalities and living conditions; examples from social history; *Festschrift* for R. Vierhaus's sixtieth birthday], ed. colleagues and students, Göttingen 1982, pp. 173–188.

9 Cf. Nipperdey, "Volksschule und Revolution," pp. 223f.

10 Thus it was no coincidence that so many teachers were among the audience of the "Young German" writers. Cf. W. Wülfing, *Junges Deutschland. Texte, Kontexte, Abbildungen, Kommentar* [Young Germany; texts, contexts, pictures, commentary], Munich and Vienna 1978, pp. 150f.; W. Hömberg, *Zeitgeist und*

Ideenschmuggel. Die Kommunikationsstrategie des Jungen Deutschland [*Zeitgeist* and idea smuggling; the Young Germans' communication strategy], Stuttgart 1975, p. 95.

11 F. A. W. Diesterweg, "Birgt die öffentliche Erziehung in der Gegenwart ein revolutionäres Prinzip in ihrem Schoß?" [Does public education in the present conceal a revolutionary principle within?], in: Diesterweg, *Sämtliche Werke*, ed. H. Deiters *et al.*, Sec. I, Vol. III, Berlin 1959 (1835), pp. 426–432.

12 Regarding the involvement of the teachers in the formation of Left Hegelian radicalism, cf. the biographical notes in: W. Eßbach, *Die Junghegelianer. Soziologie einer Intellektuellengruppe* [Young Hegelians; sociology of a group of intellectuals], Munich 1978, pp. 66–78.

13 Teachers represent an "incarnate injunction to reconstruct society," according to W. H. Riehl, *Die bürgerliche Gesellschaft* [bourgeois society], Stuttgart and Heidelberg 1851, quoted in Nipperdey, "Volksschule und Revolution," p. 224.

14 The primary school teachers in the countryside were more intensely confronted with the pauperism of the *Vormärz* than were the urban literati. On poverty, cf. H.-U. Wehler, *Deutsche Gesellschaftsgeschichte* [German social history], Vol. II: *Von der Reformära bis zur industriellen und politischen "Deutschen Doppelrevolution" 1815–1845/49* [from the reform era to the industrial and political "German double revolution"], Munich 1987, pp. 281–296.

15 The tensions between groups with a more "national" and anti-French slant and the critics of their German folksiness had riddled the opposition since the Hambach Festival, and contributed considerably to the polemic. Cf. J. Hermand, "Was ist des Deutschen Vaterland?" [What is the German's fatherland?], in A. Estermann (ed.), *Ludwig Börne 1786–1837*, Frankfurt am Main 1986, pp. 199–210.

16 Regarding the later debates, destined to become famous, in the Paulskirche (the Frankfurt church where the first constitutional assembly convened in 1848), cf. G. Wollstein, *Das "Großdeutschland" der Paulskirche. Nationale Ziele in der bürgerlichen Revolution 1848/49* [the "Greater Germany" of the Paulskirche; national goals in the 1848/49 bourgeois revolution], Düsseldorf 1977, pp. 98ff.; K.-G. Faber, "Nationalität und Geschichte in der Frankfurter Nationalversammlung," in W. Klötzer, R. Moldenhauer and D. Rebentisch (eds.), *Ideen und Strukturen der deutschen Revolution 1848* [ideas and structures of the 1848 German revolution], Frankfurt am Main 1974, pp. 103–124.

17 Cf. T. Nipperdey, "Auf der Suche nach Identität: Romantischer Nationalismus" [in search of identity: Romantic nationalism], in *Nachdenken über die deutsche Geschichte* [meditations on German history], Munich 1990, pp. 132–150, p. 146. Even Napoleon regained his heroic stature among the public; cf. W. Wülfing, K. Bruns and R. Parr, *Historische Mythologie der Deutschen* [historical mythology of the Germans], Munich 1991, pp. 18–58.

18 Regarding Saint-Simonism in Germany, cf. Sughe, *Saint-Simonismus*. More recently, these early theses have been refined; cf. W. Vordtriede, "Der Berliner Saint-Simonismus" [the Berlin variant of Saint-Simonism], in: *Heine-Jahrbuch*,

14, 1975, pp. 93–110; H. Burchhardt-Dose, *Das Junge Deutschland und die Familie. Zum literarischen Engagement in der Restaurationsepoche* [*Junges Deutschland* and the family; on literary engagement during the Restoration epoch], Frankfurt am Main 1979, especially pp. 240–249. A second wave of popularization was triggered off within the framework of discussion of early socialist blueprints by L. von Stein's *Der Sozialismus und Kommunismus des heutigen Frankreich* [socialism and communism in today's France], Leipzig 1842. Cf. R. M. Emge, *Saint-Simon, Einführung in ein Phänomen* [Saint-Simon; introduction to a phenomenon], Munich 1987, pp. 203 f. On Stein cf. E. Pankoke, *Soziale Bewegung – Soziale Frage – Soziale Politik. Grundfragen der deutschen "Sozialwissenschaft" im 19. Jahrhundert* [social movement, social question, social policy; basic questions of German "social science" in the nineteenth century], Stuttgart 1970; on the reception of the Young Hegelians, cf. C. Rihs, *L'Ecole des jeunes Hégéliens et les penseurs socialistes français* [the school of the Young Hegelians and socialist thinkers], Paris 1978.

19 Cf. R. Engelsing, "Zur politischen Bildung der deutschen Unterschichten 1798–1863" [on the political education of the German lower classes 1798–1863], in: Engelsing, *Zur Sozialgeschichte der Mittel- und Unterschichten* [on the social history of the middle and lower strata], 2nd expanded edition, Göttingen 1978, pp. 155–179.

20 H. Koopmann, notably, interprets the Young Germans in the context of the Romantic fathers who had stayed politically neutral in 1830; cf. *Das Junge Deutschland. Analyse seines Selbstverständnisses* [*Junges Deutschland*; analysis of its self-understanding], Stuttgart 1970.

21 Cf. H. R. Jauß, "Das Ende der Kunstperiode. Aspekte der literarischen Revolution bei Heine, Hugo und Stendhal" [the end of the art era; aspects of the literary revolution in Heine, Hugo and Stendhal], in: Jauß, *Literaturgeschichte als Provokation* [literary history as provocation], Frankfurt am Main 1970, pp. 107–143; P. Hohendahl, "Literarische und politische Öffentlichkeit. Die neue Kritik des Jungen Deutschlands" [literary and political public; the new critique of *Junges Deutschland*], in: Hohendahl, *Literaturkritik und Öffentlichkeit* [literary criticism and public life], Munich 1974, pp. 102–127.

22 The significance of the four leaders of the Young Germany movement can be discerned not so much from the print runs of their books as from the publicity of their periodicals. Cf. H. Brandes, *Die Zeitschriften des Jungen Deutschland. Eine Untersuchung zur literarisch-publizistischen Öffentlichkeit im 19. Jahrhundert* [the periodicals of Young Germany; an investigation into the literary-journalistic public in the nineteenth century], Opladen 1991. The range of their influence is shown above all in their reception by the young generation, which some years later was also the vehicle for the establishment of the Young Hegelian press, as for example the *Hallische Jahrbücher*. Cf. H. Rosenberg, "Arnold Ruge und die 'Hallischen Jahrbücher'" [Arnold Ruge and *Hallische Jahrbücher*], in: Rosenberg, *Politische Denkströmungen im Vormärz* [trends in political thought during the *Vormärz*], Göttingen 1972, pp. 97–115, p. 112.

23 The group character of Young Germany remains a bone of contention. The common traits developed before the prohibition decree of 1835 (cf. M. Windfuhr, "Das Junge Deutschland als literarische Opposition" [*Junges Deutschland* as literary opposition], in: *Heine-Jahrbuch*, 22, 1983, pp. 47–69) is counterposed by the competitive situation between professional writers and periodicals publishers, leading inexorably to disagreement and polemic. Internal polemic heightens publicity, thereby expanding the common market sector. Alongside that, "denunciatory" critical strategies increasingly develop in order to eliminate the competitor by "terrorist" means. Cf. I. and G. Oesterle, "Der literarische Bürgerkrieg" [the literary civil war], in: G. Mattenklott and K.R. Scherpe (eds.), *Demokratisch-revolutionäre Literatur in Deutschland: Vormärz* [democratic–revolutionary literature in Germany: *Vormärz*], Kronberg (Taunus) 1974, pp. 151–186. The same market-strategic situation leads to the development of similar writing and publication strategies.

24 Since they did not have at their disposal a common political program, the move from a principally critical to a future-oriented, more constructive phase at the beginning of the year 1835 – in the wake of the prohibition decree – magnified the existing differences. Cf. Hömberg, *Zeitgeist*, pp. 30f.

25 T. Mundt, *Madonna*, Leipzig 1835, p. 431, quoted in J. Hermand, *Das Junge Deutschland. Texte und Dokumente* [*Junges Deutschland*; texts and documents], Stuttgart 1966. Traveling became an "existential need" for the Young Germans; cf. Hömberg, *Zeitgeist*, pp. 62f.; W. Wülfing, "Reiseliteratur" [travel literature], in: H.A. Glaser (ed.), *Deutsche Literatur. Eine Sozialgeschichte,* Vol. VI: *Vormärz: Biedermeier, Junges Deutschland, Demokraten 1815–1848* [German literature; a social history; Vol. VI, *Vormärz*: Biedermeier, Young Germany, democrats 1815–1848], ed. B. Witte, Reinbek 1987, pp. 180–194. For the fundamentals on the figure of the *flâneur*, cf. W. Benjamin, *Charles Baudelaire; A Lyric Poet in the Era of High Capitalism*, London 1973. On Heine, cf. R. Hosfeld, "Welttheater als Tragikomödie. Ein denkbarer Dialog Heines mit der Moderne" [world theater as tragicomedy; an imaginary dialogue between Heine and Modernity], in: G. Höhn (ed.), *Heinrich Heine. Ästhetisch-politische Profile*, Frankfurt am Main 1991, pp. 136–154, pp. 145f.

26 T. Mundt, *Spaziergänge und Weltfahrten* [strolls and world travels], Vol. I, Altona 1838, p. 112.

27 L. Wienbarg, *Ästhetische Feldzüge* [aesthetic campaigns], ed. W. Dietze, Berlin and Weimar 1964, p. 3.

28 Cf. S. Obenaus, "Buchmarkt, Verlagswesen und Zeitschriften" [the book market, publishing and periodicals], in: H. A. Glaser (ed.), *Deutsche Literatur. Eine Sozialgeschichte*, Vol. VI: *Vormärz: Biedermeier, Junges Deutschland, Demokraten 1815–1848* [German literature; a social history; Vol. VI: *Vormärz*: Biedermeier, Young Germany, democrats 1815–1848], ed. B. Witte, Reinbek 1987, pp. 44–62. Under the compulsion of continuous production, editorial activity in particular led to new writing and publication strategies. On this, cf. Hömberg, *Zeitgeist*, p. 17.

29 T. Mundt ironically describes his reader, "who reads him in his toilet with the door closed, in order to avenge himself on his own official face of a civil servant through his forbidden dalliance," in *Zodiacus*, April 1835, p. 315, quoted in G. Oesterle, *Integration und Konflikt. Die Prosa Heinrich Heines im Kontext oppositioneller Literatur der Restaurationsepoche* [integration and conflict; the prose of Heinrich Heine in the context of oppositional literature of the restoration epoch], Stuttgart 1972, p. 106.

30 On Gutzkow's own admission, A. Ruge's *Hallische Jahrbücher* mark the transition of the opinion-forming hegemony within oppositional literature to the Young Hegelians. Cf. H. Rosenberg, "Zur Geschichte der Hegelauffassung" [on the history of the interpretation of Hegel], in: Rosenberg, *Politische Denkströmungen*, pp. 69–96; G. Meyer, "Die Anfänge des politischen Radikalismus im vormärzlichen Preußen" [the beginnings of political radicalism in Prussia during the *Vormärz*], in: Meyer, *Radikalismus, Sozialismus und bürgerliche Demokratie* [radicalism, socialism and bourgeois democracy], ed. H.-U. Wehler, Frankfurt am Main 1969, pp. 7–107. An excellent description of the Left Hegelian groupings has been provided by Eßbach, *Die Junghegelianer.*

31 The consensus within the school began to waver with the appearance of D. F. Strauss's *Das Leben Jesu. Kritisch Bearbeitet* [life of Jesus; a critical reinterpretation], Mannheim 1835. The assumption of the distinction between the "true" and the "self-misapprehending" Hegel broke the connection with the Hegelian orthodoxy of the established academics. As heterodox Hegelians, only T. Vischer and W. Vatke – a *Privatdozent* (unpaid academic similar to a "reader") celebrating his golden academic jubilee – secured academic careers. Ruge, Bauer and Nauwerk were *Privatdozente* who were dismissed or quit. During the forties, criticism of Hegel could at times further one's career. On the founding of the *Hallische Jahrbücher* as a counterpart to the *Berliner Jahrbücher für wissenschaftliche Kritik*, cf. F. W. Graf, "David Friedrich Strauss und die *Hallischen Jahrbücher*. Ein Beitrag zur positionellen Bestimmtheit der theologischen Publizistik im 19. Jahrhundert" [David Friedrich Strauss and the *Hallische Jahrbücher*; a contribution to determining the position of theological journalism during the nineteenth century], in: *Archiv für Kulturgeschichte*, 60, 1978, pp. 383–430.

32 Cf. F. Schlawe, "Die junghegelianische Publizistik" [Young Hegelian journalism], in: *Die Welt als Geschichte*, 20, 1960, pp. 30–50.

33 Cf. U. Köster, *Literatur und Gesellschaft in Deutschland 1830–1848. Dichtung am Ende der Kunstperiode* [literature and society in Germany 1830–1848; poetry at the end of the art era], Stuttgart 1984, pp. 59f.

34 Cf. R. Michels, "Zur Soziologie der Boheme und ihrer Zusammenhänge mit dem geistigen Proletariat" [on the sociology of the Bohème and its connections with the spiritual proletariat], in: Michels, *Masse, Führer, Intellektuelle. Politisch-soziologische Aufsätze 1906–1933* [masses, leaders, intellectuals; political and sociological essays 1906–1933], Frankfurt am Main and New York 1987, pp. 214–230; H. Kreuzer, *Die Boheme. Beiträge zu ihrer Beschreibung* [the Bohème; Contributions toward a description], Stuttgart 1968.

Especially in the editorial offices of the periodicals, there gathered together Bohemians and others whose talent was insufficient either for poetry or for science, a "nameless *associé* of that great invisible Heine–Börn *commandité*," according to R. Engelsing, "Zeitungen und Zeitschriften in Nordwestdeutschland 1800–1850" [newspapers and periodicals in north-west Germany 1800–1850], in: *Archiv für Geschichte des Buchwesens*, 5, 1963, col. 849–955, col. 931. Their resentment towards "better" society corresponded to that of their informers: "During the forties, communications to the periodicals originated almost exclusively from persons lacking the qualifications for the bourgeoisie and civil service positions" (col. 881). The politicization of the journalistic profession in the forties corresponded to a revaluation of personality, as a consequence of which it was turned into a moralist and "perpetrator through conviction" (col. 946).

35 On the avant-garde consciousness and the "enhancement of life feeling" that it brought about, cf. J. Hermand, "Jungdeutscher Tempelsturm" [Young Germans storm the temple], in: J. A. Kruse and B. Kortländer (eds.), *Das Junge Deutschland. Kolloquium zum 150. Jahrestag des Verbots vom 10. Dezember 1835* [Young Germany; colloquium on the 150th anniversary of the prohibition of 10 December 1835], in *Heine-Studien*, Hamburg 1987, pp. 62–82, pp. 69f.

36 The Romantics' criticism of the prosaic philistine is expanded during the periods of the "*juste-milieu*" into criticism of the business world and of the bourgeoisie. Cf. Kreuzer, *Die Boheme*, pp. 146f.

37 Cf. H. Rosenberg, "Zur Geschichte der Hegelauffassung." Regarding the conceptions of the Hegelian school after the death of Hegel, cf. especially Eßbach, *Die Junghegelianer*, pp. 116f.

38 Marx's settling of accounts with his former fellow-travelers after all bears the title: "Die heilige Familie" [the holy family], in: Marx and Engels, *Works*, Vol. II, Berlin 1959, pp. 7–223.

39 "In the field of theory, there is . . . no tolerance," A. Ruge, *Der Liberalismus und die Philosophie, Gesammelte Schriften* [liberalism and philosophy, collected writings], Vol. IV, Mannheim 1848, p. 295. On the "theoretical massacres" (Eßbach) among the radicals during the *Vormärz* cf. S. Na'aman, *Gibt es einen Wissenschaftlichen Sozialismus? Marx, Engels und das Verhältnis zwischen sozialistischen Intellektuellen und den Lernprozessen der Arbeiterbewegung* [Does a scientific socialism exist? Marx, Engels and the relationship between socialist intellectuals and the learning processes of the workers' movement], ed. M. Vester, Hanover 1979.

40 The scandal surrounding the Welcker serenade and the self-dramatization of Bruno Bauer's release have become famous. Cf. Eßbach, *Die Junghegelianer*, pp. 124f. and pp. 206f.; on the strategy of provocation, cf. H.M. Sass, Afterword on B. Bauer, *Feldzüge der Kritik* [critical campaigns], Frankfurt am Main 1968, pp. 224–268, p. 257.

41 Cf., among other things, the developmental–theoretical slant, taking as its starting point the authoritative studies of R. Koselleck, of the explications in Giesen, *Die Entdinglichung des Sozialen*, p. 72ff.

42 Cf. A. Ruge's and T. Echtermeyer's influential treatise: "Protestantismus und Romantik. Zur Verständigung über die Zeit" [Protestantism and Romanticism; toward an understanding of the age], in: *Hallische Jahrbücher*, 1839/40; moreover, H. Rosenberg, "Arnold Ruge und die 'Hallischen Jahrbücher,'" pp. 107f. Heine and *Junges Deutschland* in particular are subjected to criticism: "Resolution" and pathos were called for, i.e. Börne's "*Revoluzzertum*" [a by now disparaging term of similar connotation to "armchair revolutionary" – Translator's note] rather than Heine's "frivolous pleasure-seeking."

43 Cf. Eßbach, *Die Junghegelianer*, pp. 161f. Eßbach refers to H. Hirsch, who describes the Young Hegelians as a "working community that seeks to realize immanently the system of an objective conceptual history by dispensing with an individual writing style." Quoted from H. Hirsch, "Karl Friedrich Köppen, der intimste Berliner Freund Marxens" [Karl Friedrich Köppen, Marx's most intimate Berlin friend], in: Hirsch, *Denker und Kämpfer. Gesammelte Beiträge zur Geschichte der Arbeiterbewegung* [thinkers and fighters; collected contributions to the history of the workers' movement], Frankfurt am Main 1955, pp. 19–81, p. 46, quoted in Eßbach, *Die Junghegelianer*, p. 81, annotation 149.

44 Cf. K. Löwith (ed.), *Die Hegelsche Linke* [the Hegelian Left], introduction, pp. 7–38, Stuttgart-Bad Cannstatt 1962; H. Stuke, *Philosophie der Tat. Studien zur "Verwirklichung der Philosophie" bei den Junghegelianern und den wahren Sozialisten* [philosophy of the deed; studies on the "realization of philosophy" as conceived by the Young Hegelians and the true socialists], Stuttgart 1963. The Young Germans' equivalence of literature and life/deeds is abandoned here in favor of direct political agitation. The concept of the "party" – beyond a mere coincidence of convictions and of the dialectical–dramatic unfolding of antithetical principles – nonetheless remains bound to the short-lived alliance with liberalism; cf. T. Schieder, "Die Theorie der Partei im älteren deutschen Liberalismus" [theory of the party in older German liberalism], in: Schieder, *Staat und Gesellschaft im Wandel unserer Zeit* [state and society amid the changes of our age], Munich 1970, pp. 110–132, p. 113; Meyer, "Anfänge," pp. 11f.; Eßbach, *Die Junghegelianer*, pp. 192–203. The Left Hegelian party discussion ends in the transition to "democratic monism"; cf. P. Wende, *Radikalismus im Vormärz. Untersuchungen zur politischen Theorie der frühen deutschen Demokratie* [radicalism during the *Vormärz*; investigations into the political theory of early German democracy], Wiesbaden 1975, pp. 55f. On the systematic discussion of the currents of political thought, cf. Eder, *Geschichte als Lernprozeß?*, pp. 230–296.

45 On the rhetoric of rigor, cf. Eßbach, *Die Junghegelianer*, p. 169. The revocation of the "accommodations" of philosophy to the status quo is sharpened into an antithetics of contradiction, especially by Bakunin and E. Bauer. Cf. Wende, *Radikalismus*, p. 155.

46 Concisely formulated by Ruge and Echtermeyer: "Die Philosophie macht Partei" [philosophy becomes partisan], in "Protestantismus und Romantik," col. 417.

47 Cf. T. Schieder, "Die geschichtlichen Grundlagen und Epochen des deutschen

Parteiwesens" [historical foundations and eras of the German party system], in: Schieder, *Staat und Gesellschaft*, pp. 133–171.

48 On this cf. Eder, *Geschichte als Lernprozeß?*, pp. 180ff.

49 "The end of the theoretical movement is the practical [movement], but practice is nothing other than the movement of the mass within the confines of theory." Ruge to Prutz on 14 January 1846, quoted in Wende, *Radikalismus*, p. 159.

50 Köster points to the Romantic roots of the displacement of the level of justification to ever higher spheres. Cf. U. Köster, *Literarischer Radikalismus. Zeitbewußtsein und Geschichtsphilosophie in der Entwicklung vom Jungen Deutschland zur Hegelschen Linken* [literary radicalism; consciousness of the age and philosophy of history in the development of Young Germany into the Hegelian Left], Frankfurt am Main 1972, p. 146.

51 On this cf. Emge, *Saint-Simon*, pp. 141–180.

52 The difference between the critically educated avant-garde and the "common" education of the people that is to be enlightened guarantees the necessary distance; cf. Wende, *Radikalismus*, p. 164. The problem of first having to educate a mass that is reluctant to create a revolution also displaces the "true people" into the future, and thus acts as a goad to agitation.

53 Cf. T. Meyer, "Büchner and Weidig – Frühkommunismus und revolutionäre Demokratie. Zur Textverteilung des *Hessischen Landboten*" [early communism and revolutionary democracy; on the distribution of authorship of the *Hessischer Landbote* – i.e., the revolutionary manifesto compiled principally by Georg Büchner], in: H. Arnold (ed.), *Georg Büchner I/II, Text und Kritik*, Munich 1979, pp. 16–296; Meyer, "Die Verbreitung und Wirkung des *Hessischen Landboten*" [the dissemination and effect of the *Hessischer Landbote*], in: *Georg Büchner-Jahrbuch*, I, 1981, pp. 68–111.

54 Cf. W. Grab, "Georg Büchners *Hessischer Landbote* im Kontext deutscher Revolutionsaufrufe 1791–1848" [Georg Büchner's *Hessische Landbote* within the context of German calls to revolution], in: *Internationales Georg-Büchner Symposion 1987*, ed. B. Dedner and G. Oesterle, Frankfurt am Main 1990, pp. 65–83, p. 78.

55 Cf. E. P. Thompson, "The Moral Economy of the English Crowd in the 18th Century," in: *Past and Present*, 50, 1971, pp. 76–136.

56 Under the influence of the "new Christianity" of Saint-Simon, but also of Lamennais's "declaration of faith," the "implosion of actually transcendent expectations of salvation into the earthly-secular" plays an important role in the formation of the social movements of the *Vormärz*. Cf. W. Schieder, *Anfänge der deutschen Arbeiterbewegung. Die Auslandsvereine im Jahrzehnt nach der Juli-Revolution 1830* [beginnings of the German workers' movement; foreign societies during the decade after the 1830 July revolution], Stuttgart 1963, p. 311.

57 H. Heine, *Zur Geschichte der Religion und Philosophie in Deutschland* [on the history of religion and philosophy in Germany]. Preface to 2nd edition (1852), in: *Sämtliche Schriften*, ed. K. Briegleb, Vol. III, Munich 1971, pp. 507–513, p. 508.

58 Heine transposed the subjective divisiveness of Romanticism into a social and

political "great world cleavage." On this, cf. H. Höhn, *Heine-Handbuch. Zeit, Person, Werk* [Heine handbook; era, person, *œuvre*], Stuttgart 1987, pp. 13–16. Era and *Zeitgeist* – in relation to reality and the present – function as polemical counter-concepts to the spirit of the past; cf. H. Koopmann, *Das Junge Deutschland*, pp. 83ff.; Köster, *Literarischer Radikalismus*, pp. 3f. What counted for the Young Germans in a present overburdened by the past was only the "tendency" of a "new age" as a future incommensurable with the present; cf. Köster, *ibid.*, p. 4. The success of Young Germany in popularizing the concepts of "presence, life, movement, future" and the like, is documented in W. Wülfing, *Schlagworte des Jungen Deutschland. Mit einer Einführung in die Schlagwortforschung* [catchphrases of Young Germany; with an introduction to catchphrase research], Berlin 1982.

59 H. Laube, *Das neue Jahrhundert,* Vol. II: *Politische Briefe* [the new century, Vol. II: political letters], Leipzig 1833, p. 273. Cf. Koopmann, *Das Junge Deutschland*, pp. 81–106.

60 T. Mundt: "One must turn to the community of the future, one must write prose and poetry for the community of the future," in: Mundt (ed.), *Schriften in bunter Reihe, zur Anregung und Unterhaltung* [a colorful medley of texts, for stimulation and entertainment], reprinted Frankfurt am Main 1971, quoted in Wülfing, *Schlagworte*, p. 281. Wülfing summarizes Young Germany's consciousness of the present: "If the past is nothing but that which stands opposite the present, and the present is that which would be appropriate to the age, but which cannot realize itself because of the resistance of the past, then the future is the fulfilment of the time, and thus of the present," *ibid.*, p. 285.

61 Cf. R. Koselleck, the article "Fortschritt" [progress], in: *Geschichtliche Grundbegriffe* [basic historical concepts], Vol. II, Stuttgart 1975, pp. 363–423; R. Koselleck, C. Meier, J. Fisch and N. Bulst, the article "Revolution" in: *Geschichtliche Grundbegriffe*, 5, Stuttgart 1984, pp. 653–788; also Giesen. *Die Entdinglichung des Sozialen*, pp. 72ff.

62 H. Heine, "Reisebilder III," in: *Sämtliche Schriften* [travel images 3, collected writings], ed. K. Briegleb, Vol. II, Munich 1969, pp. 309–470, p. 376.

63 Against the background of the July 1830 revolution, the program of a philosophy only to be realized in the future does not remain restricted to the narrower circle of Left Hegelians, but is forced even by orthodox pupils. Cf. Stuke, *Philosophie der Tat*, pp. 75f. The radicalization of the program by the Young Hegelians is effected by recourse to the "esoteric doctrine" of Hegel and his early writings. On the interpretative possibilities opened up there, cf. J. Ritter, *Hegel und die französische Revolution* [Hegel and the French revolution], Frankfurt am Main 1965.

64 H. Heine, "Die Romantische Schule" [the Romantic school] (1835), in: *Sämtliche Schriften*, ed. K. Briegleb, Vol. III, Munich 1971, pp. 357–504, p. 468. On the preceding formulation of "scholars, artists, apostles," cf. Höhn, *Heine-Handbuch*, p. 262.

65 H. Laube, in a letter to Cotta in 1831, quoted in Hömberg, *Zeitgeist*, p. 27.

66 The offer of an alliance to the French intellectuals during exile in Paris, such as by Ruge and Marx in the *Deutsch-Französische Jahrbücher*, is clearly borne by a feeling of superiority founded upon one's own superior scientificity. "Behind this apparent setting at par of the German and the French socialisms, there was ultimately concealed a German claim to leadership": T. Schieder, "Sozialismus," in: *Geschichtliche Grundbegriffe*, Vol. IV, Stuttgart 1985, pp. 923–996, p. 953. At the time, the "democratic principle" was entirely capable of being tied to "constitutional monarchy."

67 Cf. K. Marx, "Zur Kritik der Hegelschen Rechtsphilosophie" [contribution towards a critique of Hegel's *Philosophy of Right*], Introduction, in: Marx and Engels, *Works*, Vol. I, Berlin 1957, p. 391.

68 This theme, developed in particular also by Mundt, Laube and v. Ungern-Sternberg, represents the most prominent victim of the discussion and of the prohibition decrees of the year 1835. The conservative criticism of the "immorality" of Young Germany was largely shared also by the liberal opposition. On this cf. J. Hermand, "Erotik im Juste-Milieu. Heines 'Verschiedene'" [eroticism in the *juste-milieu*; Heine's 'The Departed' – i.e., as in "dearly departed love"] in: W. Kuttenkeuler (ed.), *Heinrich Heine: Artistik und Engagement*, Stuttgart 1977, pp. 86–104, pp. 91f. For Heine, it is precisely frivolity that becomes "the sole possibility of humanity," remaining subversively effective both for and against the reader, according to Oesterle, *Integration und Konflikt*, p. 95. Habermas points out that the "radical motifs of a libertarian and hedonist socialism," with which Heine "liquidated the antithesis between Enlightenment and Romanticism," are still underilluminated: cf. "Heinrich Heine und die Rolle des Intellektuellen in Deutschland," in: *Merkur,* 40, 1986, pp. 453–468, p. 460. On the already displaced problematics of sexuality in Büchner, cf. P. Hohendahl, "Nachromantische Subjektivität: Büchners Dramen" [post-Romantic subjectivity: Büchner's dramas], in: *Zeitschrift für Philologie,* 108, 1989, pp. 496–511.

69 On Heine cf. H. Pepperle, "Heinrich Heine als Philosoph" [Heinrich Heine as philosopher], in: G. Höhn (ed.), *Heinrich Heine. Ästhetisch-politische Profile*, Frankfurt am Main 1991, pp.155–175; J. Hermand, "Vom 'Buch der Lieder' zu den 'Verschiedenen'" [from the "Book of Songs" to "The Departed"], in: Hohn (ed.), *ibid.*, pp. 214–235. Heine's sensualism in its most far-reaching interpretation comprises the demand for universal social happiness, and soon oversteps the bounds of Young Germany's orientation toward the *Bildungsbürgertum*: cf. Köster, *Literarischer Radikalismus*, p. 12.

70 Cf. especially Gutzkow's 1815 edition of Schleiermacher's "Vertraute Briefe an Lucinde" [intimate letters to Lucinde].

71 Marriage and sexuality became "social questions": cf. Wülfing, *Junges Deutschland*, pp.165ff.

72 G. Kühne in: *Zeitschrift für die elegante Welt* [journal for sophisticates], 36, 1836, p.174, quoted in Wülfing, *Schlagworte*, p. 232. On this, cf. also Koopmann, *Das Junge Deutschland*, p. 32; Köster, *Literarischer Radikalismus*, p.120. On the

field of tension of philosophy/actuality in Hegelianism as a catalyst for the development of Left Hegelianism, cf. Löwith, *Weltgeschichte*, pp. 15–17.

73 Cf. H. Fenske, "Ungeduldige Zuschauer. Die Deutschen und die europäische Expansion 1815–1880" [impatient audience; Germans and European expansion, 1815–1880], in: W. Reinhardt (ed.), *Imperialistische Kontinuität und nationale Ungeduld im 19. Jahrhundert* [imperialist continuity and national impatience in the nineteenth century], Frankfurt am Main 1991, pp. 87–123.

74 Wende quotes the words of K. Heinzen as one of the most clearly enunciated declarations of revolutionary intent:

> Thus the necessity that the citizens of any true state undertake an act of self-reliance, that of doing away with the form of the feudal state – the state power that is not rooted in the people, that has not the cooperation of its subjects – and giving the state a constitution that is commensurate with its requirements, must be denoted an indispensable precondition for any true state of modern times. This procedure is known by the name of revolution (1847).

Cf. P. Wende, "Der Revolutionsbegriff der radikalen Demokraten" [the radical democrats' concept of revolution], in W. Klötzer, R. Moldenhauer, and D. Rebentisch (ed.), *Ideen und Strukturen der deutschen Revolution 1848*, Frankfurt am Main 1974, pp. 57–68, quoted p. 65.

75 K. Marx, letters from the *Deutsch-französische Jahrbücher,* in: Marx and Engels, *Works*, Vol. I, Berlin 1957, p. 346.

76 Marx's formulation is famous: "The head of this emancipation is philosophy, its heart the proletariat. Philosophy cannot realize itself without the sublimation of the proletariat, the proletariat cannot sublimate itself without the realization of philosophy," in: "Zur Kritik der Hegelschen Rechtsphilosophie," p. 391.

77 W. Conze, "Vom 'Pöbel' zum 'Proletariat.' Sozialgeschichtliche Voraussetzungen für den Sozialismus in Deutschland" [from "rabble" to "proletariat"; sociohistorical preconditions for socialism in Germany], in: *Vierteljahresschrift für Sozial- und Wirtschaftsgeschichte,* 41, 1954, pp. 333–364.

78 Heine had early argued the precedence of the "social question" over the political question of the constitution, and this was then taken up by the Brockhaus encyclopedia in 1840. The political concept of democracy was displaced into

> democracy as the power of material interests and needs of the masses . . . not only the political, but also the social foundation of the state of society hitherto prevalent (must) be transformed . . . that is, not merely a complete political, but also a material and social equality between all classes of society (must) be created. This is the sense in which there has been talk of a social-democratic system of government, of a democratic and social republic, as the necessary goal of the development of the democratic principle. (Brockhaus encyclopedia, 8th edition, Vol. III, 1840, p. 372, quoted in H. L. Reimann, R. Koselleck, H. Meier, and W. Conze, article

on "Demokratie," in: *Geschichtliche Grundbegriffe*, Vol. I, Stuttgart 1972, pp. 821–899, p. 868).

At the time, the "democratic principle" was at all events compatible with "constitutional monarchy."

79 H. Heine, "Ludwig Börne. Eine Denkschrift," in: *Sämtliche Schriften*, ed. K. Briegleb, Vol. IV, Munich 1971, pp. 7–148, p. 75. On Heine, cf. K. Briegleb, "General Marx – Hund Heine. Eine Textspiegelung zur Frage: Heinrich Heine nach 1848 – ein politischer Dichter?" [General Marx – dog Heine. A mirroring of texts around the question: Heinrich Heine after 1848: a political poet?], in: *Heinrich Heine 1797–1856, Schriften aus dem Karl-Marx-Haus* [writings from the Karl-Marx house] 26, Trier 1981, pp. 153–181, pp. 164f. On the imperfect connections between radical theory and the masses, cf. Wende, *Radikalismus*, pp. 163f.

80 Letter to Gutzkow, Strasbourg 1836, in: Georg Büchner, *Sämtliche Werke und Briefe*, ed. R. W. Lehmann, Vol. II, Darmstadt 1971, p. 455.

81 The development of "emancipation" from a concept oriented to the past and directed towards movement into a teleological concept of fulfillment led to its becoming the "guiding concept of all past and future history" around 1840. K.-M. Grass and R. Koselleck, article on "Emanzipation," in: *Geschichtliche Grundbegriffe*, Vol. II, Stuttgart 1975, pp.153–197, p.169.

82 On political lyrics, cf. P. Stein, *Politisches Bewußtsein und künstlerischer Gestaltungswille in der politischen Lyrik 1750–1848* [political consciousness and the artistic will to form in political lyrics, 1750–1848], Hamburg, n.d., pp. 87–118. The discussion of the "social question" was substantially determined by the conservative model of L. v. Stein. Cf. Pankoke, *Soziale Bewegung*.

83 Cf. W. Büttner, "Der Weberaufstand in Schlesien 1844" [the 1844 weavers' uprising in Silesia], in: H. Reinalter (ed.), *Demokratische und soziale Protestbewegungen in Mitteleuropa 1815–1848/49* [democratic and social protest movements in central Europe, 1815–1848/49], Frankfurt am Main 1986, pp. 202–229.

84 K. Eder attributes these associations of tradesmen's apprentices to a diffusion of the entity of the liberal *Verein* out of a cultural elite into the bourgeois middle strata. He stresses thereby the structural change in associations, from a cultivation of sociability with an emphasis on discourse, to an equality of interests and convictions that made partisanship possible. Cf. Eder, *Geschichte als Lernprozeß?*, pp.180f. There, Eder represents the various forms of association – from the dignitaries of the autonomous communities through the radical, nationalist fraternities to the *Bund der Gerechten* ("league of the just") – which Marx and Engels joined in 1847 – as a comparatively uniform movement leading, during the Revolution of 1848, to the conglomerate *Centralmärzverein*, and fragmented further only as a result of its failure. By contrast with Eder, the present study focuses principally on the distanced, or at least ambivalent relations between intellectuals, the bourgeois opposition movement, and the peasant masses. The "implicit reader" who can be determined from the treatises

of the Left Hegelians, or the writings of the Young Germans, is simply not the *Volk* receiving the call of the subject needing emancipation, but the discerning, liberal bourgeoisie. On the radical–democratic leagues of the *Vormärz*, cf. Schnieder, *Anfänge*; E. Schraepler, *Handwerkerbünde und Arbeitervereine 1830–1853. Die politische Tätigkeit deutscher Sozialisten von Wilhelm Weitling bis Karl Marx* [tradesmen's fraternities and workers' associations; political activity of German socialists from Wilhelm Weitling to Karl Marx], Berlin and New York 1972.

85 Cf. W. Klutentreter, *Die Rheinische Zeitung von 1842/43 in der politischen und geistigen Bewegung des Vormärz* [*Rheinische Zeitung* from 1842/43 in the political and spiritual movement of the *Vormärz*], Dortmund 1966. As a consequence, the radical public was courted by a series of small newspapers and groups. Cf. B. W. Bouvier, "Die Anfänge der sozialistischen Bewegung" [beginnings of the socialist movement], in: H. Reinalter, *Demokratische und soziale Protestbewegungen in Mitteleuropa 1815–1848/49*. Frankfurt am Main 1986, pp. 265–304, pp. 292ff.

86 On the 1848 revolution, cf. T. Nipperdey, *Deutsche Geschichte 1800–1866. Bürgerwelt und starker Staat* [German history 1800–1866. Bourgeois world and strong state], Munich 1983, pp. 366–402, pp. 595–673; Wehler, *Deutsche Gesellschaftsgeschichte,* Vol. II, pp. 660ff., contains an energetic discussion of the various causes of the revolution.

87 *Ibid.*, pp. 704ff.

88 On the intense, though brief, revolutionary happiness of the German bourgeoisie, cf. T. Schieder, "Das Problem der Revolution im 19. Jahrhundert," in: Schieder, *Staat und Gesellschaft im Wandel unserer Zeit* [state and society in the transformations of our age], Munich 1970, pp.11–57, p. 15.

89 Only 6% of the deputies belonged to the radical left, and 12% to the moderate left. Figures from Wehler, *Deutsche Gesellschaftgeschichte*, Vol. II, p. 741.

90 For an exemplary treatment of the question as to whether the revolution failed principally over the national or the social issue, cf. T. Nipperdey, "Kritik oder Objektivität? Zur Beurteilung der Revolution von 1848" [criticism or objectivity? Assessing the Revolution of 1848], in: Nipperdey, *Gesellschaft, Kultur, Theorie*, Göttingen 1976, pp. 259–278; and D. Langewiesche, "Republik, konstitutionelle Monarchie und 'soziale Frage'" [republic, constitutional monarchy and 'social question'], in: *Historische Zeitschrift*, 230, 1980, pp. 529–548.

91 The victory of the forces of reaction saved the reputation of the intellectuals and prevented the "revolution of the intellectuals," i.e. the professorial Frankfurt Parliament, from carrying out the "betrayal of the revolution," according to L. Namier, *1848: The Revolution of the Intellectuals*, Oxford 1946, pp. 123f.

6 The nation–state up to the founding of empire: the code of *Realpolitik*

1 Cf. H. Schleier, "Die kleindeutsche Schule (Droysen, Sybel, Treitschke)," in: J. Streisand (ed.), *Studien über die Geschichtswissenschaft von 1800–1871*, Vol. I: *Die deutsche Geschichtswissenschaft vom Beginn des 19. Jahrhunderts bis zur*

Reichsgründung von oben [German historical scholarship in the nineteenth century up to the founding of the Reich from above], East Berlin 1969, pp. 271–310; G.G. Iggers, *Deutsche Geschichtswissenschaft. Eine Kritik der traditionellen Geschichtsauffassung von Herder bis zur Gegenwart* [German historical scholarship; a critique of the traditional understanding of history, from Herder to the present], Munich 1971, pp. 120–163; W. Hardtwig, "Von Preußens Aufgabe in Deutschland zu Deutschlands Aufgabe in der Welt. Liberalismus und borussianisches Geschichtsbild zwischen Revolution und Imperialismus" [from Prussia's mission in Germany to Germany's mission in the world; Liberalism and Borussian views of history, between revolution and imperialism], in: Hardtwig, *Geschichtskultur und Wissenschaft* [culture of history and knowledge], Munich 1990, pp. 103–160.

2 Cf. K. Obermann, "Die deutschen Historiker in der Revolution von 1848/9," in: Streisand, *Studien*, Vol. I, pp. 219–240.

3 Cf. H. Seier on Sybel: "Ein Leben ohne Krise" [a life without crisis], "Heinrich von Sybel," in: H.-U. Wehler (ed.), *Deutsche Historiker*, Vol. II, Göttingen 1971, pp. 24–38, p. 26.

4 Maximilian II of Bavaria, for example, founded a Historical Commission of the Bavarian Academy, and took Ranke's advice to appoint his student, Sybel – who was known for his anti-Catholic beliefs – to a professorship. Ranke himself advised Frederick William IV and Maximilian II. Frederick William of Prussia had Sybel's argument against Ficker read to him out loud. Duncker was an adviser to the Crown Prince of Bavaria, etc.

5 See Ringer, *Die Gelehrten*, pp. 12–22.

6 In the nineteenth century, historical scholarship generally understood itself as the "tone-setting and pathbreaking element" of the public political realm. The new term *Historiker* characterized precisely this instrumentalization of history for current action: cf. W. Hardtwig, "Erinnerung, Wissenschaft, Mythos. Nationale Geschichtsbilder und politische Symbole in der Reichsgründungsära und im Kaiserreich" [memory, scholarship, myth; national historical images and political symbols in the era of the *Reichsgründung* and the Wilhelmine empire], in: Hardtwig, *Geschichtskultur*, pp. 224–263, here pp. 231f. As distinct from the Romantics and the *Vormärz* intellectuals, the Borussian historians were "classical," i.e., state-affirming, intellectuals. On the difference between Romantic, classical, tragic, and critical intellectuals, cf. Dahrendorf, *Gesellschaft und Demokratie*, pp. 311–324.

7 Precisely the "conservative (constitutional) Liberals" proved to be, after the Revolution of 1848, the "actual carriers of the German 'cultural nation,' and viewed the goal of the nation–state as the cultural nation's fulfillment, substantiating all this largely in an idea of imperial history," according to Dann, "Nationalismus," p. 109.

8 The "transpolitical" idea of education (Koselleck), which became especially obvious in the political sphere in 1848, was to be recuperated after the Revolution in a "scientific" form, i.e. that of historical scholarship. Cf: R. Koselleck, "Einleitung – Zur anthropologischen und semantischen Struktur der

Bildung" (on the anthropological and semantic structure of education) in: Koselleck (ed.), *Bildungsbürgertum im 19. Jahrhundert*, Part 2: *Bildungsgüter und Bildungswissen* [educational goods and educational knowledge], Stuttgart 1990, pp. 11–47.

9 Cf. Iggers, *Deutsche Geschichtswissenschaft*, p. 118.

10 The newly established institutions of education and publishing advanced disciplinary integration and created bases for school education. Cf. W. Weber, *Priester der Klio. Historisch-sozialwissenschaftliche Studien zur Herkunft und Karriere deutscher Historiker und zur Geschichte der Geschichtswissenschaft 1800–1970* [Priests of Klio (the Muse of History); historical and social-science studies on the origins and careers of German historians, and the history of historical scholarship, 1800–1970], Frankfurt am Main 1984.

11 On Sybel as a Protestant in the Catholic Rhineland, with access to the Rhineland Liberals around Mevissen etc., cf. V. Dotterweich, *Heinrich von Sybel. Geschichtswissenschaft in politischer Absicht (1817–1861)* [Sybel: historical research in the service of politics], Göttingen 1978, p. 30. On Treitschke as an admirer of Prussia in Saxonian Dresden, cf. G. G. Iggers, "Heinrich v. Treitschke," in: H.-U. Wehler (ed.), *Deutsche Historiker*, Vol. II, Göttingen 1971, pp. 66–80, here p. 66.

12 Cf. D. Langewiesche, "Bildungsbürgertum und Liberalismus im 19. Jahrhundert," in: J. Kocka (ed.), *Bildungsbürgertum im 19. Jahrhundert*, Part 4: *Politischer Einfluß und gesellschaftliche Formation* [political influence and societal formation], Stuttgart 1989, pp. 95–121, here pp. 98f.

13 For the end of the nineteenth century, with the relative values unlikely to have changed, Ringer provides the following estimate: between 6,000 and 40,000 Marks annually. By comparison, a teacher earned 1,500 Marks: *Die Gelehrten*, p. 44.

14 *Ibid.*

15 Cf. Dotterweich, *Heinrich von Sybel*, p. 32.

16 *Ibid.*, p. 91.

17 Cf. G. List, "Historische Theorie und nationale Geschichte zwischen Frühliberalismus und Reichsgründung" [historical theory and national history between early Liberalism and the *Reichsgründung*], in: F. Faulenbach (ed.), *Geschichtswissenschaft in Deutschland*, Munich 1974, p. 35–53, pp. 41f.

18 Organs of "Borussianism" arose especially with the *Preußische Jahrbuch*, founded in 1858 and edited by R. Haym, and the *Historische Zeitschrift*, founded in 1859 and edited by v. Sybel. Cf. T. Schieder, "Die deutsche Geschichtsschreibung im Spiegel der *Historischen Zeitschrift*" [German historical writing as mirrored in *H.Z.*], in: *Historische Zeitschrift*, 189, 1959, pp. 1–73, pp. 2ff.

19 Cf. R. Koselleck, "Die Verfügbarkeit der Geschichte" [the availability of history], in: Koselleck, *Vergangene Zukunft*, Frankfurt am Main 1979, pp. 260–276 (English translation in: Koselleck, *Futures Past: On the Semantics of Historical Time*, Cambridge, MA 1985).

20 J. G. Droysen, "Zur Charakterisierung der europäischen Krisis (1854)" [on the character of the European crisis], in: Droysen, *Politische Schriften*, ed. F. Gilbert, Munich 1933, pp. 307–342, here p. 324.

21 Droysen, *ibid.*, p. 328. The ability to increase becomes the determining principle: "The restless increase of its stuff [historical work], is the measure of its increase": "Grundriß der Historik" [outline of historical studies], in: Droysen, *Historik*, reprint of the 1882 edition, Darmstadt 1967, para. 50, p. 347.

22 In the 1850s, the self-reinforcing fragmentation of the *Bürgertum* heralds the "fall from grace" of Liberalism. Cf. L. Gall, "'Sündenfall' des liberalen Denkens oder Krise der bürgerlichen Bewegung? Zum Verhältnis von Liberalismus und Imperialismus in Deutschland" ["Fall from grace" of liberal thinking, or crisis of the bourgeois movement? On the relation of liberalism and imperialism in Germany], in: K. Holl and G. List (eds.), *Liberalismus und imperialistischer Staat. Imperialismus als Problem liberaler Parteien in Deutschland 1890–1914* [imperialism as a problem of the liberal parties in Germany], Göttingen 1975, pp. 148–158. The often-harsh distance assumed to Bismarck remains an "episode"; cf. H. Seier, "Liberalismus und Staat in Deutschland zwischen Revolution und Reichsgründung," in: W. Klötzer, R. Moldenhauer and D. Rebentisch (eds.), *Ideen und Strukturen der deutschen Revolution 1848*, Frankfurt am Main 1974, pp. 69–84, here p. 74.

23 This distinction was further advanced through the professionalization of historical research, and through the development of seminar technique and practices of source verification. Unlike Ranke, Sybel and Treitschke no longer believed without reservations in the ability of the general lay public to independently develop a view of history. Cf. W. Hock, *Liberales Denken im Zeitalter der Paulskirche. Droysen und die Frankfurter Mitte* [liberal thinking in the age of the Paulskirche; Droysen and the Frankfurt centrists], Münster 1957, pp. 48f.

24 "The historian must be a critical researcher, a political expert, and a performing artist," according to Sybel, quoted in W. Bußmann, "Heinrich von Sybel," in: Bußmann, *Wandel und Kontinuität in Politik und Geschichte* [continuity and change in politics and history], ed. W. Pöls, Boppard am Rhein 1973, pp. 409–20, here p. 414.

25 Cf. T. Nipperdey, *Deutsche Geschichte 1866–1918*, Vol. I: *Arbeitswelt und Bürgergeist* [working world and bourgeois ethic], Munich 1990, p. 592.

26 F. Paulsen as quoted by Nipperdey, *ibid.*, p. 596; cf. also p. 636.

27 Seier, "Heinrich von Sybel," p. 31.

28 Cf. Dotterweich, *Heinrich von Sybel*, pp. 364–366; G. Koch, "Der Streit zwischen Sybel und Ficker und die Einschätzung der mittelalterlichen Kaiserpolitik in der modernen Historiographie" [the argument between Sybel and Ficker and their views of medieval German imperial policy in modern historiography], in: Streisand (ed.), *Studien*, Vol. I, pp. 311–336.

29 Cf. A. Rapaport, *Fights, Games, and Debates*, Ann Arbor 1974, pp. 245–309; B. Giesen, "Konflikttheorie," in: R. König and G. Endruweit (eds.), *Handbuch der modernen soziologischen Theorie*, Stuttgart 1992.

30 Cf. Münch, *Die Kultur der Moderne*, Vol. II, pp. 721ff. On the solitude and freedoms of German scholarship, cf. the still impressive Dahrendorf, *Gesellschaft und Demokratie*, pp. 183f.

31 W. v. Humboldt had already created the metaphor of a nation as its biography: cf. Hardtwig, "Preußens Aufgabe," pp. 110f. In general, cf. Koselleck, "Einleitung."

32 The historian's resigned, quiet work in the archives bespeaks the "honorable, sustained work" of the Prussian people in the "laborious school [of the] state" (Treitschke). On the poetic realism of Treitschke's metaphorics as stimulated by G. Freytag, cf. W. Bußmann, *Heinrich von Treitschke. Sein Welt- und Geschichtsbild* [his world and historical picture], Göttingen 1952, pp. 279f., quotations *ibid.* According to H. White, "embourgeoisement," i.e. the tacit agreement of the hard-working citizen with the present order, is a central effect of the subtly elaborated "writing style" of Droysen and the techniques of contemporary novelists: "Droysens Historik: Geschichtsschreibung als bürgerliche Wissenschaft" [historical writing as a bourgeois scholarship], (English translation in: White, *The Content of the Form. Narrative Discourse and Historical Representation*, Baltimore and London 1987). This "bourgeois" ethos serves as one of the foils to contemporary judgments of Bismarck's "frivolous lack of plans or principles" (Sybel); cf. Bußmann, *Heinrich von Treitschke*, p. 47.

33 Cf. Hardtwig, "Preußens Aufgabe," p. 109.

34 H. v. Treitschke, *Aufsätze, Reden, Briefe*, Vol. I [assorted writings], Meersburg 1929, p. 27.

35 E. Troeltsch, *Naturrecht und Humanität* [natural law and humanity], (1925) reprint, Aalen 1966, p. 15.

36 Within this horizon, every convert to or against Prussia and Bismarck and/or the Habsburgs and their empire became a "quantité négligeable"; cf. H. Schulze, *Der Weg zum Nationalstaat. Die deutsche Nationalbewegung vom 18. Jahrhundert bis zur Reichsgründung* [the road to the nation–state; the German national movement from the eighteenth century to the *Reichsgründung*], Munich 1985, p. 121.

37 "We may say with certainty that with each passing year, history assumes the same position for public opinion, and as a ferment of general education in Germany, that philosophy held twenty years ago." Sybel to G. Waitz, 28 May 1857, quoted by Dotterweich, *Heinrich von Sybel*, p. 337.

38 Cf. Nipperdey, *Deutsche Geschichte 1800–1866*, pp. 513ff., here pp. 532ff.

39 Among the already-classic works by Reinhart Koselleck, cf. "Historia magistra vitae. Über die Auflösung des Topos im Horizont neuzeitlich bewegter Geschichte" [. . . on the dissolution of topos within the horizon of a history infused with the modern spirit], and "Die Verfügbarkeit der Geschichte" [the availability of history], both in: Koselleck, *Vergangene Zukunft*, pp. 38–66 and pp. 260–276 (English translation in Koselleck, *Futures Past*).

40 Cf. R. Koselleck, "Standortbindung und Zeitlichkeit. Ein Beitrag zur historio-

graphischen Erschließung der Welt" [locational formation and temporality; a contribution to the historiographic enclosure of the world], in: Koselleck, *Vergangene Zukunft*, pp. 176–207.

41 Among others, cf. H. White, *Metahistory. The Historical Imaginations in Nineteenth Century Europe*, Baltimore and London 1973; R. Koselleck, H. Lutz, and J. Rüsen (eds.), *Formen der Geschichtsschreibung*, Munich 1982; and Giesen, *Die Entdinglichung des Sozialen*, pp. 84f.

42 Exactly this is the significance of Droysen's "first great fundamental principle" of historical scholarship: "That which is given in historical research is not things past . . . but that which still remains of them in the here and now": J. G. Droysen, "Grundriß der Historik," para. 5, p. 327. In this process, "discursive portrayal" as the preferred form of historiography explicitly relates historical cognition to current debates on public matters. On Droysen's "presentism," cf. White, "Droysens Historik," pp. 108–131, pp. 116f.

43 Cf. J. Rüsen, "Politisches Denken und Geschichtswissenschaft bei J.G. Droysen" [political thought and historical scholarship], in: K. Kluxen and W. J. Mommsen, *Politische Ideologien und nationalstaatliche Ordnung. Studien zur Geschichte des 19. und 20. Jahrhunderts. Festschrift für Theodor Schieder zu seinem 60. Geburtstag* [political ideologies and nation–state order . . . Festschrift for T. S.], Munich and Vienna 1968, pp. 171–188; W. J. Mommsen, "Objektivität und Parteilichkeit im historiographischen Werk Sybels und Treitschkes" [objectivity and partisanship in Sybel and Treitschke], in: R. Koselleck, W. J. Mommsen and J. Rüsen (eds.), *Objektivität und Parteilichkeit*, Munich 1977, pp. 134–158. On the alternative political positions possible within this particular timeframe, cf. J. Rüsen, "Der Historiker als 'Parteimann des Schicksals.' Georg Gottfried Gervinus und das Konzept der objektiven Parteilichkeit im deutschen Historismus" [the historian as "partisan of destiny"; G. G. G. and the concept of objective partisanship in German historicism], in: Koselleck, Mommsen and Rüsen (eds.), *Objektivität und Parteilichkeit*, pp. 77–125. The tension between historiography and primary historical scholarship is then resolved by Theodor Mommsen in favor of research; portrayal is sacrificed to research. Cf. H. Berding, "Theodor Mommsen. Das Problem der Geschichtsschreibung" [T. M. The problem of writing history], in: P. Alter, W.J. Mommsen, and T. Nipperdey (eds.), *Geschichte und politisches Handeln. Studien zu europäischen Denkern der Neuzeit. Theodor Schieder zum Gedächtnis* [history and political action; studies of European thinkers in the modern age; in memory of T.S.], Stuttgart 1985, pp. 243–260.

44 Through the central category of "the work of history," the work of the historian, in carrying it forth into its "ethical interpretation," acquires downright "reality-altering potency," according to W. Hardtwig, "Geschichtsreligion – Wissenschaft als Arbeit – Objektivität" [historical religion; science as work; objectivity] in: *Historische Zeitschrift*, 252, 1991, pp. 1–32, here p. 26.

45 J. G. Droysen, "Enzyklopädie und Methodologie der Geschichte," in: Droysen, *Historik*, Darmstadt 1967, p. 287.

46 Students of Hegel, like Droysen, in particular retain the fundamental teleological ideational tropes. Cf. J. Rüsen, *Begriffene Geschichte. Genesis und Begründung der Geschichtstheorie J.G. Droysens* ["comprehended history"; genesis and substantiation of Droysen's theory of history], Paderborn 1969. For a general look at the "vulgar Hegelian" elements of contemporary discourse, cf. W. Bußmann, "Zur Geschichte des deutschen Liberalismus im 19. Jahrhundert," in: Bußmann, *Wandel und Kontinuität*, pp. 103–133, pp. 129f.

47 For Droysen the meaning of history is that "it, and only it, can give the state, the people, the army and so forth the image of itself"; it is the "foundation for political training and education. The statesman is the practical historian": "Grundriß der Historik," para. 93, pp. 364f.; Treitschke strove for a "common national historical tradition for all educated person": *Deutsche Geschichte im 19. Jahrhundert*, Vol. I, reprint Königstein (Taunus) and Düsseldorf 1981, p. v.

48 "Germany's unity could not be created from freedom, from national decisions. This would rather require a power against other powers, to break down their objections, to protect us from their interests." J. G. Droysen, "Preußen und das System der Großmächte" (1849) [Prussia and the system of great powers], in: Droysen, *Politische Schriften*, pp. 212–229, here p. 229.

49 J. Rüsen, "Johann Gustav Droysen," in: H.-U. Wehler (ed.), *Deutsche Historiker*, Vol. I, Göttingen 1971, pp. 7–23, p. 15.

50 Seier, "Heinrich von Sybel."

51 According to G. G. Iggers, the ultimately metahistoriographical faith in the compatibility of power with reason and morality is exactly what blinds German historians to the "demonic aspect of power": *Deutsche Geschichtswissenschaft*, pp. 120–162, especially pp. 126f. On Droysen's conception, cf. G. Birtsch, *Die Nation als sittliche Idee. Der Nationalstaatsbegriff in Geschichtsschreibung und politischer Gedankenwelt J.G. Droysens* [the nation as an idea of values; the conception of the nation–state in Droysen], Cologne 1964, pp. 82f. On the quite early tendencies to replace the natural-law construction of the state concept with a historical and realistic one, cf. Seier, "Liberalismus und Staat."

52 L. A. v. Rochau, *Grundsätze der Realpolitik* [principles of *Realpolitik*], ed. H.-U. Wehler, Frankfurt am Main, Berlin and Vienna 1972, p. 25; nearly identical wording can be found in: Droysen, "Grundriß der Historik," para. 71, p. 352.

53 F. G. Droysen, "Zur Charakterisierung der europäischen Krisis," p. 323. Diagnosed in this manner, the "will to power" (Rüsen) is declared pathological. Cf. Rüsen, *Begriffene Geschichte*, pp. 74f., pp. 89f.

54 For Sybel, "practical, lasting" success is the "highest judge," the "quintessential deciding authority." Cf. H. Seier, *Die Staatsidee Heinrich von Sybels in den Wandlungen der Reichsgründerzeit 1862/71* [the idea of state of H. v. S. through changes in the era of the foundation of the *Reich* 1862–71], Lübeck and Hamburg 1961, p. 39, quotation *ibid.* "The [national] revolution is still only a question of appropriateness. As soon as it has prospects for success, it must be dared." H. v. Treitschke, *Letters 1913*, Vol. II, p. 351, quoted in Bußmann, "Geschichte des deutschen Liberalismus," p. 125.

55 Hence Rochau, already in 1853: "Thus it is a simply unreasonable demand that

power should be subordinate to right [or law: *Recht*]. Power obeys only greater power," in: *Grundsätze*, p. 26. Later, H. v. Treitschke: "There are no absolute limits on state power," in: "Die Freiheit" [freedom], in: *Historische und politische Aufsätze*, Vol. III, 5th edition, Leipzig 1886, pp. 3–42, p.17. Cf. K.-G. Faber, "Realpolitik als Ideologie. Die Bedeutung des Jahres 1866 für das politische Denken in Deutschland" [*Realpolitik* as ideology; the meaning of 1866 (Austro–Prussian War) for political thought in Germany], in: *Historische Zeitschrift*, 203, 1966, pp. 1–45.

56 "It is a natural law that Germany *should* form a homogeneous, indestructible body, but whether Germany *will* form a homogeneous and indestructible body is up to an act of the nation's freedom." G. Thaulow, *Das europäische Gleichgewicht durch den Prager Frieden vom 23. August 1866* [the European balance through the Peace of Prague], Kiel 1867, quoted in: Faber, "Realpolitik als Ideologie," p. 21. In the 1860s, the metaphor of historical development as "being according to natural law" came to dominate, and "theoretical idealism [allied itself with] practical naturalism," according to Faber, *ibid.*, p. 21. On the replacement of organic metaphor through the "will" to state, cf. Bußman, *Heinrich von Treitschke*, pp. 236f.

57 According to Dahlmann,

> unity [should] open the way to power for the force of the German people [*deutsche Volkskraft*]. The way to power is the only way that will satisfy and nourish a boiling urge to freedom that has not yet recognized itself . . . Germany as Germany must finally enter the ranks of the political great powers of this part of the Earth. That can only happen through Prussia, and Prussia cannot recover without Germany, or Germany without Prussia. . . (1849, in the National Assembly, quoted by Hardtwig, "Preußens Aufgabe," p. 119).

More generally, cf. Wollstein, *Das "Großdeutschland" der Paulskirche.*

58 Cf. Treitschke, *Deutsche Geschichte*, Vol. I, p. 301.

59 Cf. Birtsch, *Die Nation*, p. 48, note 69.

60 For Droysen, the "national parliament" is a "base of power," much like "military duty" and "unprecedented victories," and thus, according to Hardtwig, must function "primarily in the service of national power, and not in the service of bourgeois rights of freedom or of coparticipation in any acts under the authority of the state." In: Hardtwig, "Preußens Aufgabe," p. 121.

61 "The historical state, in the midst of becoming, should be designed so that it produces enough commonalities among its residents to suffice for the achievement of state goals, for the realization of education, values, and freedom. The state need not be the nation, but it must be able to become the nation." Sybel, lectures (1864), quoted by Seier, *Die Staatsidee Heinrich von Sybels*, pp. 65f. On the following passage, cf. Seier, *ibid.*, pp. 59–75.

62 "Should the state have a nationality of similar kind as its foundation, it can all the same remove itself from that nationality at times, by creating it anew." Sybel, lectures, (1847–48), quoted by Seier, *ibid.*, pp. 64f.

63 "Sovereignty must exist somewhere in the state, at a particular address – the final, decisive word must be somewhere." Sybel, lectures, folio 135, quoted by Seier, *ibid.*, p. 45.

64 This is the common denominator of "positive" conceptions of the state, which in older historiography won for national liberalism the attribution of "classical Liberalism": cf. H. Rosenberg, *Rudolf Haym und die Anfänge des klassischen Liberalismus* [R.H. and the beginnings of classical liberalism], Munich and Berlin 1933.

65 On Droysen's combination of internal with external power development, cf. Birtsch, *Die Nation*, pp. 101f.

66 "Nothing seems more deplorable to me than the lack of insight and continuity of insight into foreign relations, so thoroughly determined as they are by nature and history. If one is ambitious enough about the assignment, then the history of the foreign relations of Prussia is the only, and also the best, instruction for practical use." J.G. Droysen, *Briefwechsel* [letters and responses], ed. R. Hübner, Stuttgart 1929, Vol. II, pp. 126f. On Droysen's plan to "work out maxims for action in foreign policy," cf. Hardtwig, "Preußens Aufgabe," pp. 111f., also pp. 124f., pp. 133f.

67 *Ibid.*, pp. 148f.; and E. Fehrenbach, "Rankerenaissance und Imperialismus in der wilhelminischen Zeit" [the "Ranke renaissance" and imperialism in the Wilhelmine age], in: F. Faulenbach (ed.), *Geschichtswissenschaft in Deutschland*, Munich 1974, pp. 54–65.

68 On the concept of civilization, cf. the classic deliberations by N. Elias, in: *The Civilizing Process*, 2 vols., New York 1978.

69 Cf. Nipperdey, *Deutsche Geschichte 1800–1866*, pp. 656f., 684f., 704f.; Schulze, *Der Weg zum Nationalstaat*, pp. 109f.; W. Siemann, *Gesellschaft im Aufbruch. Deutschland 1849–1971* [society in break-up], Frankfurt am Main 1990, pp. 268f.

70 The "movement . . . towards the concentration of great masses" noted by Treitschke bespeaks "an urge to expel foreign-like elements of people (*fremdartige Volkselemente*)" so that the state becomes "that which it should be by nature, the unified, organized *Volk*." Quotes from H. v. Treitschke, *Zehn Jahre deutsche Kämpfe* [ten years of German struggles], 2nd edition, Berlin 1879, p. 114; and "Die Freiheit," p. 8.

71 Cf. J. G. Droysen, "Zur Charakterisierung der europäischen Krisis." Precisely in the face of the thoroughgoing crisis of an emerging "world system of states" (p. 330), "only the non-Roman German, only the Protestant spirit, has the inner freedom, and the urgent impulse, to accomplish what is necessary" (p. 335), i.e. to prepare the power resources that will grow "from the strongest natural combinations . . . from the most direct impulses that rule over emotion" (p. 332), so as to avoid, for the best reasons of state, the "Austrian solution to the German question" (p. 334), of a "sick man" of Germany (p. 329). "It is up to Prussia to achieve and preserve the position that our people will take up in the coming future of the world" (p. 336). Droysen observed, in 1849, that Austria had

"turned away from Germany in its political forms, much as in its intellectual movement – it does not even have a university system in common with us – and has also become separate from the rest of Germany in its material interests" (pp. 220f.). Austria "lived from Germany's decline; its greatness was determined by our powerlessness. Austria's politics was and remains one of keeping Germany from becoming itself" (p. 213). J.G. Droysen, "Preußen und das System der Großmächte."

72 On Protestantism as the core of Prusso-German identity, cf. Hardtwig, "Preußens Aufgabe," pp. 152f.

73 H. v. Sybel, *Die Politischen Parteien der Rheinprovinz in ihrem Verhältnis zur preußischen Verfassung* [the political parties of the Rhine province in their relation to the Prussian constitution], Düsseldorf 1847, p. 16.

74 Cf. Dotterweich, *Heinrich von Sybel*, p. 58.

75 H. v. Sybel, *Die politischen Parteien*, p. 16.

76 Dotterweich, *Heinrich von Sybel*, p. 69.

77 Sybel, lectures (1847–48), quoted by Dotterweich, *ibid.*, p. 72.

78 Heine, who was a cosmopolitan as well as a democrat and a Jew, became the favorite target of national ideas of homogenization. Treitschke, who can hardly dispute the status of Heine's lyric, ultimately accuses him of having never written a drinking song, demonstrating thus that he could not possibly be a true German poet. Cf. H. Treitschke, *Deutsche Geschichte im 19. Jahrhundert* [German history of the nineteenth century], Vol. IV, reprint Königstein (Taunus) and Düsseldorf 1981, p. 423. On the "Berlin anti-Semitism debate" set off by Treitschke, cf. H. Berding, *Moderner Antisemitismus in Deutschland*, Frankfurt am Main 1988, pp. 113f.

79 Quoted in J. Hejderhoff and P. Wentzcke (eds.), *Deutscher Liberalismus im Zeitalter Bismarcks. Eine politische Briefsammlung* [German liberalism in Bismarck's time; a collection of political letters], Vol. I, Bonn and Leipzig 1925, p. 494.

80 Cf. E. Fehrenbach, "Die Reichsgründung in der deutschen Geschichtsauffassung" [the founding of the *Reich* in German historical understanding], in: T. Schieder and E. Deuerlein (eds.), *Reichsgründung 1870/71*, Stuttgart 1970, pp. 259–290, here pp. 260f.

81 Even and precisely Bismarck's "game" with national and political motifs was "taken as proof that for every Prussian statesman, without exception, the question of German unity inevitably becomes one of a school of liberalism – not of the anarchic and revolutionary, but of the positivist and state-supporting liberalism." H. v. Sybel, "Das neue Deutschland und Frankreich" (1866), in: Sybel, *Vorträge und Aufsätze* [lectures and essays], Berlin 1874, p. 297; on this, cf. Seier, "Liberalismus und Staat," p. 76.

82 Cf. Seier, *Die Staatsidee Heinrich von Sybels*, p. 193. The power-political cunning over "digestibility" provided the underlying motivation. For Treitschke, for example, "language is no political principle." Cf. Bußmann, *Heinrich von Treitschke*, pp. 316ff.

83 For example T. Vischers: cf. F. Meinecke, "3 Generationen Gelehrtenpolitik" [three generations of scholarly politics], in: *Historische Zeitschrift*, 125, 1922, pp. 248–283, pp. 262f.

84 Cf. Meinecke, *ibid.*; E. Deuerlein, "Die Konfrontation von Nationalstaat und national Bestimmter Kultur" [the confrontation between nation–state and nationally defined culture], in: T. Schieder and E. Deuerlein (eds.), *Reichsgründung 1870/71*, Stuttgart 1970, pp. 226–258; U. Köster, "Elitekultur – Kulturelite. Repräsentative Kultur und Sezessionsbewegung im Kaiserreich" [elite culture and cultural elite; representative culture and secessionary movements in the empire], in: *Ploetz*: *Das deutsche Kaiserreich. 1867/71 bis 1918. Bilanz einer Epoche* [the German Empire, 1867/71–1918; balance of an era], ed. D. Langewiesche, Freiburg and Würzburg 1984, pp. 181–188.

85 Other concepts, like "society" and "culture," took its place, and other academic disciplines, such as the just-emerging sociology, took over the leading function held by historical scholarship.

86 F. Nietzsche, "David Strauss – Der Bekenner und Schriftsteller" [D. S. – confessor and man of letters], in: *Unzeitmäßige Betrachtungen* [untimely observations], Munich 1964, pp. 7–72, p. 7.

Epilogue: German identity between 1945 and 1990

1 On the trope of "negative nationalism" cf. W. Reese-Schäfer, "Universalismus, negativer Nationalismus und die neue Einheit der Deutschen" [universalism, negative nationalism, and the new unity of the Germans], in: P. Braitling and W. Reese-Schäfer (eds.), *Universalismus, Nationalismus und die neue Einheit der Deutschen*, Frankfurt am Main 1991, pp. 39–54, here p. 46.

2 One need only recall the various succeeding waves of Hesse enthusiasm.

3 Quite some time ago, Georg Simmel pointed out the function of negative identification in processes of group formation in "Der Streit" [the argument], in: Simmel, *Soziologie. Untersuchungen über die Formen der Vergesellschaftung* [examinations of the forms of socialization], 4th edition, Berlin 1958, pp. 186–255. Carl Schmitt's idea of the primacy of defining the enemy (or war) in identifying friends (or peace) might also be mentioned in this connection: Schmitt, *Der Begriff des Politischen* (1932), Berlin 1987. Cf. also Reese-Schäfer, "Universalismus," pp. 44ff.

4 Odo Marquard therefore spoke of "disobedience after the fact": *Abschied vom Prinzipiellen*, pp. 9ff.

5 Jürgen Habermas in particular emphasizes the parallels to the Young Hegelians, Habermas, *The Philosophical Discourse of Modernity: Twelve Lectures*, Cambridge, MA 1989.

6 On the new social movements cf. the various works by K. Eder, e.g. "Soziale Bewegungen und kulturelle Evolution. Überlegungen zur Rolle der neuen sozialen Bewegungen in der kulturellen Evolution der Moderne" [social movements and cultural evolution; on the role of new social movements in the cultural evolution of Modernity], in: J. Berger (ed.), *Die Moderne – Kontinuität und*

Zäsuren [Modernity: continuity and caesuras], *Soziale Welt*, special issue No. 4, Göttingen 1986, pp. 335–357; see also K.P. Japp, "Neue soziale Bewegungen und die Kontinuität der Moderne," in: J. Berger (ed.), *ibid.*, pp. 311–333; and B. Giesen, "Der Herbst der Moderne? Zum zeitdiagnostischen Potential neuer sozialer Bewegungen" [the autumn of Modernism? On the age-diagnostic potential of new social movements], in: J. Berger (ed.), *ibid.*, pp. 359–376.

7 The *Historikerstreit* can also be read as an example of this definition of identity, and that applies to all sides in that debate. Cf. *Historikerstreit. Die Dokumentation der Kontroverse um die Einzigartigkeit der nationalsozialistischen Judenvernichtung* [*Historikerstreit*: a documentation of the controversy surrounding the uniqueness of the National Socialists' decimation of the Jews], 2nd edition, Munich and Zurich 1987. [The heated and charged *Historikerstreit* has involved a highly public series of exchanges among scholars and publicists, starting in 1986, over historically revisionist views of the Third *Reich* and its aftermath. The debate was sparked by historian Ernst Nolte and his theses, published in the *Frankfurter Allgemeine Zeitung*, that, among other things, the Nazi movement and its crimes must be understood as a response to, and a parallel adoption of, Bolshevik practice. Jürgen Habermas fired a countering broadside, in defense of the "Holocaust nation's" uniqueness, appearing in *Die Zeit*, the flagship of German liberalism. The German print media was promptly filled with protestations pro and con. The debate revived again following German unification, and with the resurgence of a xenophobic nationalism in 1991–93, as a series of exchanges over totalitarianisms left and right. Its most recent incarnation has revolved around the German reception of Daniel J. Goldhagen's *Hitler's Willing Executioners*, New York 1995. – Translator's note.]

8 On this cf. J. Weiß, "Wiederverzauberung der Welt? Bemerkungen zur Wiederkehr der Romantik in der gegenwärtigen Kulturkritik" [A reenchantment of the world? Observations on the return of Romanticism in current cultural criticism], in: F. Neidhardt *et al.* (eds.), *Kultur und Gesellschaft*, *Kölner Zeitschrift für Soziologie und Sozialpsychologie*, Special Issue No. 27, Opladen 1986.

9 The "correct" categorization of this series of events is still a matter of debate. While Jürgen Habermas speaks of a "compensatory ('catch-up') revolution," Hermann Lübbe prefers the term "anti-revolution." Cf. J. Habermas, "Nachholende Revolution und linker Revisionsbedarf. Was heißt Sozialismus heute?" [compensatory revolution and the leftist need for revision; what does socialism mean today?], in: Habermas, *Die Moderne – ein unvollendetes Projekt. Philosophisch-politische Aufsätze 1977–1990* [Modernity: an uncompleted project; essays], Leipzig 1990, pp. 213–241; and H. Lübbe, "Die Nostalgie des Urbanen und die europäische Anti-Revolution des Jahres 1989" [the nostalgia of urbanity and the European anti-revolution of 1989], in: Lübbe, *Freiheit statt Emanzipationszwang. Die liberale Tradition und das Ende der marxistischen Illusion* ["freedom instead of forced emancipation"; liberal tradition and the end of the Marxist illusion], Osnabrück 1991, pp. 75–90.

10 Although naturally one should by no means overlook the unintended side effects that massive emigration had on the collapse of this regime. It accelerated the regime's loss of face, and the new possibility of emigration simultaneously lowered the risks of protest. Cf. K.-J. Opp, "DDR 89. Zu den Ursachen einer spontanen Revolution" [GDR '89; on the causes of a spontaneous revolution], in: *Kölner Zeitschrift für Soziologie und Sozialpsychologie*, 43, 2, 1991, pp. 302–321.

11 An interesting alternative, but one running contrary to all traditional fronts, and therefore doomed to finding no echo, was formulated in this connection by Ulrich Oevermann. He demanded national unity precisely as a means for finally taking the blame for the Holocaust: "Zwei Staaten oder Einheit? Der 'dritte Weg' als Fortsetzung des deutschen Sonderweges" [Two states or unity?; the "third path" as a continuation of the German *Sonderweg*], in: *Merkur*, 40, 1990, pp. 91–106.

12 On this particular learning process, cf. K.O. Hondrich, *Lehrmeister Krieg* ["Headmaster War"], Reinbek 1992. For a stronger focus on the "leftist scene," cf. C. Stephan and C. Leggewie, "Abschied vom linken Gewissen" [farewell to leftist conscience], in: *Journal Frankfurt*, 14–27 Feb. 1991, pp. 32f.

Bibliography

Alexander, J. C. "Core Solidarity, Ethnic Outgroup, and Social Differentiation: A Multidimensional Model of Inclusion in Modern Societies." In: Dofny, J. and Akiwowo, A. (Eds.) *National and Ethnic Movements*. Beverly Hills and London 1980, pp. 5–28.

Fin de siècle. Social Theory. London and New York 1995.

Alexander, J.C. and Colomy, P. (Eds.) *Differentiation Theory and Social Change*. New York and Oxford 1990.

Anderson, B. *Imagined Communities.* 2nd expanded edn. London 1991.

Anonymous. "Von den Vortheilen für Industrie, Moralität, Patriotismus und Bevölkerung, wenn die Bauerngüter getheilt werden." In: *Neues Hannoverisches Magazin*, 5, 1795, pp. 1243–1248 and 1249–1270.

"Moralische Schilderung des ehemals altfränkischen itzt ***artigen Frauenzimmers. Von einem altväterschen, aber redlich denkenden Patrioten entworfen, An. 1740." In: *Schweizerisches Museum*, 3, 1, 1784, pp. 740–752.

"Rede, gehalten in der vaterländischen Gesellschaft zu B. . ." In: *Neues Hannoverisches Magazin*, 7, 6, 1796, pp. 97–116.

Archer, M. *Culture and Agency. The Place of Culture in Social Theory*. Cambridge 1990.

Arndt, E. M. "Über den Volkshaß und über den Gebrauch einer fremden Sprache" (1803). Reprinted in: Vogt, H. (Ed.) *Nationalismus gestern und heute*. Opladen 1967, pp. 102–105.

Bade, K. J. (Ed.) *Deutsche im Ausland – Fremde in Deutschland. Migration in Geschichte und Gegenwart*. Munich 1992.

Banton, M. *Racial and Ethnic Competition*. Cambridge 1983.

Barth, F. (Ed.) *Ethnic Groups and Boundaries: The Social Organization of Cultural Difference*. Boston 1969.

Barthes, R. *Mythologies*. Paris 1957.

Baudrillard, J. *Les Stratégies fatales*. Paris 1983.

Bauman, Z. *Legislators and Interpreters. On Modernity, Postmodernity and Intellectuals*. Ithaca, NY 1987.

Baumgart, F. "Lehrer und Lehrervereine während der Revolution von 1848/49." In: *Mentalitäten und Lebensverhältnisse. Beispiele aus der Sozialgeschichte. R. Vierhaus zum 60. Geburtstag*. Festschrift. Ed. colleagues and students. Göttingen 1982, pp. 173–188.

Behler, E. *Friedrich Schlegel in Selbstzeugnissen und Bilddokumenten.* Reinbek 1988.

Ben-David, J. *The Scientist's Role in Society – A Comparative Study.* 2nd edn. London 1984.

Bendix, R. *Nation-Building and Citizenship*. 2nd expanded edn. Berkeley 1977.

Kings or People: Power and the Mandate to Rule. Berkeley 1978.

Freiheit und historisches Schicksal. Frankfurt am Main 1982.

"Strukturgeschichtliche Voraussetzungen der nationalen und kulturellen Identität in der Neuzeit." In: Giesen, B. (Ed.) *Nationale und kulturelle Identität. Studien zur Entwicklung des kollektiven Bewußtseins in der Neuzeit.* Frankfurt am Main 1991, pp. 39–55.

Benjamin, W. *Charles Baudelaire: a lyric poet in the era of high capitalism.* London 1973.

Berding, H. "Theodor Mommsen. Das Problem der Geschichtsschreibung." In: Alter, P., Mommsen, W. J. and Nipperdey, T. (Eds.) *Geschichte und politisches Handeln. Studien zu europäischen Denkern der Neuzeit. Theodor Schieder zum Gedächtnis.* Stuttgart 1985, pp. 243–260.

Moderner Antisemitismus in Deutschland. Frankfurt am Main 1988.

Berding, H., Etienne, F., and Ullmann, H.-P. (Eds.) *Deutschland und Frankreich im Zeitalter der Französischen Revolution*. Frankfurt am Main 1989.

Berding, H. and Schimpf, D. "Assimilation und Identität. Probleme des jüdischen Schul- und Erziehungswesens in Hessen-Kassel im Zeitalter der Emanzipation." In: Giesen, B. (Ed.) *Nationale und kulturelle Identität. Studien zur Entwicklung des kollektiven Bewußtseins in der Neuzeit*. Frankfurt am Main 1991, pp. 350–387.

Berger, P. L. and Luckmann, T. *The Social Construction of Reality: a Treatise in the Sociology of Knowledge.* Garden City, NY 1966.

Bergmann, J. R. "Deskriptive Praktiken als Gegenstand und Methode der Ethnomethodologie." In: Herzog, M. and Graumann, C. F. (Eds.) *Sinn und Erfahrung. Phänomenologische Methoden in den Humanwissenschaften.* Heidelberg 1991, pp. 86–102.

Beyer, C. S. L. v. "Ueber Kosmopolitismus und Patriotismus." In: *Deutsche Monatsschrift*, 1, 1795, pp. 223–230.

Birtsch, G. *Die Nation als sittliche Idee. Der Nationalstaatsbegriff in Geschichtsschreibung und politischer Gedankenwelt J. G. Droysens.* Cologne 1964.

Bitterli, U. *Alte Welt – neue Welt. Formen des europäisch-überseeischen Kontakts vom 15. bis zum 18. Jahrhundert*. Munich 1986.

Bödeker, H. E. "Aufklärung als Kommunikationsprozeß." In: Vierhaus, R. (Ed.) *Aufklärung als Prozeß.* Hamburg 1988, pp. 89–111.

Boon, J. A. *Other Tribes, Other Scribes. Symbolic Anthropology in the Comparative Study of Cultures, Histories, Religions, and Texts*. Cambridge 1982.

Bouvier, B. W. "Die Anfänge der sozialistischen Bewegung." In: Reinalter, H. (Ed.) *Demokratische und soziale Protestbewegungen in Mitteleuropa 1815–1848/49*. Frankfurt am Main 1986, pp. 265–304.

Brandes, B. E. *Über den Einfluß und die Wirkungen des Zeitgeistes auf die höheren Stände Deutschlands.* Part 2. Hanover 1810.

Brandes, H. *Die Zeitschriften des Jungen Deutschland. Eine Untersuchung zur literarisch-publizistischen Öffentlichkeit im 19. Jahrhundert*. Opladen 1991.

Brentano, C. *Ausgewählte Werke*. Ed. M. Morris. Vol. III. Leipzig 1904.

Briegleb, K. "General Marx – Hund Heine. Eine Textspiegelung zur Frage: Heinrich Heine nach 1848 – ein politischer Dichter?" In: *Heinrich Heine 1797–1856, Schriften aus dem Karl-Marx-Haus* 26, Trier 1981, pp. 153–181.

Brubaker, W. R. *Citizenship and Nationhood in France and Germany*. Cambridge, MA 1992.

Nationalism Reframed. Nationhood and the National Question in the New Europe. Cambridge, MA 1996.

Brubaker, W. R. (Ed.) *Immigration and the Politics of Citizenship in Europe and North America*. Washington, DC 1989.

Brunschwig, H. *Gesellschaft und Romantik in Preußen im 18. Jahrhundert. Die Krise des preußischen Staates am Ende des 18. Jahrhunderts und die Entstehung der romantischen Mentalität*. Frankfurt am Main, Berlin and Vienna 1975 (1976).

Büchner, G. *Sämtliche Werke und Briefe*. Ed. R. W. Lehmann. Vol. II. Darmstadt 1971.

Burchhardt-Dose, H. *Das Junge Deutschland und die Familie. Zum literarischen Engagement in der Restaurationsepoche.* Frankfurt am Main 1979.

Burke, K. "The Virtues and Limitations of Debunking." In: Burke. *The*

Philosophy of Literary Form. Berkeley and Los Angeles 1973, pp. 168–190.

Büsch, J. G. "Von dem Unnatürlichen in dem Umgange der Gelehrten und Ungelehrten." In: Büsch. *Vermischte Abhandlungen.* Part 2, Hamburg 1777, pp. 509–524.

Bußmann, W. *Heinrich von Treitschke. Sein Welt- und Geschichtsbild.* Göttingen 1952.

"Zur Geschichte des deutschen Liberalismus im 19. Jahrhundert." In: Bußmann. *Wandel und Kontinuität in Politik und Geschichte.* Ed. W. Pöls. Boppard am Rhein 1973, pp. 103–133.

"Gustav Freytag. Maßstäbe seiner Zeitkritik." In: Bußmann. *Wandel und Kontinuität in Politik und Geschichte.* Ed. W. Pöls. Boppard am Rhein 1973, pp. 135–162.

"Heinrich von Sybel." In: Bußmann. *Wandel und Kontinuität in Politik und Geschichte.* Ed. W. Pöls. Boppard am Rhein 1973, pp. 409–420.

Büttner, W. "Der Weberaufstand in Schlesien 1844." In: Reinalter, H. (Ed.) *Demokratische und soziale Protestbewegungen in Mitteleuropa 1815–1848/49.* Frankfurt am Main 1986, pp. 202–229.

Chatterjee, P. *Nationalist Thought and the Colonial World – A Derivative Discourse?* London 1986.

Cohen, A. P. *The Symbolic Construction of Community.* London 1985.

Collins, R. "A Micro-Macro Theory of Intellectual Creativity: The Case of German Idealist Philosophy." In: *Sociological Theory*, 5, 1987, pp. 47–69.

Culture, Communication and National Identity: The Case of Canada. Toronto 1990.

"On the Sociology of Intellectual Stagnation: The Late Twentieth Century in Perspective." In: *Theory, Culture and Society*, 9, 1992, pp. 73–96.

Connor, W. *Ethnonationalism. The Quest for Understanding.* Princeton, NJ 1994.

Conze, W. "Vom 'Pöbel' zum 'Proletariat.' Sozialgeschichtliche Voraussetzungen für den Sozialismus in Deutschland." In: *Vierteljahresschrift für Sozial- und Wirtschaftsgeschichte*, 41, 1954, pp. 333–364.

"Nation und Gesellschaft – Zwei Grundbegriffe der revolutionären Epoche." In: *Historische Zeitschrift*, 198, 1964, pp. 1–16.

Coulmas, F. *Sprache und Staat. Studien zur Sprachplanung.* Berlin and New York 1985.

Die Wirtschaft mit der Sprache. Frankfurt am Main 1992.

Crouch, C. and Pizzorno, A. (Eds.) *The Resurgence of Class Conflict in Western Europe since 1968.* 2 Vols. London 1978.

Dahrendorf, R. *Gesellschaft und Demokratie in Deutschland*. Munich 1965. (Available in English as *Society and Democracy in Germany*. Garden City, NY 1967).

Dann, O. "Nationalismus und sozialer Wandel in Deutschland 1806–1850." In: Dann. (Ed.) *Nationalismus und sozialer Wandel*. Hamburg 1978, pp.77–128.

"Einleitung." In: Dann. (Ed.) *Lesegesellschaften und bürgerliche Emanzipation – Ein europäischer Vergleich*. Munich 1981, pp. 9–28.

Debray, R. *Teachers, Writers, Celebrities. The Intellectuals of Modern France*. London 1981.

Degenkolbe, G. "Über logische Strukturen und gesellschaftliche Funktionen von Leerformeln." In: *Kölner Zeitschrift für Soziologie und Sozialpsychologie*, 17, 1965, pp. 327–338.

Deleuze, G. *Différence et répétition*. Paris 1968.

Deuerlein, E. "Die Konfrontation von Nationalstaat und national bestimmter Kultur." In: Schieder, T. and Deuerlein, E. (Eds.) *Reichsgründung 1870/71*. Stuttgart 1970, pp. 226–258.

Deutsch, K. W. *Nationalism and Social Communication*. Cambridge, MA 1953.

Nationalism and its Alternatives. New York 1969.

Diesterweg, F. A. W. "Birgt die öffentliche Erziehung in der Gegenwart ein revolutionäres Prinzip in ihrem Schoß?" In: Diesterweg. *Sämtliche Werke*. Ed. H. Deiters *et al.* Sec. I, Vol. III. Berlin 1959 (1835) pp. 426–432.

Dotterweich, V. *Heinrich von Sybel. Geschichtswissenschaft in politischer Absicht (1817–1861)*. Göttingen 1978.

Droysen, J. G. *Briefwechsel*. Ed. R. Hübner. Vol. II. Stuttgart 1929.

"Preußen und das System der Großmächte" (1849). In: Droysen. *Politische Schriften*. Ed. F. Gilbert. Munich 1933. pp. 212–229.

"Zur Charakterisierung der europäischen Krisis" (1854). In: Droysen. *Politische Schriften*. Ed. F. Gilbert. Munich 1933, pp. 307–342.

"Enzyklopädie und Methodologie der Geschichte." In: Droysen. *Historik*. Reprint of the 1882 edn. Darmstadt 1967.

"Grundriß der Historik." In: Droysen. *Historik*. Reprint of the 1882 edn. Darmstadt 1967.

Düding, D. *Organisierter gesellschaftlicher Nationalismus 1808–1847. Bedeutung und Funktion der Turner- und Sängervereine für die deutsche Nationalbewegung*. Munich 1984.

Düding, D., Friedmann, P., and Münch, P. (Eds.) *Öffentliche Festkultur. Politische Feste in Deutschland von der Aufklärung bis zum Ersten Weltkrieg*. Reinbek 1988.

Dülmen, R. van. *Die Gesellschaft der Aufklärer*. Frankfurt am Main 1986.

Dux, G. *Die Logik der Weltbilder. Sinnstrukturen im Wandel der Geschichte*. Frankfurt am Main 1981.

Eckermann, J. P. *Gespräche mit Goethe*. Berlin 1956.

Eco, U. "A Map of the Empire in 1:1 Scale". In: Eco. *Diario minimo*. Milan 1963.

Eder, K. *Die Entstehung staatlich organisierter Gesellschaften. Ein Beitrag zu einer Theorie sozialer Evolution*. Frankfurt am Main 1980.

Geschichte als Lernprozeß? Zur Pathogenese politischer Modernität in Deutschland. Frankfurt am Main 1985.

"Soziale Bewegungen und kulturelle Evolution. Überlegungen zur Rolle der neuen sozialen Bewegungen in der kulturellen Evolution der Moderne." In: Berger, J. (Ed.) *Die Moderne – Kontinuität und Zäsuren* (*Soziale Welt*, Special Issue No. 4). Göttingen 1986, pp. 335–357.

Die Vergesellschaftung der Natur. Frankfurt am Main 1988.

The New Politics of Class. Social Movements and Cultural Dynamics in Advanced Societies. London, Newbury Park and New Delhi 1993.

Eisenstadt, S. N. "The Axial Age: The Emergence of Transcendental Visions and the Rise of Clerics." In: *European Journal of Sociology*, 23, 2, 1982, pp. 299–314.

"Die Konstruktion nationaler Identitäten in vergleichender Perspektive." In: Giesen, B. (Ed.) *Nationale und kulturelle Identität. Studien zur Entwicklung des kollektiven Bewußtseins in der Neuzeit*. Frankfurt am Main 1991, pp. 21–38.

Eisenstadt, S. N. (Ed.) *Power, Trust, and Meaning. Essays in Sociological Theory and Analysis*. Chicago 1995.

(Ed.) *Kulturen der Achsenzeit. Ihre Ursprünge und ihre Vielfalt*. 2 Vols. Frankfurt am Main 1987.

(Ed.) *Kulturen der Achsenzeit II. Ihre institutionelle und kulturelle Dynamik*. 3 Vols. Frankfurt am Main 1992.

Eisenstadt, S. N. and Rokkan, S. (Eds.) *Building States and Nations*. 2 Vols. Beverly Hills 1973.

Eisenstein, E. L. *The Printing Press as an Agent of Change – Communications and Cultural Transformations in Early-Modern Europe*. Cambridge 1982.

Elias, N. *The Civilizing Process*. 2 Vols. New York 1978.

The Court Society. New York 1983.

The Germans. Studies of Power, Struggles and the Development of Habitus in the Nineteenth and Twentieth Centuries. New York 1996.

Emge, R. M. *Saint-Simon. Einführung in ein Phänomen*. Munich 1987.

Empson, W. *Some Versions of Pastoral*. London 1986.

Engelhardt, U. *Bildungsbürgertum. Begriffs- und Dogmengeschichte eines Etiketts*. Stuttgart 1986.

Engelsing, R. "Zeitungen und Zeitschriften in Nordwestdeutschland 1800–1850." In: *Archiv für Geschichte des Buchwesens*, 5, 1963, cols. 849–955.

Der Bürger als Leser. Stuttgart 1974.

"Die Perioden der Lesergeschichte in der Neuzeit." In: Engelsing. *Zur Sozialgeschichte deutscher Mittel- und Unterschichten*. 2nd expanded ed. Göttingen 1978, pp. 112–154.

"Zur politischen Bildung der deutschen Unterschichten 1789–1863." In: Engelsing. *Zur Sozialgeschichte deutscher Mittel- und Unterschichten*. 2nd expanded edn. Göttingen 1978, pp. 115–179.

Eßbach, W. *Die Junghegelianer. Soziologie einer Intellektuellengruppe*. Munich 1978.

Esser, H. "Ethnische Difierenzierung und moderne Gesellschaft." In: *Zeitschrift für Soziologie*, 17, 1988, pp. 235–248.

Faber, K.-G. "Realpolitik als Ideologie. Die Bedeutung des Jahres 1866 für das politische Denken in Deutschland." In: *Historische Zeitschrift*, 203, 1966, pp. 1–45.

"Nationalität und Geschichte in der Frankfurter National-versammlung." In: Klötzer, W., Moldenhauer, R. and Rebentisch, D. (Eds.) *Ideen und Strukturen der deutschen Revolution 1848*. Frankfurt am Main 1974, pp. 103–124.

Fehrenbach, E. "Die Reichsgründung in der deutschen Geschichtsauffassung." In: Schieder, T. and Deuerlein, E. (Eds.) *Reichsgründung 1870/71*. Stuttgart 1970, pp. 259–290.

"Rankerenaissance und Imperialismus in der wilhelminischen Zeit." In: Faulenbach, F. (Ed.) *Geschichtswissenschaft in Deutschland*. Munich 1974, pp. 54–65.

Fenske, H. "Ungeduldige Zuschauer. Die Deutschen und die europäische Expansion 1815–1880." In: Reinhardt, W. (Ed.) *Imperialistische Kontinuität und nationale Ungeduld im 19. Jahrhundert*. Frankfurt am Main 1991, pp. 87–123.

Fertig, L. "Die Hofmeister. Befunde, Thesen, Fragen." In: Hermann, U. (Ed.) *Die Bildung des Bürgers. Die Formierung der bürgerlichen Gesellschaft und die Gebildeten im 18. Jahrhundert*. Weinheim and Basel 1982, pp. 322–328.

Fichte, J. G. "Reden an die deutsche Nation." In: *Johann Gottlieb Fichtes sämtliche Werke*. Ed. I.H.Fichte. Vol. VII, Berlin 1845/46, pp. 257–502.

Finkielkraut, A. *La Défaite de la pensée*. Paris 1987.

Foerster, C. "Sozialstruktur und Organisationsformen des deutschen Preß- und Vaterlandsvereins von 1832/33." In: Schieder, W. (Ed.) *Liberalismus in der Gesellschaft des deutschen Vormärz*. Göttingen 1983, pp. 147–166.

Francis, E. *Interethnic Relations. An Essay in Sociological Theory*. New York 1976.

Frank, M. *Einführung in die frühromantische Ästhetik*. Frankfurt am Main 1989.

Freyre, G. *Herrenhaus und Sklavenhütte. Ein Bild der brasilianischen Gesellschaft*. Stuttgart 1982.

Fuchs, P. "Historisch-systematische Analyse des Nationencodes in der deutschen Öffentlichkeit zwischen 1770 und 1850." A working paper in the research project "Nation als Publikum." MS. University of Gießen 1989.

Gall, L. " 'Sündenfall' des liberalen Denkens oder Krise der bürgerlichen Bewegung? Zum Verhältnis von Liberalismus und Imperialismus in Deutschland." In: Holl, K. and List, G. (Eds.) *Liberalismus und imperialistischer Staat. Imperialismus als Problem liberaler Parteien in Deutschland 1890–1914*. Göttingen 1975, pp. 148–158.

Bürgertum in Deutschland. Berlin 1989.

Garfinkel, H. *Studies in Ethnomethodology*. Englewood Cliffs, NJ 1967.

Garve, C. "Ueber die Maxime Rochefoucaulds: das bürgerliche Air verliehrt sich zuweilen bey der Armee, niemahls am Hofe." In: Garve. *Versuche über verschiedene Gegenstände aus der Moral, der Literatur und dem gesellschaftlichen Leben*. Part I, Breslau 1792, pp. 295–452.

"Clubs." In: Batscha, Z. *et al.* (Eds.) *Von der ständischen zur bürgerlichen Gesellschaft*. Frankfurt am Main 1981, pp. 279–288.

Gay, P. *The Enlightenment: An Interpretation*. New York 1969.

Geertz, C. "After the Revolution: The Fate of Nationalism in the New States." In: Geertz. *The Interpretation of Cultures*. New York 1973, pp. 234–254.

"The Integrative Revolution: Primordial Sentiment and Civil Politics in the New States." In: Geertz. *The Interpretation of Cultures*. New York 1973, pp. 255–310.

Works and Lives: The Anthropologist as Author. Cambridge 1988.

Gehlen, A. "Deutschtum und Christentum bei Fichte." In: Gehlen. *Gesamtausgabe*. Vol. II. Frankfurt am Main 1980, pp. 215–293.

Moral und Hypermoral. Eine pluralistische Ethik. Wiesbaden 1986.

Geiger, T. *Aufgaben und Stellung der Intelligenz in der Gesellschaft*. Stuttgart 1949.

Gellner, E. "Nationalism." In: Gellner. *Thought and Change*. London 1964, pp. 147–178.

Nations and Nationalism. Oxford 1983.

Gennep, A. van. *The Rites of Passage*. London 1960.

Gerth, H. *Bürgerliche Intelligenz um 1800*. Göttingen 1976.

Geschichtliche Grundbegriffe. 5 vols. Stuttgart 1972–1985.

Gessinger, J. *Sprache und Bürgertum. Sozialgeschichte sprachlicher Verkehrsformen im Deutschland des 18. Jahrhunderts.* Stuttgart 1980.

Giddens, A. *A Contemporary Critique of Historical Materialism.* Vol. I: *Power, Property and the State.* London 1981.

The Nation–State and Violence. Cambridge 1981.

Giesecke, M. *Der Buchdruck in der frühen Neuzeit. Eine historische Fallstudie über die Durchsetzung neuer Informations- und Kommunikationstechnologien.* Frankfurt am Main 1991.

Giesen, B. "Der Herbst der Moderne? Zum zeitdiagnostischen Potential neuer sozialer Bewegungen." In: Berger, J. (Ed.) *Die Moderne – Kontinuität und Zäsuren* (*Soziale Welt*, Special Issue No. 4) Göttingen 1986, pp. 359–376.

"Code, Process and Situation in Cultural Selection." In: *Cultural Dynamic*, 4, 2, 1991, pp. 172–185.

Die Entdinglichung des Sozialen. Eine evolutionstheoretische Perspektive auf die Postmoderne. Frankfurt am Main 1991.

"Konflikttheorie." In: König, R. and Endruweit, G. (Eds.) *Handbuch der modernen soziologischen Theorie.* Stuttgart 1992.

Giesen, B. (Ed.) *Nationale und kulturelle Identität. Studien zur Entwicklung des kollektiven Bewußtseins in der Neuzeit.* Frankfurt am Main 1992.

Giesen, B., and Eisenstadt, S. N. "The Construction of Collective Identity." In: *Arch. europ. sociol.*, XXXVI, pp. 72–102.

Giesen, B., and Junge, K. "Vom Patriotismus zum Nationalismus. Zur Evolution der 'Deutschen Kulturnation.'" In: Giesen, B. (Ed.) *Nationale und kulturelle Identität. Studien zur Entwicklung des kollektiven Bewußtseins in der Neuzeit.* Frankfurt am Main 1991, pp. 255–303.

Giesen, B., Junge, K., and Kritschgau, C. "Vom Patriotismus zum völkischen Denken: Intellektuelle als Konstrukteure der deutschen Identität." In: H. Berding (Ed.) *Nationales Bewußtsein und kollektive Identität. Studien zur Entwicklung des kollektiven Bewußtseins in der Neuzeit 2.* Frankfurt am Main 1994, pp. 345–393.

Glasersfeld, E. v. *Wissen, Sprache und Wirklichkeit. Arbeiten zum radikalen Konstruktivismus.* Braunschweig and Wiesbaden 1987.

Goffman, E. "The Lecture." In: Goffman. *Forms of Talk.* Pennsylvania 1981, pp. 160–195.

Goody, J. *The Domestication of the Savage Mind.* Cambridge 1977.

Görres, J. "Teutschland und die Revolution" (1819). In: Görres. *Politische Schriften.* Ed. M. Görres. Vol. IV, Munich 1856, pp. 65–244.

Gouldner, A. *The Future of Intellectuals and the Rise of the New Class: A*

Frame of Reference, Theses, Conjectures, Arguments, and an Historical Perspective on the Role of Intellectuals and Intelligentsia in the International Class Contest of the Modern Era. New York 1979.

Grab, W. "Georg Büchners *Hessischer Landbote* im Kontext deutscher Revolutionsaufrufe 1791–1848." In: *Internationales Georg-Büchner Symposion 1987*. Ed. B. Dedner and G. Oesterle. Frankfurt am Main 1990, pp. 65–83.

Grabes, H. "England oder die Königin? Öffentlicher Meinungsstreit und nationale Identität unter Mary Tudor." In: Giesen, B. (Ed.) *Nationale und kulturelle Identität. Studien zur Entwicklung des kollektiven Bewußtseins in der Neuzeit*. Frankfurt am Main 1991, pp. 121–168.

Graf, F. W. "David Friedrich Strauss und die *Hallischen Jahrbücher*. Ein Beitrag zur positionellen Bestimmheit der theologischen Publizistik im 19. Jahrhundert." In: *Archiv für Kulturgeschichte*, 60, 1978, pp. 383–430.

Gramsci, A. *Zu Politik, Geschichte und Kultur*. Frankfurt am Main 1980.

Grass, K.-M. and Koselleck, R. "Emanzipation." In: *Geschichtliche Grundbegriffe*. Vol. II. Stuttgart 1975, pp. 153–197.

Grathoff, R. *Milieu und Lebenswelt*. Frankfurt am Main 1989.

Greene, G. *Journey Without Maps.* Harmondsworth 1978.

Greenfeld, L. *Nationalism. Five Roads to Modernity*. Cambridge, MA 1992.

Grimm, J. "Deutsche Grenzalterthümer." In: Grimm. *Abhandlungen zur Mythologie und Sittenkunde. Kleinere Schriften*. Vol. II. Berlin 1965, pp. 30–74.

Habermas, J. "Können komplexe Gesellschaften eine vernünftige Identität ausbilden?" In: Habermas. *Zur Rekonstruktion des Historischen Materialismus*. Frankfurt am Main 1976, pp. 92–126.

"Heinrich Heine und die Rolle des Intellektuellen in Deutschland." In: *Merkur*, 40, 1986, pp. 453–468.

The Structural Transformation of the Public Sphere: An Inquiry into a Category of Bourgeois Society. Cambridge, MA 1989.

The Philosophical Discourse of Modernity: Twelve Lectures. Cambridge, MA 1989.

"Nachholende Revolution und linker Revisionsbedarf. Was heißt Sozialismus heute?" In: Habermas. *Die Moderne – ein unvollendetes Projekt. Philosophisch-politische Aufsätze 1977–1990*. Leipzig 1990, pp. 213–241.

Haferkorn, H.J. "Zur Entstehung der bürgerlich-literarischen Intelligenz und des Schriftstellers in Deutschland zwischen 1750 und 1800." In: Lutz, B. (Ed.) *Deutsches Bürgertum und literarische Intelligenz 1750–1800. Literaturwissenschaft und Sozialwissenschaften* 3. Stuttgart 1974, pp. 113–275.

Hahn, A. "Konsensfiktionen in Kleingruppen. Dargestellt am Beispiel von jungen Ehen." In: Neidhardt, F. (Ed.) *Gruppensoziologie. Perspektiven und Materialien*. Special Issue no. 25 of *Kölner Zeitschrift für Soziologie und Sozialpsychologie*, Opladen 1983, pp. 210–232.

Hammar, T. *Democracy and the Nation State – Aliens, Denizens and Citizens in a World of International Migration* (Research in Ethnic Relation Series). Aldershot 1990.

Hardtwig, W. "Von Preußens Aufgabe in Deutschland zu Deutschlands Aufgabe in der Welt. Liberalismus und borussianisches Geschichtsbild zwischen Revolution und Imperialismus." In: Hardtwig. *Geschichtskultur und Wissenschaft*. Munich 1990, pp. 103–160.

"Erinnerung, Wissenschaft, Mythos. Nationale Geschichtsbilder und politische Symbole in der Reichsgründungsära und im Kaiserreich." In: Hardtwig. *Geschichtskultur und Wissenschaft*. Munich 1990, pp. 224–263.

"Geschichtsreligion – Wissenschaft als Arbeit – Objektivität." In: *Historische Zeitschrift*, 252, 1991, pp. 1–32.

Harman, L. D. *The Modern Stranger – On Language and Membership*. Berlin, New York and Amsterdam 1988.

Havelock, E. A. *Preface to Plato*. Cambridge, MA 1982 (1963).

Hechter, M. *Internal Colonialism. The Celtic Fringe in British National Development, 1536–1966*. Berkeley and Los Angeles 1975.

"Group Formation and the Cultural Division of Labor." In: *American Journal of Sociology*, 84, 1978, pp. 293–318.

"Internal Colonialism Revisited." In: Tiryakian, E.A. and Rogowski, R. (Eds.) *New Nationalisms of the Developed West*. London 1985, pp. 17–26.

Heine, H. "Reisebilder III." In: *Sämtliche Schriften*. Ed. K. Briegleb. Vol. II. Munich 1969, pp. 309–470.

"Zur Geschichte der Religion und Philosophie in Deutschland." Preface to 2nd Edition (1852). In: *Sämtliche Schriften*. Ed. K. Briegleb. Vol. III. Munich 1971, pp. 507–513.

"Ludwig Börne. Eine Denkschrift." In: *Sämtliche Schriften*. Ed. K. Briegleb. Vol. IV. Munich 1971, pp. 7–148.

"Die Romantische Schule" (1835). In: *Sämtliche Schriften*. Ed. K. Briegleb. Vol. III. Munich 1971, pp. 357–504.

Hejderhoff, J., and Wentzcke, P. (Eds.) *Deutscher Liberalismus im Zeitalter Bismarcks. Eine politische Briefsammlung*. Vol. I. Bonn and Leipzig 1925.

Herder, J. G., "Briefe zur Beförderung der Humanität." In: Herder. *Johann Gottfried Herders sämtliche Werke*. Ed. B. Suphan. Vol. XVII, 7th letter. Berlin 1881, pp. 28–33.

"Ideen zur Philosophie der Geschichte der Menschheit." In: *Johann Gottfried Herders sämtliche Werke.* Ed. B. Suphan. Vol. XIII. Berlin 1887.

"Auch eine Philosophie zur Bildung der Menschheit. Beytrag zu vielen Beyträgen des Jahrhunderts" (1774). In: *Johann Gottfried Herders sämtliche Werke*. Ed. B. Suphan, Vol. V. Berlin 1891, pp. 475–594.

Hermand, J. *Das Junge Deutschland. Texte und Dokumente*. Stuttgart 1966.

"Erotik im Juste-Milieu. Heines 'Verschiedene,'" in: Kuttenkeuler, W. (Ed.) *Heinrich Heine: Artistik und Engagement*, Stuttgart 1977, pp. 86–104.

"Was ist des Deutschen Vaterland?" In: Estermann, A. (Ed.) *Ludwig Börne 1786–1837*. Frankfurt am Main 1986, pp. 199–210.

"Jungdeutscher Tempelsturm." In: Kruse, J.A. and Kortländer, B. (Eds.) *Das Junge Deutschland. Kolloquium zum 150. Jahrestag des Verbots vom 10. Dezember 1835*. Series: *Heine-Studien*. Hamburg 1987, pp. 65–82.

"Vom 'Buch der Lieder' zu den 'Verschiedenen.'" In: Höhn, G. (Ed.) *Heinrich Heine. Ästethisch-politische Profile*. Frankfurt am Main 1991, pp. 214–235.

Hill, C. "Protestantismus, Pamphlete, Patriotismus und öffentliche Meinung im England des 16. und 17. Jahrhunderts." In: Giesen, B. (Ed.) *Nationale und kulturelle Identität. Studien zur Entwicklung des kollektiven Bewußtseins in der Neuzeit*. Frankfurt am Main 1991, pp. 100–120.

Hirsch, E. D. *Cultural Literacy. What Every American Needs to Know*. New York 1988.

Hirsch, H. "Karl Friedrich Köppen, der intimste Berliner Freund Marxens." In: Hirsch. *Denker und Kämpfer. Gesammelte Beiträge zur Geschichte der Arbeiterbewegung*. Frankfurt am Main 1955, pp. 19–81.

Hirschman, A. O. *Exit, Voice and Loyalty – Responses to Declines in Firms, Organizations, and States*. Cambridge, MA 1970.

Historikerstreit. Die Dokumentation der Kontroverse um die Einzigartigkeit der nationalsozialistischen Judenvernichtung. 2nd edn. Munich and Zürich 1987.

Hobsbawm, E. J. *Nations and Nationalism since 1870: Programme, Myth, Reality*. Cambridge 1991.

Hock, W. *Liberales Denken im Zeitalter der Paulskirche. Droysen und die Frankfurter Mitte*. Münster 1957.

Hocks, P. and Schmidt, P. *Literarische und politische Zeitschriften 1789–1805*. Stuttgart 1975.

Hoffmann-Axthelm, I. *Geisterfamilie – Studien zur Geselligkeit der Frühromantik*. Frankfurt am Main 1973.

Hohendahl, P. "Literarische und politische Öffentlichkeit. Die neue Kritik des Jungen Deutschlands." In: Hohendahl. *Literaturkritik und Öffentlichkeit*. Munich 1974, pp. 102–127.

"Nachromantische Subjektivität: Büchners Dramen." In: *Zeitschrift für Philologie*, 108, 1989, pp. 496–511.

Höhn, H. *Heine-Handbuch. Zeit, Person, Werk*. Stuttgart 1987.

Hölderlin, F. Letter to his brother of 12.2.1789. In: Hölderlin. *Sämtliche Werke*. Ed. F. Beißner, Vol. VI.1, Stuttgart 1954, No. 152, p. 264.

Hömberg, W. *Zeitgeist und Ideenschmuggel. Die Kommunikationsstrategie des Jungen Deutschland*. Stuttgart 1975.

Hondrich, K. O. *Lehrmeister Krieg*. Reinbek 1992.

Honigsheim, P. "Soziologie der Kunst, Musik und Literatur." In: Eisermann, G. (Ed.) *Die Lehre von der Gesellschaft*. Stuttgart 1958, pp. 338–373.

Hosfeld, R. "Welttheater als Tragikomödie. Ein denkbarer Dialog Heines mit der Moderne." In: Höhn, G. (Ed.) *Heinrich Heine. Ästhetisch-politische Profile*. Frankfurt am Main 1991, pp. 136–154.

Hroch, M. "Das Erwachen kleiner Nationen als Problem der komparativen Forschung." In: Winkler, H. A. (Ed.) *Nationalismus*. 2nd expanded edn. Königstein (Taunus) 1985, pp. 155–172.

Iggers, G. G. *Deutsche Geschichtswissenschaft. Eine Kritik der traditionellen Geschichtsauffassung von Herder bis zur Gegenwart*. Munich 1971, pp. 120–163.

"Heinrich v. Treitschke." In: Wehler, H.-U. (Ed.) *Deutsche Historiker*. Vol. II, Göttingen 1971, pp. 66–80.

Jahn, F. L. "Einleitung in die allgemeine Volkstumskunde." In: Jahn. *Deutsches Volkstum*. Leipzig 1936, pp. 27–45.

Japp, K. P. "Neue soziale Bewegungen und die Kontinuität der Moderne." In: Berger, J. (Ed.) *Die Moderne – Kontinuität und Zäsuren* (*Soziale Welt*, Special Issue No. 4). Göttingen 1986, pp. 311–333.

Jauß, H. R. "Das Ende der Kunstperiode. Aspekte der literarischen Revolution bei Heine, Hugo und Stendhal." In: Jauß. *Literaturgeschichte als Provokation*. Frankfurt am Main 1970, pp. 107–143.

Jeismann, M. *Das Vaterland der Feinde*. Stuttgart 1992.

Kaiser, G. *Pietismus und Patriotismus im literarischen Deutschland: Ein Beitrag zum Problem der Säkularisierung*. Wiesbaden 1961.

Kant, I. "Beantwortung der Frage: Was ist Aufklärung?" In: Kant. *Werke*. Ed. E. Cassirer. Vol. IV. Berlin 1922.

"Kritik der Urtheilskraft." In: Kant. *Werke*. Vol. V. Berlin 1968, pp. 165–485.

Kedourie, E. *Nationalism*. London 1966.

Kiesel, H. and Münch, P. *Gesellschaft und Literatur im 18. Jahrhundert. Voraussetzungen und Entstehung des literarischen Markts in Deutschland*. Munich 1977.

Kleist, H. v. "Katechismus der Deutschen, abgefaßt nach dem Spanischen zum Gebrauch für Kinder und Alte." In: Kleist. *Sämtliche Werke und Briefe*. Ed. H. Sembdner. Vol. II. 2nd edn. Munich 1961, pp. 350–360.

Kluckhohn, P. "Voraussetzungen und Verlauf der romantischen Bewegung." In: Steinbüchel, T. (Ed.) *Romantik. Ein Zyklus Tübinger Vorlesungen*. Tübingen and Stuttgart 1958, pp. 13–26.

Klutentreter, W. *Die Rheinische Zeitung von 1842/43 in der politischen und geistigen Bewegung des Vormärz*. Dortmund 1966.

Knigge, A. Frhr. v. *Über den Umgang mit Menschen* (1788). Ed. G. Ueding, 3rd edn., Frankfurt am Main 1982.

Koch, G. "Der Streit zwischen Sybel und Ficker und die Einschätzung der mittelalterlichen Kaiserpolitik in der modernen Historiographie." In: Streisand, J. (Ed.) *Studien über die Geschichtswissenschaft von 1800–1871*. Vol. I: *Die deutsche Geschichtswissenschaft vom Beginn des 19. Jahrhunderts bis zur Reichsgründung von oben*. East Berlin 1969, pp. 311–336.

Kocka, J. "Bürgertum und Bürgerlichkeit als Probleme der deutschen Geschichte vom späten 18. zum frühen 20. Jahrhundert." In: Kocka. (Ed.) *Bürger und Bürgerlichkeit im 19. Jahrhundert*. Göttingen 1987, pp. 21–63.

Kohl, K.-H. *Entzauberter Blick. Das Bild vom Guten Wilden und die Erfahrungen der Zivilisation*. Frankfurt am Main 1986.

Kohn, H. *Die Slawen und der Westen*. Vienna 1956.

The Mind of Germany. London 1965.

Konrád, G., and Szelényi, I. *The Intellectuals on the Road to Class Power*. New York 1979.

Koopmann, H. *Das Junge Deutschland. Analyse seines Selbstverständnisses*. Stuttgart 1970.

Koselleck, R. "Fortschritt." In: *Geschichtliche Grundbegriffe*. Vol. II. Stuttgart 1975, pp. 363–423.

"Die Verfügbarkeit der Geschichte." In: Koselleck. *Vergangene Zukunft*, Frankfurt am Main 1979, pp. 260–276. (English translation in: Koselleck. *Futures Past: On the Semantics of Historical Time*. Cambridge, MA 1985).

"Die Kriegerdenkmäler als Identitätsstiftung für Überlebende." In: Marquard, O., and Stierle, K.-H. (Eds.) *Identität*. Munich 1979, pp. 255–276.

"*Historia magistra vitae*. Über die Auflösung des Topos im Horizont neuzeitlich bewegter Geschichte." In: Koselleck. *Vergangene Zukunft*,

Frankfurt am Main 1979, pp. 38–66. (English translation in: Koselleck. *Futures Past: On the Semantics of Historical Time*. Cambridge, MA 1985).

"Standortbindung und Zeitlichkeit. Ein Beitrag zur historiographischen Erschließung der Welt." In: Koselleck. *Vergangene Zukunft*. Frankfurt am Main 1979, pp. 176–207.

Preußen zwischen Reform und Revolution. Allgemeines Landrecht, Verwaltung und soziale Bewegung 1791–1848, 2nd edn. Stuttgart 1981.

"Sprachwandel und Ereignisgeschichte." In: *Merkur*, 43, 1989, pp. 657–673.

"Einleitung – Zur anthropologischen und semantischen Struktur der Bildung." In: Koselleck. (Ed.) *Bildungsbürgertum im 19. Jahrhundert*. Part 2: *Bildungsgüter und Bildungswissen*. Stuttgart 1990, pp. 11–47.

Koselleck, R. (Ed.) *Bildungsbürgertum im 19. Jahrhundert*. Part 2: *Bildungsgüter und Bildungswissen*. Stuttgart 1990.

Koselleck, R., Lutz, H. and Rüsen, J. (Ed.) *Formen der Geschichtsschreibung*. Munich 1982.

Koselleck, R., Meier, C., Fisch, J., and Bulst, N. "Revolution." In: *Geschichtliche Grundbegriffe*. 5, Stuttgart 1984, pp. 653–788.

Köster, U. *Literarischer Radikalismus. Zeitbewußtsein und Geschichtsphilosophie in der Entwicklung vom Jungen Deutschland zur Hegelschen Linken*. Frankfurt am Main 1972.

Literatur und Gesellschaft in Deutschland 1830–1848. Dichtung am Ende der Kunstperiode. Stuttgart 1984.

"Elitekultur – Kulturelite. Repräsentative Kultur und Sezessionsbewegung im Kaiserreich." In: *Ploetz: Das deutsche Kaiserreich. 1867/71 bis 1918. Bilanz einer Epoche*. Ed. von D. Langewiesche, Freiburg and Würzburg 1984, pp. 181–188.

Kreuzer, H. *Die Boheme. Beiträge zu ihrer Beschreibung*. Stuttgart 1968.

"Krieg." In: *Deutsche Encyclopädie oder Allgemeines Real-Wörterbuch aller Künste und Wissenschaften*. Ed. H. M. G. Köster and J. F. Roos, Vol. XXIII, Frankfurt am Main 1804, pp. 170–188.

Kristeva, J. *Fremde sind wir uns selbst*. Frankfurt am Main 1990.

Krockow, C. Graf v. *Nationalismus als deutsches Problem*. Munich 1970.

Krohn, W., and Küppers, G. (Eds.) *Emergenz: Die Entstehung von Ordnung, Organisation und Bedeutung*. Frankfurt am Main 1992.

Kuhn, T. *Die Entstehung des Neuen*. Frankfurt am Main 1978.

Kunisch, J. "Von der gezähmten zur entfesselten Bellona. Die Umwertung des Krieges im Zeitalter der Revolutions- und Freiheitskriege." In: *Kleist-Jahrbuch 1988/89*. Ed. H.J. Kreutzer. Berlin 1988, pp. 44–63.

Lakoff, G. *Women, Fire, and Dangerous Things. What Categories Reveal about the Mind*. Chicago and London 1987.

Langewiesche, D. "Republik, konstitutionelle Monarchie und soziale Frage." In: *Historische Zeitschrift*, 230, 1980, pp. 529–548.

"Bildungsbürgertum und Liberalismus im 19. Jahrhundert." In: Kocka, J. (Ed.) *Bildungsbürgertum im 19. Jahrhundert.* Part 4: *Politischer Einfluß und gesellschaftliche Formation.* Stuttgart 1989, pp. 95–121.

Laube, H. *Das neue Jahrhundert*, Vol. II: *Politische Briefe.* Leipzig 1833.

Lepenies, W. *Melancholie und Gesellschaft.* Frankfurt am Main 1969.

Aufstieg und Fall der Intellektuellen in Europa. Frankfurt am Main and New York 1992.

Lepsius, M. R. "Zur Soziologie des Bürgertums und der Bürgerlichkeit." In: Kocka, J. (Ed.) *Bürger und Bürgerlichkeit im 19. Jahrhundert*, Göttingen 1987, pp. 79–100.

"Der Europäische Nationalstaat: Erbe und Zukunft." In: Lepsius. *Interessen, Ideen und Institutionen.* Opladen 1990, pp. 256–269.

"Kritik als Beruf. Zur Soziologie der Intellektuellen." In: Lepsius. *Interessen, Ideen und Institutionen.* Opladen 1990, pp. 270–285.

Ideen, Interessen und Institutionen. Opladen 1990.

"Ein Unbekanntes Land." In: Giesen, B. and Leggewie, C. (Ed.) *Experiment Vereinigung.* Berlin 1991, pp. 71–76.

Lerner, D. *The Passing of Traditional Society. Modernizing the Middle East.* New York 1958.

Lévi-Strauss, C. *Tristes Tropiques.* London 1955.

"Les Organisations dualistes existent-elles?" In: Lévi-Strauss. *Anthropologie structurale.* Vol. I. Paris 1958, pp. 148–180.

Lipset, S. M. *Political Man.* New York 1960.

The First New Nation – The United States in Historical and Comparative Perspective. New York 1979.

List, G. "Historische Theorie und nationale Geschichte zwischen Frühliberalismus und Reichsgründung." In: Faulenbach, F. (Ed.) *Geschichtswissenschaft in Deutschland.* Munich 1974, pp. 35–53.

Lovejoy, A. *The Great Chain of Being.* Cambridge, MA 1982.

Löwenthal, R. "Neues Mittelalter oder anomische Kulturkrise." In: Löwenthal. *Gesellschaftswandel und Kulturkrise.* Frankfurt am Main 1979, pp. 37–57.

Löwith, K. *Weltgeschichte und Heilsgeschehen.* Stuttgart 1953.

Löwith, K. (Ed. and Introduction). *Die Hegelsche Linke.* Stuttgart and Bad Cannstatt 1962, p. 7–38.

Lübbe, H. "Die Nostalgie des Urbanen und die europäische Anti-Revolution des Jahres 1989." In: Lübbe. *Freiheit statt Emanzipationszwang. Die liberale Tradition und das Ende der marxistischen Illusion.* Osnabrück 1991, pp. 75–90.

Luckmann, T. *Die unsichtbare Religion.* Frankfurt am Main 1991.

Luckmann, T., and Berger, P. L. *The Social Construction of Reality: a Treatise in the Sociology of Knowledge.* Garden City, NY 1966.

Luhmann, N. "Diskussion als System." In: Habermas, J. and Luhmann, N. *Theorie der Gesellschaft oder Sozialtechnologie?* Frankfurt am Main 1971, pp. 316–341.

"Über die Funktion der Negation in sinnkonstituierenden Systemen." In: Luhmann. *Soziologische Aufklärung.* Vol. III, Opladen 1981, pp. 35–49.

Mann, M. *The Sources of Social Power.* Vol. I: *A History of Power from the Beginning to AD 1760.* Cambridge 1986.

Mannheim, K. *Essays on the Sociology of Culture.* London 1956.

Ideology und Utopia: An Introduction to the Sociology of Knowledge. San Diego 1985.

Marquard, O. "Über einige Beziehungen zwischen Ästhetik und Therapeutik in der Philosophie des 19. Jahrhunderts." In: Marquard. *Schwierigkeiten mit der Geschichtsphilosophie.* Frankfurt am Main 1973, pp. 85–106.

"Inkompetenzkompensationskompetenz. Über Kompetenz und Inkompetenz der Philosophie." In: Marquard. *Abschied vom Prinzipiellen.* Stuttgart 1981, pp. 23–38.

"Kunst als Antifiktion – Versuch über den Weg der Wirklichkeit ins Fiktive." In: Marquard. *Aesthetica und Anaesthetica.* Paderborn 1989, pp. 82–99.

Marx, K. Letters from the *Deutsch-französische Jahrbüchern.* In: Marx and Engels, *Works.* Vol. I, Berlin 1957.

"Zur Kritik der Hegelschen Rechtsphilosophie." Introduction, In: Marx and Engels, *Works.* Vol. I, Berlin 1957.

"Die heilige Familie." In: Marx and Engels, *Works.* Vol. II, Berlin 1959, pp. 7–223.

Mason, E. C. *Deutsche und englische Romantik.* Göttingen 1966.

Maturana, H. R. *Erkennen: Die Organisation und Verkörperung von Wirklichkeit. Arbeiten zum Radikalen Konstruktivismus.* Braunschweig and Wiesbaden 1982.

Maturana, H. R., and Verela F. J. *Autopoiesis and Cognition.* Dordrecht 1980.

Mead, G. H. *Mind, Self, and Society. From the Standpoint of a Social Behaviorist.* Chicago 1967.

Meinecke, F. *Weltbürgertum und Nationalstaat. Studien zur Genesis des deutschen Nationalstaats.* Munich and Berlin 1908.

"3 Generationen Gelehrtenpolitik." In: *Historische Zeitschrift*, 125, 1922, pp. 248–283.

Mennemeier, F. N. "Fragment und Ironie beim jungen Friedrich Schlegel.

Versuch der Konstruktion einer nicht geschriebenen Theorie" (1968). In: Peter, K. (Ed.) *Romantikforschung seit 1945*. Königstein (Taunus) 1990, pp. 229–250.

Menzel, U. "Das Ende der 'Dritten Welt' und das Scheitern der großen Theorien. Zur Soziologie einer Disziplin in auch selbstkritischer Absicht." In: *Politische Vierteljahresschrift*, 32, 1991, pp. 4–33.

Merritt, R. L. "Nation-Building in America: The Colonial Years." In: Deutsch, K. W. *et al. Nation-Building*. New York 1963, pp. 56–72.

Meyer, G. "Die Anfänge des politischen Radikalismus im vormärzlichen Preußen." In: Meyer. *Radikalismus, Sozialismus und bürgerliche Demokratie*. Ed. H.-U. Wehler, Frankfurt am Main 1969, pp. 7–107.

Meyer, T. "Büchner und Weidig – Frühkommunismus und revolutionäre Demokratie. Zur Textverteilung des *Hessischen Landboten*." In: Arnold, H. (Ed.) *Georg Büchner I/II, Text und Kritik*. Munich 1979, pp. 16–296.

"Die Verbreitung und Wirkung des *Hessischen Landboten*." In: *Georg Büchner-Jahrbuch*, I, 1981, pp. 68–111.

Michels, R. "Historisch-kritische Untersuchungen zum politischen Verhalten der Intellektuellen." In: Michels. *Masse, Führer, Intellektuelle. Politisch-soziologische Aufsätze 1906–1933*. Frankfurt am Main and New York 1987, pp. 189–213.

"Zur Soziologie der Boheme und ihrer Zusammenhänge mit dem geistigen Proletariat." In: Michels. *Masse, Führer, Intellektuelle. Politisch-soziologische Aufsätze 1906–1933*. Frankfurt am Main and New York 1987, pp. 214–230.

Möller, H. *Vernunft und Kritik – Deutsche Aufklärung im 17. und 18. Jahrhundert*. Frankfurt am Main 1986.

Mommsen, W. J. "Objektivität und Parteilichkeit im historiographischen Werk Sybels und Treitschkes." In: Koselleck, R., Mommsen, W. J. and Rüsen, J. (Eds.) *Objektivität und Parteilichkeit*. Munich 1977, pp. 134–158.

Moser, C. F. v. *Von dem deutschen Nationalgeist*. 1766.

Mosse, G. L. *Die Nationalisierung der Massen. Politische Symbolik und Massenbewegung in Deutschland von den napoleonischen Kriegen bis zum 3. Reich*. Frankfurt am Main and Berlin 1976.

Mühlmann, W. E. *Homo Creator. Abhandlungen zur Soziologie, Anthropologie und Ethnologie*. Wiesbaden 1962.

"Chiliasmus, Nativismus, Nationalismus." In: *Soziologie und moderne Gesellschaft. Verhandlungen des 14. Deutschen Soziologentages*. Stuttgart 1966, pp. 228–242.

Mühlmann, W. E. (Ed.) *Chiliasmus und Nativismus*. Berlin 1961.

Müller, A. "Die Elemente der Staatskunst." In: Peter, K. (Ed.) *Die politische Romantik in Deutschland. Eine Textsammlung.* Stuttgart 1985, pp. 280–300.

Münch, R. *Theorie des Handelns.* Frankfurt am Main 1982.

Die Struktur der Moderne. Frankfurt am Main 1984.

Die Kultur der Moderne. 2 Vols. Frankfurt am Main 1986.

Dialektik der Kommunikationsgesellschaft. Frankfurt am Main 1991.

Mundt, T. *Madonna.* Leipzig 1835.

Spaziergänge und Weltfahrten. Vol. I, Altona 1838.

Mundt, T. (Ed.) *Schriften in bunter Reihe, zur Anregung und Unterhaltung.* Reprint, Frankfurt am Main 1971.

Na'aman, S. *Gibt es einen Wissenschaflichen Sozialismus? Marx, Engels und das Verhältnis zwischen sozialistischen Intellektuellen und den Lernprozessen der Arbeiterbewegung.* Ed. M. Vester, Hanover 1979.

Nagel, J. and Olzak, S. "Ethnic Mobilization in New and Old States: An Extension of the Competition Model." In: *Social Problems,* 30, 1982, pp. 127–143.

Nairn, T. *The Break-up of Britain.* London 1977.

Namier, L. *1848: The Revolution of the Intellectuals.* Oxford 1946.

Nedelmann, B. "Georg Simmel – Emotion und Wechselwirkung in intimen Gruppen." In: Neidhardt, F. (Ed.) *Gruppensoziologie. Perspektiven und Materialien. Kölner Zeitschrift für Soziologie und Sozialpsychologie,* Special Issue no. 25, Opladen 1983, pp. 174–209.

"Profane und heilige 'Soziale Welt' (Jahrgang 1989)." In: *Soziologische Revue,* Yr. 15, 1992, pp. 139–152.

Newman, G. *The Rise of English Nationalism. A Cultural History 1740–1830.* New York 1987.

Nielsen, F. "Toward a Theory of Ethnic Solidarity in Modern Societies." In: *American Sociological Review,* 50, 1985, pp. 133–149.

Nietzsche, F. "David Strauss – der Bekenner und Schriftsteller." In: *Unzeitgemäße Betrachtungen.* Munich 1964, pp. 7–72.

Nipperdey, T. "Nationalidee und Nationaldenkmal in Deutschland im 19. Jahrhundert." In: Nipperdey. *Gesellschaft, Kultur, Theorie,* Göttingen 1976, pp. 133–173.

"Der Verein als soziale Struktur in Deutschland im späten 18. und frühen 19. Jahrhundert." In: Nipperdey. *Gesellschaft, Kultur, Theorie.* Göttingen 1976, pp. 174–205.

"Volksschule und Revolution im Vormärz. Eine Fallstudie zur Modernisierung II." In: Nipperdey. *Gesellschaft, Kultur, Theorie.* Göttingen 1976, pp. 206–227.

"Kritik oder Objektivität? Zur Beurteilung der Revolution von 1848."

In: Nipperdey. *Gesellschaft, Kultur, Theorie*. Göttingen 1976, pp. 259–278.

Deutsche Geschichte 1800–1866. Bürgerwelt und starker Staat. Munich 1983.

"Probleme der Modernisierung in Deutschland." In: Nipperdey. *Nachdenken über die deutsche Geschichte*. Munich 1990, pp. 52–70.

"Auf der Suche nach Identitat: Romantischer Nationalismus." In: *Nachdenken über die deutsche Geschichte*. Munich 1990, pp. 132–150.

Deutsche Geschichte 1866–1918. Vol. I: *Arbeitswelt und Bürgergeist*. 2nd Ed. Munich 1990.

Nora, P. (Ed.) *Realms of Memory: Rethinking the French Past*. Vol. I: *Conflicts and Divisions*. New York 1996.

Novalis. "Fragmente und Studien 1797–1798." No. 37. In: Novalis. *Werke*. Ed. G. Schulz, Munich 1969.

"Vermischte Bemerkungen (Blütenstaub)." 1797–1798. In: Novalis. *Schriften. Die Werke Friedrich von Hardenbergs*. Ed. P. Kluckhohn and R. Samuel (Critical Edn.) Vol. II, 3rd expanded and revised edn. Darmstadt 1977, section VI, HKA No. 267, 280, 347.

Schriften. Die Werke Friedrich von Hardenbergs. Ed. P. Kluckhohn and R. Samuel (Critical Edn.) Vol. III, 3rd expanded and revised edn. Darmstadt 1977, section IX, HKA No. 50.

Obenaus, S. "Buchmarkt, Verlagswesen und Zeitschriften." In: Glaser, H. A. (Ed.) *Deutsche Literatur. Eine Sozialgeschichte*. Vol. VI: *Vormärz: Biedermeier, Junges Deutschland, Demokraten 1815–1848*. Ed. B. Witte. Reinbek 1987, pp. 44–62.

Obermann, K. "Die deutschen Historiker in der Revolution von 1848/49." In: Streisand, J. (Ed.) *Studien über die Geschichtswissenschaft von 1800–1871*. Vol. I: *Die deutsche Geschichtswissenschaft vom Beginn des 19. Jahrhunderts bis zur Reichsgründung von oben*. East Berlin 1969, pp. 219–240.

Oehler, K. "Idee und Grundriß der Peirceschen Semiotik." In: Krampen, M., Posner, R. and Uexküll, T. v. (Eds.) *Die Welt als Zeichen. Klassiker der modernen Semiotik*. Berlin 1981, pp. 15–49.

Oesterle, G. *Integration und Konflikt. Die Prosa Heinrich Heines im Kontext oppositioneller Literatur der Restaurationsepoche*. Stuttgart 1972.

"F. Schlegel in Paris oder die romantische Gegenrevolution." In: Fink, G.-L. (Ed.) *Die deutsche Romantik und die Französische Revolution. Actes du Colloque International, Collection Recherches Germaniques*, 3. Strasbourg 1989, pp. 163–179.

Oesterle, I. and G. "Der literarische Bürgerkrieg." In: Mattenklott, G. and

Scherpe, K. R. (Eds.) *Demokratisch-revolutionäre Literatur in Deutschland: Vormärz*. Kronberg (Taunus) 1974, pp. 151–186.

Oevermann, U. "Zwei Staaten oder Einheit? Der 'dritte Weg' als Fortsetzung des deutschen Sonderweges." In: *Merkur*, 44, 1990, pp. 91–106.

Ong, W. J. *Ramus, Method, and the Decay of Dialog*. Cambridge, MA 1958.

Orality and Literacy – The Technologizing of the Word. London 1982.

Opp, K.-J. "DDR 89. Zu den Ursachen einer spontanen Revolution." In: *Kölner Zeitschrift für Soziologie und Sozialpsychologie*, 43, 2, 1991, pp. 302–321.

Packard, V. *A Nation of Strangers*. New York 1972.

Palm, G. F. "Politische-Moralische Reflexionen." In: *Neues Hannoverisches Magazin*, 4, 1794, pp. 353–368.

Pankoke, E. *Soziale Bewegung – Soziale Frage – Soziale Politik. Grundfragen der deutschen "Sozialwissenschaft" im 19. Jahrhundert*. Stuttgart 1970.

Patriotisches Archiv für Deutschland. 5, 1786.

Paz, O. *El Laberinto de la soledad*. Ed. Enrico Mario Santi. Madrid 1993.

Peirce, C.S. "Syllabus of Certain Topics of Logic," Ms. not yet fully available in English; German complete version ed. and translated by H. Pape: *Phänomen und Logik der Zeichen*. Frankfurt am Main 1983.

Pepperle, H. "Heinrich Heine as Philosoph." In: Höhn, G. (Ed.) *Heinrich Heine. Ästhetisch-politische Profile*. Frankfurt am Main 1991, pp. 155–175.

Plessner, H. *Die verspätete Nation*. Stuttgart 1959.

Prignitz, C. *Vaterlandsliebe und Freiheit. Deutscher Patriotismus von 1750–1850*. Wiesbaden 1981.

Rapaport, A. *Fights, Games and Debates*. Ann Arbor 1974.

Reese-Schäfer, W. "Universalismus, negativer Nationalismus und die neue Einheit der Deutschen." In: Braitling, P., and Reese-Schäfer, W. (Eds.) *Universalismus, Nationalismus und die neue Einheit der Deutschen*. Frankfurt am Main 1991, pp. 39–54.

Reimann, H. L., Koselleck, R., Meier, H., and Conze, W. "Demokratie." In: *Geschichtliche Grundbegriffe*. Vol. I. Stuttgart 1972, pp. 821–899.

Riehl, W. H. *Die bürgerliche Gesellschaft*. Stuttgart and Heidelberg 1851.

Rihs, C. *L'Ecole des jeunes Hégéliens et les penseurs socialistes français*. Paris 1978.

Ringer, F. K. *Die Gelehrten. Der Niedergang der deutschen Mandarine 1890–1933*. Munich 1987.

Ritter, J. *Hegel und die französische Revolution*. Frankfurt am Main 1965.

Rochau, L.A. v. *Grundsätze der Realpolitik*. Ed. by H.-U. Wehler, Frankfurt am Main, Berlin and Vienna 1972.

Rokkan, S. *et al.* "Nationbuilding – A Review of Recent Comparative Research and a Selected Bibliography of Analytical Studies." In: *Current Sociology*, 19, 1971, pp. 1–86.

Rosenberg, H. *Rudolf Haym und die Anfänge des klassischen Liberalismus*. Munich and Berlin 1933.

"Zur Geschichte der Hegelauffassung." In: Rosenberg. *Politische Denkströmungen im Vormärz*. Göttingen 1972, pp. 69–96.

"Arnold Ruge und die 'Hallischen Jahrbücher.'" In: Rosenberg. *Politische Denkströmungen im Vormärz*. Göttingen 1972, pp. 97–115.

Roth, G. and Schwedler, H. (Ed.) *Self-Organizing Systems. An Interdisciplinary Approach*. Frankfurt am Main 1981.

Ruge, A. *Der Liberalismus und die Philosophie, Gesammelte Schriften*. Vol. IV. Mannheim 1848.

Ruge, A. and Echtermeyer, T. "Protestantismus und Romantik. Zur Verständigung über die Zeit." In: *Hallische Jahrbücher*, 1839/40.

Rüschemeyer, D. "Bourgeoisie, Staat und Bildungsbürgertum. Idealtypische Modelle für die vergleichende Erforschung von Bürgertum und Bürgerlichkeit." In: Kocka, J. (Ed.) *Bürger und Bürgerlichkeit im 19. Jahrhundert*. Göttingen 1987, pp. 101–120.

Rüsen, J. "Politisches Denken und Geschichtswissenschaft bei J.G. Droysen." In: Kluxen, K. and Mommsen, W.J. *Politische Ideologien und nationalstaatliche Ordnung. Studien zur Geschichte des 19. und 20. Jahrhunderts. Festschrift für Theodor Schieder zu seinem 60. Geburtstag*. Munich and Vienna 1968, pp. 171–188.

Begriffene Geschichte. Genesis und Begründung der Geschichtstheorie J. G. Droysens. Paderborn 1969.

"Johann Gustav Droysen." In: Wehler, H.-U. (Ed.) *Deutsche Historiker*. Vol. I. Göttingen 1971, pp. 7–23.

"Der Historiker als 'Parteimann des Schicksals.' Georg Gottfried Gervinus und das Konzept der objektiven Parteilichkeit im deutschen Historismus." In: Koselleck, R., Mommsen, W.J., and Rüsen, J. (Eds.) *Objektivitat und Parteilichkeit*. Munich 1977, pp. 77–125.

Sahlins, M. *Historical Metaphors and Mythical Realities*. Ann Arbor, MI 1981.

Said, E. *Orientalism*. New York 1978.

Sass, H. M. Afterword on B. Bauer, *Feldzüge der Kritik*. Frankfurt am Main 1968, pp. 224–268.

Schelling, F.W.J. "Über das Verhältnis der bildenden Künste zur Natur"

(1807). In: Schelling. *Ausgewählte Schriften*. Vol. II: *Schriften 1801–1803*. Frankfurt am Main 1985.

Schelsky, H. *Einsamkeit und Freiheit*. Hamburg 1963.

Die Arbeit tun die anderen. Klassenkampf und Priesterherrschaft der Intellektuellen. Opladen 1975.

Schieder, T. "Die deutsche Geschichtsschreibung im Spiegel der *Historischen Zeitschrift*." In: *Historische Zeitschrift*, 189, 1959, pp.1–73.

"Das Problem der Revolution im 19. Jahrhundert." In: Schieder. *Staat und Gesellschaft im Wandel unserer Zeit*. Munich 1970, pp. 11–57.

"Die Theorie der Partei im älteren deutschen Liberalismus." In: Schieder, *Staat und Gesellschaft im Wandel unserer Zeit*. Munich 1970, pp. 110–132.

"Die geschichtlichen Grundlagen und Epochen des deutschen Parteiwesens." In: Schieder. *Staat und Gesellschaft im Wandel unserer Zeit*. Munich 1970, pp. 133–171.

"Sozialismus." In: *Geschichtliche Grundbegriffe*. Vol. IV. Stuttgart 1985, pp. 923–996.

Schieder, W. *Anfänge der deutschen Arbeiterbewegung. Die Auslandsvereine im Jahrzehnt nach der Juli-Revolution 1830*. Stuttgart 1963.

Schilling, H. "Die Geschichte der nördlichen Niederlande." In: *Geschichte und Gesellschaft*, 8, 1982, pp. 475–517.

"Nationale Identität und Konfession in der europäischen Neuzeit." In: Giesen, B. (Ed.) *Nationale und kulturelle Identität. Studien zur Entwicklung des kollektiven Bewußtseins in der Neuzeit*. Frankfurt am Main 1991, pp. 192–252.

Schlawe, F. "Die junghegelianische Publizistik." In: *Die Welt als Geschichte*, 20, 1960, pp. 30–50.

Schlegel, F. v. "Über das Studium der griechischen Poesie." In: Schlegel. *Schriften zur Literatur*. Ed. W. Rasch. Munich 1972, pp. 84–192.

Schleier, H. "Die kleindeutsche Schule (Droysen, Sybel, Treitschke)." In: Streisand, J. (Ed.) *Studien über die Geschichtswissenschaft von 1800–1871*. Vol. I: *Die deutsche Geschichtswissenschaft vom Beginn des 19. Jahrhunderts bis zur Reichsgründung von oben*. East Berlin 1969, pp. 271–310.

Schluchter, W. *Religion und Lebensführung*, 2 Vols. Frankfurt am Main 1988.

Schmid, M. *Leerformeln und Ideologiekritik*. Tübingen 1972.

Schmidt, S.J. (Ed.) *Der Diskurs des Radikalen Konstruktivismus*. Frankfurt am Main 1987.

Schmitt, C. "Nehmen/Teilen/Weiden." In: Schmitt. *Verfassungsrechtliche Aufsätze aus den Jahren 1924–1954.* Berlin 1985, pp. 489–504.

Der Begriff des Politischen (1932). Berlin 1987.

Schmitt-Sasse, J. "Der Patriot und sein Vaterland. Aufklärer und Reformer im sächsischen Rétablissement." In: Bödeker, H. E., and Herrmann, U. (Eds.) *Aufklärung als Politisierung – Politisierung als Aufklärung.* Hamburg 1987, pp. 237–252.

Schraepler, E. *Handwerkerbünde und Arbeitervereine 1830–1854. Die politische Tätigkeit deutscher Sozialisten von Wilhelm Weitling bis Karl Marx.* Berlin and New York 1972.

Schulte-Sasse, J. "Das Konzept bürgerlich-literarische Öffentlichkeit und die historischen Gründe seines Zerfalls." In: Bürger, C. *et al.* (Eds.) *Aufklärung und literarische Öffentlichkeit.* Frankfurt am Main 1980, pp. 83–115.

Schulze, H. *Der Weg zum Nationalstaat. Die deutsche Nationalbewegung vom 18. Jahrhundert bis zur Reichsgründung.* Munich 1985.

Schumpeter, J. A. *Capitalism, Socialism, and Democracy.* 5th edn. London 1976.

Schütz, A. "Der Fremde." In: Schütz. *Gesammelte Aufsätze.* Vol. III. The Hague 1972, pp. 53–69.

Seier, H. *Die Staatsidee Heinrich von Sybels in den Wandlungen der Reichsgründerzeit 1862/71.* Lübeck and Hamburg 1961.

"Heinrich von Sybel." In: Wehler, H.-U. (Ed.) *Deutsche Historiker.* Vol. II. Göttingen 1971, pp. 24–38.

"Liberalismus und Staat in Deutschland zwischen Revolution und Reichsgründung." In: Klötzer, W., Moldenhauer, R., and Rebentisch, D. (Eds.) *Ideen und Strukturen der deutschen Revolution 1848.* Frankfurt am Main 1974, pp. 69–84.

Seton-Watson, H. *Nations and States: An Enquiry into the Origins of Nations and the Politics of Nationalism.* Boulder, CO 1977.

Shils, E. "Intellectuals, Public Opinion and Economic Development." In: *World Politics*, 10, 1958, pp. 232–255.

"Intellectuals, Tradition, and the Tradition of Intellectuals: Some Preliminary Considerations." In: Shils. *Center and Periphery. Essays on Macrosociology.* Chicago 1975, pp. 21–35.

"Personal, Primordial, Sacred and Civil Ties." In: Shils. *Center and Periphery. Essays on Macrosociology.* Chicago 1975, pp. 111–126.

Tradition. Chicago 1981.

Siemann, W. *Gesellschaft im Aufbruch. Deutschland 1849–1971.* Frankfurt am Main 1990.

Simmel, G. *Der Krieg und die geistige Entscheidung*. Munich 1917.
"Der Streit." In: Simmel. *Soziologie. Untersuchungen über die Formen der Vergesellschaftung*. 4th edn. Berlin 1958, pp. 186–255.
"Exkurs über den Fremden." In: Simmel. *Soziologie. Untersuchungen über die Formen der Vergesellschaftung*. 4th edn. Berlin 1958, pp. 509–512.
Smith, A. D. *Theories of Nationalism*. London 1971.
The Ethnic Origins of Nations. Cambridge, MA 1986.
National Identity. Reno, Las Vegas and London 1991.
Soeffner, H.-G. *Die Ordnung der Rituale. Die Auslegung des Alltags 2*. Frankfurt am Main 1992.
Staël, Madame de. *Über Deutschland*. Ed. M. Bosse. Frankfurt am Main 1985.
Stein, L. v. *Der Sozialismus und Kommunismus des heutigen Frankreich*. Leipzig 1842.
Stein, P. *Politisches Bewußtsein und künstlerischer Gestaltungswille in der politischen Lyrik 1750–1848*. Hamburg, n.d., pp. 87–118.
Stephan, C. and Leggewie, C. "Abschied vom linken Gewissen." In: *Journal Frankfurt*, 14–27 Feb. 1991, pp. 32f.
Stichweh, R. *Der frühmoderne Staat und die europäische Universität*. Frankfurt am Main 1991.
Stolleis, M. *Geschichte des öffentlichen Rechts in Deutschland*. Munich 1988.
Strauss, D. F. *Das Leben Jesu. Kritisch bearbeitet*. Mannheim 1835.
Stuke, H. *Philosophie der Tat. Studien zur "Verwirklichung der Philosophie" bei den Junghegelianern und den wahren Sozialisten*. Stuttgart 1963.
Sughe, W. *Saint-Simonismus und Junges Deutschland. Das Saint-Simonistische System in der deutschen Literatur der ersten Hälfte des 19. Jahrhunderts*. Berlin 1935.
Sybel, H. v. *Die politischen Parteien der Rheinprovinz in ihrem Verhältnis zur preußischen Verfassung*. Düsseldorf 1847.
"Das neue Deutschland und Frankreich" (1866). In: Sybel. *Vorträge und Aufsätze*. Berlin 1874.
Teller, W. A. "Ueber Patriotismus." In: *Berlinische Monatsschrift*, 22, 1793, pp. 431–447.
Tenbruck, F. *Die unbewältigten Sozialwissenschaften oder die Abschaffung des Menschen*. Graz 1984.
"Der Fortschritt der Wissenschaft als Trivialisierungsprozeß." In: Tenbruck. *Die kulturellen Grundlagen der Gesellschaft*. Opladen 1989, pp. 143–174.

"Modernisierung – Vergesellschaftung – Gruppenbildung – Vereinswesen." In: Tenbruck. *Die kulturellen Grundlagen der Gesellschaft*. Opladen 1989, pp. 215–226.

"Der Traum der säkularen Ökumene. Sinn und Grenze der Entwicklungsvision." In: Tenbruck. *Die kulturellen Grundlagen der Gesellschaft*. Opladen 1989, pp. 291–307.

Thadden, R. v. *Nicht Vaterland, nicht Fremde. Essays zu Geschichte und Gegenwart*. Munich 1989.

"Aufbau nationaler Identität. Deutschland und Frankreich im Vergleich." In: Giesen, B. (Ed.) *Nationale und kulturelle Identität. Studien zur Entwicklung des kollektiven Bewußtseins in der Neuzeit*. Frankfurt am Main 1991, pp. 493–510.

Thaulow, G. *Das europäische Gleichgewicht durch den Prager Frieden vom 23. August 1866*. Kiel 1867.

Thompson, E. P. "The Moral Economy of the English Crowd in the 18th Century." In: *Past and Present*, 50, 1971, pp. 76–136.

Tiryakian, E.A. "Nationalism, Modernity, and Sociology." In: *Sociologia Internationalis*, I, 1988, pp. 1–17.

Todorov, T. *Die Eroberung Amerikas. Das Problem des Anderen*. Frankfurt am Main 1985.

Tönnies, F. *Gemeinschaft und Gesellschaft. Grundbegriffe der reinen Soziologie* (1887). Berlin 1912.

Treitschke, H. v. *Zehn Jahre deutsche Kämpfe*. 2nd edn. Berlin 1879.

"Die Freiheit." In: *Historische und politische Aufsätze*. Vol. III. 5th edn. Leipzig 1886, pp. 3–42.

Aufsätze, Reden, Briefe. Vol. I. Meersburg 1929.

Deutsche Geschichte im 19. Jahrhundert. Vol. I. Reprint. Königstein (Taunus) and Düsseldorf 1981.

Deutsche Geschichte im 19. Jahrhundert. Vol. 4. Reprint. Königstein (Taunus) and Düsseldorf 1981.

Troeltsch, E. *Naturrecht und Humanität* (1925). Reprint. Aalen 1966.

Turner, V. T. *Das Ritual. Struktur und Anti-Struktur*. Cologne 1989.

Tyrell, H. "Romantische Liebe – Überlegungen zu ihrer 'quantitativen Bestimmtheit.'" In: Baecker, D. *et al.* (Eds.) *Theorie als Passion. Niklas Luhmann zum 60. Geburtstag*. Frankfurt am Main 1987, pp. 570–599.

Valéry, P. *Herr Teste*. Frankfurt am Main 1984.

Vierhaus, R. "Umrisse einer Sozialgeschichte der Gebildeten in Deutschland." In: Vierhaus. *Deutschland im 18. Jahrhundert*. Göttingen 1987, pp. 167–182.

"Patriotismus." In: Vierhaus. *Deutschland im 18. Jahrhundert*. Göttingen 1987, pp. 96–109.

"Heinrich von Kleist und die Krise des preußischen Staates um 1800." In: Vierhaus. *Deutschland im 18. Jahrhundert*. Göttingen 1987, pp. 216–234.

Staaten und Stände. Vom Westfälischen bis zum Hubertusburger Frieden 1648 bis 1763. Frankfurt am Main and Berlin 1990.

Villaume, P. "Patriotismus und Konstitutionalismus." In: Batscha, Z. *et al.* (Eds.) *Von der ständischen zur bürgerlichen Gesellschaft*. Frankfurt am Main 1981, pp. 267–276.

Vogt, H. (Ed.) *Nationalismus gestern und heute*. Opladen 1967.

Vordtriede, W. "Der Berliner Saint-Simonismus." In: *Heine-Jahrbuch*, 14, Hamburg 1975, pp. 93–110.

Walker, M. *German Home-Towns*. Ithaca, NY 1971.

Weber, M. "Der Nationalstaat und die Volkswirtschaftspolitik." In: Weber. *Gesammelte politische Schriften*. Tübingen 1988, pp. 1–25.

Weber, W. *Priester der Klio. Historisch-sozialwissenschaftliche Studien zur Herkunft und Karriere deutscher Historiker und zur Geschichte der Geschichtswissenschaft 1800–1970*. Frankfurt am Main 1984.

Wegmann, N. *Diskurse der Empfindsamkeit. Zur Geschichte eines Gefühls in der Literatur des 18. Jahrhunderts*. Stuttgart 1988.

Wehler, H.-U. *Deutsche Gesellschaftsgeschichte*. Vol. I: *Vom Feudalismus des Alten Reiches bis zur defensiven Modernisierung der Reformära 1700–1815*. Munich 1987.

Deutsche Gesellschaftsgeschichte. Vol. II: *Von der Reformära bis zur industriellen und politischen "Deutschen Doppelrevolution" 1815–1848/49*. Munich 1987.

Weingart, P., Kroll, J., and Bayertz, K. *Rasse, Blut und Gene. Geschichte der Eugenetik und Rassenhygiene in Deutschland*. Frankfurt am Main 1988.

Weiß, J. "Wiederverzauberung der Welt? Bemerkungen zur Wiederkehr der Romantik in der gegenwärtigen Kulturkritik." In: Neidhardt, F. *et al.* (Eds.) *Kultur und Gesellschaft. Kölner Zeitschrift für Soziologie und Sozialpsychologie,* Special Issue No. 27, Opladen 1986, pp. 286–301.

Welke, M. "Gemeinsame Lektüre und frühe Formen von Gruppenbildungen im 17. und 18. Jahrhundert: Zeitungslesen in Deutschland." In: Dann, O. (Ed.) *Lesegesellschaften und bürgerliche Emanzipation. Ein europäischer Vergleich*. Munich 1981, pp. 29–53.

Wende, P. "Der Revolutionsbegriff der radikalen Demokraten." In: Klötzer, W., Moldenhauer, R. and Rebentisch, D. (Eds.) *Ideen und Strukturen der deutschen Revolution 1848*. Frankfurt am Main 1974, pp. 57–68.

Radikalismus im Vormärz. Untersuchungen zur politischen Theorie der frühen deutschen Demokratie. Wiesbaden 1975.

White, H. *Tropics of Discourse. Essays in Cultural Criticism*. Baltimore and London 1978.

Metahistory. The Historical Imagination in Nineteenth Century Europe. Baltimore and London 1987.

"Droysens Historik: Geschichtsschreibung als bürgerliche Wissenschaft." In: White. *Die Bedeutung der Form*. Frankfurt am Main 1990, pp. 108–131. (English translation in: White. *The Content of the Form. Narrative Discourse and Historical Representation*. Baltimore and London 1987).

Wiedemann, C. "Römische Staatsnation und griechische Kulturnation." In: *Akten des VII. Internat. Germanisten-Kongresses Göttingen 1985*, Tübingen 1986, pp.173–178.

"'Supplement seines Daseins?' Zu den kultur- und identitätsgeschichtlichen Voraussetzungen deutscher Schriftstellerreisen nach Rom–Paris–London seit Winckelmann." In: Wiedemann (Ed.) *Rom–Paris–London. Erfahrung und Selbsterfahrung deutscher Schriftsteller und Künstler in den fremden Metropolen – Ein Symposion*. Stuttgart 1988, pp. 1–20.

Wienbarg, L. *Ästhetische Feldzüge*. Ed. W. Dietze. Berlin and Weimar 1964.

Williams, R. *The Long Revolution*. Harmondsworth 1961.

Windfuhr, M. "Das Junge Deutschland als literarische Opposition." In: *Heine-Jahrbuch*, 22, 1983, pp. 47–69.

Winkler, H. A. "Der deutsche Sonderweg. Eine Nachlese." In: *Merkur*, 35, 1981, pp. 793–804.

Woesler, W. "Die Idee der deutschen Nationalliteratur in der zweiten Hälfte des 18. Jahrhunderts." In: Garber, K. (Ed.) *Nation und Literatur im Europa der Frühen Neuzeit, Akten des I. Internationalen Osnabrücker Kongresses zur Kulturgeschichte der Frühen Neuzeit*. Tübingen 1989, pp. 716–733.

Wollstein, G. *Das "Großdeutschland" der Paulskirche. Nationale Ziele in der bürgerlichen Revolution 1848/49*. Düsseldorf 1977.

Wülfing, W. *Junges Deutschland. Texte, Kontexte, Abbildungen, Kommentar*. Munich and Vienna 1978.

Schlagworte des Jungen Deutschland. Mit einer Einführung in die Schlagwortforschung. Berlin 1982.

"Reiseliteratur." In: Glaser, H. A. (Ed.) *Deutsche Literatur. Eine Sozialgeschichte*. Vol. 6: *Vormärz: Biedermeier, Junges Deutschland, Demokraten 1815–1848*. Ed. B. Witte. Reinbek 1987, pp. 180–194.

Wülfing, W., Bruns, K., and Parr, R. *Historische Mythologie der Deutschen*. Munich 1991.

Zapf, W. "Der Untergang der DDR und die soziologische Theorie der Modernisierung." In: Giesen, B. and Leggewie, C. (Eds.) *Experiment Vereinigung*, Berlin 1991, pp. 38–51.

Zerubavel, E. *The Fine Line. Making Distinctions in Everyday Life.* New York 1991.

Zilsel, E. *Die sozialen Ursprünge der neuzeitlichen Wissenschaft*. Frankfurt am Main 1976.

Zimmer, H. *Auf dem Altar des Vaterlandes. Religion und Patriotismus in der deutschen Kriegslyrik des 19. Jahrhunderts*. Frankfurt am Main 1971.

Index